CW00548596

CHANGING BOR
A KINGDOM UNLO⎣

Commendations

"With a wealth of experience working on borders in the UK and around the world I can think of no better person to write about the subject and explore the practical and policy issues involved than Tony Smith. Interweaving his own story and drawing on his experience this book will be important reading for anyone interested in this topic."

Rt Hon Theresa May MP, former UK Home Secretary and Prime Minister

"A brilliant insight into the personal and professional life of an immigration officer, from starting on the first rung to the top job and a ringside role in dealing with the fallout from some of the worst terrorist atrocities in history."

Charles Hymas, Home Affairs Editor, Daily Telegraph

"Tony Smith's rise through the ranks of the Immigration Service to the top of the Border Force is the thread weaving together this fascinating memoir-cum-social history of immigration control, and of London, from the 1970s to today. It is a trenchant and fair-minded account of a service struggling with many conflicting pressures and generally dealing with them in a humane manner, with just a hint of nostalgia for the simplicity and common sense of the old days."

David Goodhart, journalist, author, commentator UK Policy Exchange

"A candid account of life at the sharp end by a man who rose from the front line to very top of the UK Border Force. If you want a rigorous and humane immigration system, read this book!"

Sir Mark Sedwill, former UK Cabinet Secretary and National Security Advisor

"Tony Smith is one of the world's foremost authorities on border management and controls. I should know. As Commissioner of U.S. Customs and Border Protection (CBP), I saw Tony in action in the immediate aftermath of 9/11. Tony was a key part of the Canadian team that worked with me and others at CBP as part of the Smart Border Accords, a binational effort that included some of the most innovative measures ever taken by two countries to keep their mutual border open and moving, despite the threats posed by global terrorism. We proved that with smart border approaches, we could both secure, but also facilitate the movement of people and goods across our mutual border. Later, Tony led the creation of the U.K. Border Force that built on the notion that, like the U.S., better border security can be achieved by eliminating the fragmentation of responsibilities of multiple border agencies (Customs, immigration, agriculture and environmental protection, etc.) and consolidating the personnel and functions into one agency, one single border agency to protect and manage all aspects of the border. More recently, Tony and I have served as the co-chairs of the International Summit on Borders which has allow him to share his wealth of knowledge broadly to border officials of many nations. A colleague and friend, Tony's memoirs of *Changing Borders,* and what changed them, is a must read for anyone interested in border control and government policies relating to border management and immigration."

Robert Bonner, Former Commissioner, U.S. Customs and Border Protection.

Tony Smith CBE

Former Head of the UK Border Force

Changing Borders

A Kingdom Unlocked

From Immigration Service to Border Force

Quadrant Books

First published in 2021 by Quadrant Books
A member of the Memoirs Group
Suite 2, Top Floor, 7 Dyer Street, Cirencester, Gloucestershire, GL7 2PF

Copyright ©Tony Smith CBE 2022
Tony Smith CBE has asserted his right under the Copyright Designs and Patents
Act 1988 to be identified as the author of this work.

The moral right of the author has been asserted by them in
accordance with the Copyright, Designs and Patents Act, 1988
All rights reserved.

No part of this publication may be reproduced, stored in a retrieval
system, or transmitted in any form or by any means, without the prior
permission in writing of the publisher, nor be otherwise circulated in
any form of binding or cover other than that in which it is published
and without a similar condition including this condition being imposed
on the subsequent purchaser

Reasonable efforts have been made to find the copyright holders of
any third party copyright material. An appropriate acknowledgement can
be inserted by the publisher in any subsequent printing or edition

A catalogue record for this book is available from the British Library

Changing Borders: a Kingdom Unlocked

Paperback ISBN: 978-1-86151-062-4

Typeset by Ray Lipscombe, Cirencester
Printed and bound in Great Britain

This book is dedicated to the fine body of men and women, past and present, who work day and night, all year round, to protect our borders. May the Force be with you.

INTRODUCTION

There are few topics that foster more argument than immigration and border control. Some people want open borders and the complete free movement of people. Others want to build walls and fences to keep people out. Tensions run high on both sides and can divide governments and nations alike.

For those working at the sharp end of immigration and border control, it is like walking a tightrope.

This is the story of a lifetime in border control – from a young immigration officer starting out on the line at Heathrow in the seventies, through to reaching the dizzy heights of becoming Head of the UK Border Force after the London 2012 Olympics and beyond. It picks up the story of border control from one of my predecessors – TWE Roche – who wrote about the history of the UK Immigration Branch from 1066 to 1969 in his book "The Key in the Lock".

In Part One, my story winds through the tightening of immigration controls on Aliens and Commonwealth citizens in the 1970s under the Immigration Act 1971, through to the complete abolition of immigration controls on European Union citizens in the 1990s. It describes the growth of organised immigration crime rings in the 1980s, through to the huge surge in asylum applications at the UK Border in the 2000s.

In Part Two, we see how immigration control and terrorist travel became inextricably linked after the 9/11 attacks in 2001, and how border controls adapted to the birth of "home grown terrorism" after the 7/7 attacks in London four years later. As far as I know, I am the only person to have been Director of Ports of Entry in two different countries – Canada and the UK – during times of terrorist attack. Looking back, I suppose it was inevitable that I would end up leading the UK border security programme for the London 2012 Olympic Games, in the hope that lightning could surely not strike thrice in my extraordinary career.

In Part Three, I cover a range of high-profile border related events that have happened since I retired from public service in 2013. From the disappearance of flight MH370 in Malaysia in 2014 to the birth of the Australian Border Force in 2015; from the Paris and Berlin attacks to the EU Migrant Crisis in 2016; from the Windrush scandal in 2018 through to Brexit and the Irish Border in 2019; and from migrant boats in the English Channel to the impact of COVID-19 at the border in 2020 to date.

There is never a dull moment in the world on border control.

In writing this book I was encouraged by many literary experts to focus solely upon the subject of border control, rather than on my personal story. But in my case, the two are inextricably linked. The Border Force (or the Immigration Service as it was once known) is my extended family. I have spent nearly 50 years of my life working in this business, and I'm not done yet. And - as the story shows -my personal life would not have turned out as it did, had I not embarked on this extraordinary journey in the first place.

This is my story. In writing it, I have named many people, ranging from friends and colleagues through to senior civil servants and politicians. Of course, their perspective and memories of some events may differ from mine. But throughout my life I have always tried to treat everybody with respect regardless of their status, political opinion, or background. It has been an honour and a privilege to know and work with them all.

CONTENTS

PART ONE
The Early Years – 1972-1999

PART TWO
North America and beyond – 2000-2013

PART THREE
Life on the outside – 2013-2021

11 September 2001: Calgary, Canada

The phone in the hotel room rang. "Hey Tony – you awake yet?"

"Well, if I wasn't already, I am now Jaise. What's up?"

"Turn on your TV and take a look."

"Holy shit!"

The second plane smashed into the Twin Towers. Smoke and screams were emanating from the TV.

"What are we going to tell the conference?" I mumbled, still trying to come to terms with the fact that the USA was under attack. And most of the US and Canadian Border Agency leaders were here in Calgary, with me.

"Well, when you've figured that Tony, the guys are gonna want to know what they should do."

"About what?" I asked.

"About the border. Word is that the US have closed their border and three hundred flights are being diverted to Canada."

"Blimey!" I said, reverting to my native tongue as my mind raced around the scenario.

"Blimey for sure Tony – you had best get down to the lobby. In case you forgot, you are the Director of Ports and Borders in this country."

PART ONE

The Early Years – 1972-1999

CHAPTER 1

My First Immigration Service Interview, Adelaide House, London Bridge

"So why do you want to be an Immigration Officer, son? Do you know what you're letting yourself in for?"

I gulped and took a deep breath. I didn't know. Why did I want to be an Immigration Officer? Did I even know what an Immigration Officer was?

I just wanted a job really. It was the Summer of 1972. I was 18 years old and about to leave school. I needed a job. The careers teacher at school told me to try the civil service. After filling out a few forms and passing a test, here I was – somewhere in the "Port of London". Or rather in a dark and dingy office at London Bridge, being glared at by a bloke who must be at least 70 years old. An Inspector from the "Immigration Service" who looked as though he was about to eat me for breakfast.

"Well sir, I have worked hard at school and I got my "O" levels and my "A" levels. My careers teacher told me I could be an EO in the Civil Service if I got two "A" levels. So here I am."

The Inspector stood up and gazed out of the small window across the Thames towards London Bridge station.

"The Civil Service? This isn't the bloody *Civil Service* son. This is the *Immigration Service*. You will be an Immigration Officer, not an Executive Officer. An IO, not an EO. We are a different breed entirely. And I need to know if you've got what we need."

I wasn't sure if I did have what he needed. He looked at me over his horn-rimmed spectacles. I knew he was pretty high up in the organisation. I didn't know how high up. The letter inviting me to the interview had said, "HM Inspector, Immigration Branch, London." I knew that an IO was about the same grade as an EO, and I had learned that the next grade up to this was a Higher Executive Officer or a Chief Immigration Officer. And this guy was higher than that. Although he had obviously spent a big chunk of his life getting to this level. He looked like an old sea captain. No uniform, just a plain grey suit, white shirt, and dark tie. But there was something in the ruddy complexion that indicated a history of life at sea, a face coloured by wind and rain, and probably fuelled by a fair degree of alcohol along the way. This face had spent most of its life outdoors, certainly not sitting in an office reading and writing, which is what I thought people at the Home Office did.

"You're a London lad, aren't you?"

Not hard to spot. I was born in St Thomas's, just up the river from where we stood. Not quite within the sound of Bow Bells, but close enough.

Mum and Dad had met in Central London. Dad (Ron) was one of a family of 12 siblings brought up in Newbury, Berkshire. Most of the boys served in the armed forces, during or after World War 2. Dad became a member of the Royal Horse Guards, doing regular shifts keeping guard on horseback outside Horseguards Parade in Whitehall in his fine ceremonial uniform. Mum (Meg) was living nearby – her father was a canon who had been posted to the Society for the Propagation of the Gospel in Lambeth when she was 14, and she was educated at the famous Greycoat school in Westminster. She took great pleasure in strolling down Whitehall after school with her schoolmates to show off her handsome soldier boyfriend, who sat proudly on horseback trying not to react to the pointing and giggling schoolgirls in front of him. Dad always spoke fondly about his time in the Royal Horseguards, not least escorting the young Princess Elizabeth to her wedding at Westminster Abbey in 1947 as an "outrider".

The story of Ron and Meg Smith is strong enough to merit a book of its own. The fact that they fell in love so young and stayed together for their entire lives, through thick and thin, is an inspiration. Their courtship survived his posting to Berlin, and they married in 1952. I came along about 18 months later.

Life was tough for us in those early days. After demob Dad moved into the grocery trade and Mum became a secretary. They rented a maisonette in West Drayton, where I first went to school, then Dad got a job as a van salesman with Mr Kipling Cakes in Hammersmith. We moved to a one-bedroomed flat in Shepherds Bush when my younger brother (Michael) and I were still small. Mike and I had the bedroom, and Mum and Dad slept on a sofa bed, which they made up every night in the living room. There was an indoor toilet, but no bathroom. Bathing took place in turn in a tin bath filled by a hot water tap and hosepipe run from the kitchen tap, then drained by baling with a bucket into the kitchen sink. We were on the third floor, so washing was suspended on sticks and lines from the window to dry. Our "garden" was a communal yard behind the flats, where we frequently got into trouble for smashing windows with our football. I attended Victoria Junior Boys School in Shepherds Bush, and thus began my lifetime association with Queens Park Rangers football club.

I was fortunate enough to pass the eleven plus and secure a place at St Clement Danes Grammar School in Du Cane Road,

Shepherds Bush. Du Cane Road was also famous for housing Hammersmith hospital and Wormwood Scrubs prison. Dad told me that the word in Newbury was that the only time old Grandad Smith ever bought a round in his local was when he heard that one of his vast array of grandchildren had made it to grammar school. A rare occurrence in those days.

Although we weren't angels at Clement Danes – and there were a few devils amongst us – our boys were generally well disciplined and well behaved. A few turned out to be criminals in later life, but nothing like the number from local Comprehensives, which were riddled with bullying and gang wars. I did suffer the odd battering from the bullies at Christopher Wren – I had to walk past there on my way to school and back – but nothing serious. And I learned to look after myself in the odd playground brawl. This was standard practice in the back streets of Shepherds Bush in those days, so nothing much out of the ordinary.

I went through most of the fashion phases of the sixties and seventies. This included the famous "skinhead" era, where we wore boots, turned-up jeans and braces. I became one of the "Loft boys" at QPR and got involved in a fair few skirmishes when it was fashionable for away fans to try to "take the Loft". Fans were not segregated in those days, so it was quite common for one group of fans to rampage round the ground to the other end looking for trouble. Policing tactics were different too – they would just wade in wielding truncheons, grab a few of us, and march us unceremoniously out of the ground. This happened to me a few times and on one such occasion I was forced to crawl out underneath the turnstile. The arresting officer chose to kick me on the derrière as I went through, causing me to hit my head on the turnstile, much to the amusement of his mates (and mine).

These days there would be all kinds of complaints and investigations for things like that, but for us it was just part of the growing up process. It certainly did me no harm. If anything, it taught me right from wrong, and the importance of some form of authority to instil a sense of discipline in young men. Political correctness is all well and good in the right measure, but I spent a great deal of my career working in law enforcement with some excellent police officers, some of whom were often afraid to exercise their powers to the full extent for fear of political recrimination.

Along the scale of good boys and bad ones, I suppose I was around the middle. I worked hard in class and enjoyed my fair share of mischief too. I can remember those famous cross-country runs that took us out of the school gates, right along Du Cane Road, right again between the hospital and the prison, and up to Wormwood Scrubs. The course then took us on a full circuit of the Scrubs and back to the school, the same way we came. I was never a great runner, and a group of us noticed that there was a café along the route which would be a useful hiding place, so whilst our esteemed classmates were struggling round the Scrubs in the wind and rain, my mates and I were diving into the café for pie and mash and a cuppa, then re-joining the pack on their way back. This worked well for a few weeks until somebody told the PE teacher, who caught us red-handed one day. We were all subjected to a severe dose of "the slipper" – so severe that I really did find it hard to sit down for a few days afterwards.

Corporal punishment was quite normal in school in those days, and almost expected for those boys who broke the rules. I am sure one or two of the teachers were sadists. One took great pleasure in requiring transgressors to kneel in front of the class with their arms raised. As soon as the arms grew weary and started to drop, he would bring both his palms down simultaneously on the poor lad's ears. Others thought nothing of throwing chalk and board wipers at boys caught talking during lessons, and the worst offenders were sent off to see the headmaster for a caning. Whilst these practices were clearly wrong – and have (rightly) been banished from the classroom nowadays – I have to say that I don't think they caused us any serious harm. In many respects they kept us in order, for most of the time.

My mind wandered back to the interview.

"Yes sir. I have just left school and I need to get a job now."

"So, you want to work in London then?" He looked at me quizzically – almost suggesting that I must be a bit crazy to limit my horizons to my home city.

"Yes sir. I am getting married, and I need to get a house of my own. So, I need to start working now".

I had met Marilyn when I was 14 years old. She went to Burlington Girls' school, which was next door to Clement Danes. She came from a local family in Shepherds Bush, and we hung around together, riding round the streets of W12 on our bicycles. We had our first date at the Hammersmith Empire, where we watched "The Sound of Music", and we started going to the Hammersmith Palais together when we were old enough. It was common for teenagers to get engaged in those days – not just me, but most of my mates too. Except the nerds who applied to UCAS to go to University.

I did manage to pass six 'O' levels, which was enough to secure a place in the sixth form. However, my main passes were in English, French and Maths, which was not the right combination for "A" level. I was told I had to opt for the arts or the sciences. Given my dismal performance in Physics, I thought the arts were a better bet, so I took English, French, and British Constitution.

My best A level score was in the latter; again ironic, given that I was to go on to serve in the highest levels of government in later life. In fact, I went on to manage a fair number of people with university degrees from places like Oxford and Cambridge, belying the myth that it is impossible to reach the upper echelons of the UK Civil Service without the right "old school tie". Although that, of course, depended to a great extent upon who was on the selection committee.

By the time the sixth form came around, our parents could hear wedding bells in the distance. So could we. Most of my mates were getting engaged to their childhood sweethearts by the age of 18 and were already working full-time. Only a small number of them remained in school, and none were the brightest or the best.

I remember one classmate in particular, called Graham. He had just scraped into the sixth form, and he was in my French class at "A" level. It became a standard joke that whenever he was singled out to translate a French word into English, Graham would just stare blankly at the teacher until he gave up and asked someone else. Graham was a good-looking lad with an eye for the ladies and it was common knowledge amongst us that he spent most evenings partying, rather than preparing for his French classes. During one lesson the teacher invited us to translate "balayeuse". Even the nerds in the class looked at each other blankly when Graham's hand shot up. "Yes Graham?" enquired the teacher. "Road sweeping machine, sir" came the prompt reply. I almost fell off my chair, as did most of the class. I never quite know how he did it, but to this day I still smile to myself when I drive past a road sweeping machine and recall that moment.

"Well, I don't know why you are here. We're a mobile grade son. We work all over in the country. We go where the Chief Inspector wants us to go. If he wants you in Liverpool, or Belfast, or Prestwick, then that's where you will go. And wives? Well, it takes a certain type of wife to put up with the lifestyle of an IO. You'll have to work shifts. All hours. Night shifts. If you are lucky, you'll get to do crossings. You might even get sent abroad. Would your girlfriend be happy with that, son? It's a man's world in the Immigration Service."

I started to feel a bit sick. I hadn't expected this at all. I thought I would get a job at London Airport. Marilyn would not want to leave London; it would be hard enough to get her out of

W12. She needed the comfort of her close-knit family. That was her life. Her Mum didn't know how to get across the river when Hammersmith Bridge was closed. I did not want to be stuck on some ferry in Belfast with all these sailor men with big red noses at some ungodly hour. I wanted to play football with my mates and see my girl at night-time. And go to QPR. Sod this for a game of soldiers.

The Inspector stared at me and sighed. "Look son it's your life. I must decide whether you've got what it takes to be an IO. I've read your file. Sure, you can read and write. And sure, we can knock you into shape. But you have to have the heart for this job – and I'm not sure you have."

I knew he was right. This Immigration Officer thing was not for me. I got home, got my pen and paper out, and wrote to the Home Office. Please give me a job in London that is not in the Immigration Service.

Four weeks later I was reporting to the Immigration and Nationality Department of the Home Office at Princeton House, High Holborn. I was to become an Executive Officer in B1 Division, dealing with applications from "aliens" wanting to extend their stay in the country. The Immigration Service was no more than a bad dream.

Little did I know then that I would not only spend most of my working life in the Immigration Service, but would go on to become the only Immigration Officer to rise up through the ranks to become interim Director General (Grade 2) level of the UK Border Force – two grades above the post that was once known as the "Chief Inspector" of the Immigration Service.

CHAPTER 2

Granting Extensions of Stay: the Aliens Department and the birth of Lunar House, Croydon

I reported to the Immigration and Nationality Department at Princeton House in High Holborn on 16 October 1972. This was my first "real" job. Of course, I had taken temporary work before this. My first job was working in Harry's Greengrocers in the Shepherds Bush Road. Thursday night, Friday night and all-day Saturday for twenty-seven shillings and sixpence, plus tips. I had also worked in Woolworths in Ealing as a warehouse assistant, and in Lloyds Bank as a clerk. But these were all temporary roles. This was different. The Home Office was a career.

I was ushered into a room with about 16 other new recruits, where we were gradually sifted into groups. Some were headed to other bits of the Home Office. We were whittled down into smaller groups until we were in pairs. I was twinned with a stunning blonde called Janet. Like me, Janet was getting engaged, but neither of us could deny the mutual attraction that prevailed between us. Janet was a posh bird from Weybridge. I was a working-class lad from Shepherds Bush. This was the first time that it dawned on me that there might be another world out there beyond Marilyn and West London.

Janet and I did go out together once or twice. There was clearly something between us, but we were both committed elsewhere and chose to follow our heads rather than our hearts. A dilemma that was to come back to haunt me in later life.

We went through our EO training at Princeton House, in High Holborn. We were taught about Home Office files. How to write minutes on the minute sheet of the file, which was always attached to the left-hand side of the file with an India tag, inserted through a hole two thirds of the way up the page. Not half-way, not three quarters; two thirds. The right-hand side of the file was reserved for documents received from, or sent to, the applicant. This invariably included a "pouch" which contained the applicant's passport. Holes and India tags also attached these. This was fine until the tag broke off and the passport fell out in a cabinet somewhere, thus necessitating a call to the "Special Search" team who spent their working lives searching cabinets for lost passports so that some poor foreigner could get their passport back to travel.

During my training the Aliens Branch, together with the rest of the Immigration & Nationality Department, was relocated to a grand spanking new building in Croydon, Lunar House, in Wellesley Road. Lunar House and its sister building next door, Apollo House, were a classic example of 1970s architecture, 20 floors high with a three-storey "podium" attached, complete with a pond and fountains below. In fact, it occurs to me that even 50 years later the pond was never filled with water, more with dirt and grime that whistled in the wind between the stilts upon which the building was built. I have traversed the world and have seldom found anywhere as windy as the car parks below Lunar House and Apollo House, which were strong enough to knock the hapless officials who worked there completely off their feet on a bad day.

We had by now moved from Shepherds Bush to South Ealing, and the journey from West London to Croydon was much harder than getting to Central London by tube. I had a motor scooter in those days and can vividly remember navigating my way round the South Circular Road to Croydon on it in the freezing cold and rain, then having to sit by the radiator in the office to thaw out.

After I passed my driving test, I could only afford an old clapped-out Austin A40. That was good enough at least to keep me warm on the journey; but the clutch was on the way out, and I couldn't afford a new one. It got to the point where I had to alter my journey home and go via Streatham rather than Wimbledon, in the certain knowledge that the car would not be able to get up Wimbledon Hill.

After six weeks of training, we were divided into groups led by Higher Executive Officers (HEOs). I was sent to Group 13 in B1 Division (Aliens). Janet was sent to Group 8 (also Aliens). Others went to B3 Division (Commonwealth). There was a different set of rules for Commonwealth and Aliens in those days, with Commonwealth citizens receiving much more favourable treatment – at least until the passing of the Immigration Act 1971, which came into force on 1 January 1973. Alien files were green, and Commonwealth files were yellow.

I soon got to understand the hierarchy of the grading structure. The Home Office was then (and still is) hugely "gradist". As an EO, I was a manager. I oversaw the Clerical Officers (COs) in my group. The COs did not have "A" levels. They only had "O" levels. They had to work at CO level for a few years, then seek promotion to EO. But CO was not the lowest entry level to the Home Office. That was reserved for the Clerical Assistants (CAs). The CAs had neither "O" levels nor "A" levels. They reported to the COs. The COs reported to the EOs, and the EOs reported to the group leader, who was the HEO. (These grades still exist today, save for the fact that the word "Clerical" became outmoded and was replaced with the term "Administrative". Thus, CAs became AAs and COs became AOs).

So here was my first taste of management. I was an 18-year-old kid straight out of school managing COs and CAs who were generally older than me, and more experienced – but obviously not as clever as me, because I had "A" levels.

Grade determined roles and responsibilities. The CAs put files together, logged them in and out of the group, and made the tea. They were not allowed to write on the files. The COs could write on the files, but only to implement an EO's decision and to make any enquiries the EO wanted. The EO decided who got an extension of stay in the country, and nearly everyone did, but occasionally some poor alien got refused. The EO could not refuse an extension to an alien without referring the case to the HEO. If the HEO agreed, then the alien was refused. The passport was marked with a refusal (a secret signal which amounted to underlining the date of expiry of leave in the passport) and the alien was sent a letter telling them to appeal or leave the country.

"Stats" were completed every Friday by each group. Each EO had to declare the number of cases they had cleared over the week, and the number of refusals they had issued. This was my first taste of performance management in the Home Office.

I quickly learned how to find favour in this system: aim for 80 files per week and three refusals. Clear more than that, and you are not taking enough care with each case. Clear less, and you are not pulling your weight. Refuse more, and you are a "head-hunter". Refuse less, and you are a "screaming liberal". I later learned that measuring performance in the UK immigration system was something that would continue to haunt the Department in its various manifestations throughout my entire career.

My early days in Group 13 provided me with my first taste of working in a team. School was never really like that. It was more like every boy for himself, except for sport, where you represented the school against other schools. My game was always football. St Clement Danes was a very good footballing school in those days. I was never good enough to make the first eleven, who reached the national schools cup final when I was in the fifth form. I turned out for the thirds. I also played Sunday morning football in the West London Sunday league – we had a pretty good side that went on to win the West London First Division title and the Open cup in later years. This enabled me to keep in touch with my mates from West London and gave me a social outlet outside the workplace, which was something I always found valuable.

My HEO was a spinster called Muriel who had been in the Department for years. She had worked her way slowly up to HEO level, and it was clear that she had now reached the pinnacle of her career.

The atmosphere in Group 13 was a bit like school though. The HEO had her own desk at the front of the room, while the EOs sat in a group of four desks facing each other, working on our files under her watchful gaze. The COs and CAs came next, all in the line of sight of the HEO.

There were two young EOs there, Angie and Geoff. Angie was a great character who worked hard and really wanted to be an IO (I wondered why, given my recent experiences of the IS). Geoff was a brash Yorkshireman who hated the IS with a vengeance and vowed never to join. The fourth desk was vacant when I got there, but it was later filled by an IO from Heathrow called Andy Michael. Andy went on to become a legend in the IS and he holds the dubious distinction of being the first IO to have introduced a young Tony Smith into the ways of the UK Immigration Service.

The interaction between Andy and Muriel was a source of great entertainment. Muriel was very prim and proper, always punctual and extremely organised. She had her own individual tea service on her desk – matching teapot, teacup, saucer, milk jug and sugar bowl – and she would tiptoe out to the kitchen every 90 minutes or so to wash up her gear and make her next cup. I soon learned that a good time to refer a case to Muriel was shortly after her latest brew. She did like a little natter over a cup of tea.

Potential refusals were usually based on an inadequate amount of documentation to support the applicant's case. Students needed to submit a letter from a college showing that they were registered for full time study at a "bona fide" educational institution. They also needed to produce evidence of funds, usually in the form of a bank statement. There was little investigative work involved in this. It might be appropriate to telephone a college for an "attendance check", but without any field investigations it was hard to tell whether these were genuine students or illegal workers simply using the "student" cover to get an extension of stay stamped in their passport. Abuse of the student rules was a continual challenge for the Department, and in later years it was something that brought me into contact with international organised crime gangs.

Muriel's first test was always to look at the photograph in the passport. If somebody "looked nice" then there was very little chance of Muriel agreeing to a refusal. But if they looked mean they would have a mountain to climb to get her approval for a further extension. It soon dawned upon me that the process by which foreign nationals got to stay in the UK back then was often based on the whim of the senior caseworker, and I was amazed that people's lives could be affected by something as simple as how they looked on the day that their passport photo was taken. When the International Civil Aviation Organisation (ICAO) started to issue rules about the standard of passport photos – including a prohibition on smiling, to satisfy facial recognition systems – it occurred to me that Muriel's refusal rate would likely have been a lot higher if she had worked in a later era.

Andy's approach was quite different. He was loud and brash, far from punctual, and generally everything Muriel wasn't. He used colourful Cockney language (which I understood well but made Muriel shiver). He was mostly concerned about how the applicant got past immigration at the border in the first place – something that did not occur to the EO caseworkers, who had never worked at the ports. In those days, all foreign visitors and students were interviewed by Immigration Officers upon arrival at the UK border. They needed to satisfy the IO that they were genuinely seeking entry for the period of the visit as stated by them, and that they would depart the country within the period of leave given. So, by definition, the mere act of seeking an extension of stay after admission was potentially a breach of contract, whether or not the applicant qualified under the rules.

Immigration Officers prided themselves upon their investigative skills to get to the truth. They were used to human interaction, rather than process by correspondence and codification. They believed that there was no substitute for the "face to face" encounter with an applicant. Many argued that they had a "sixth sense" which enabled them to identify the genuine from the bogus. Documentation was only a part of the story. The whole was carried in the body language, the profile, the eyes, and the bags.

This dilemma would come back to haunt the Department in years to come. Many Directors and Senior Directors who entered the Department from outside did not recognise this as a critical piece of the process. Reputations were forged by developing codified systems to fit modern IT solutions and save money. It became sexy to dumb down the role of the Immigration Officer, preferring instead to opt for automated procedures that would put the system "online" and remove face to face interviews wherever possible. In the end, I found myself as the lone voice in the UKBA Senior Management Team in arguing against this obsession, where investigation and enforcement was dumbed down in favour of more efficient process flows and codification. Ultimately this was one of the major contributing factors to the

"Windrush scandal" of 2018, where innocent and legitimate long-term migrants from the West Indies suddenly found themselves being served with deportation notices, simply because there was no government record to confirm their lawful status in the UK. Whereas any self-respecting Immigration Officer back in the day would have been able to establish lawful status via a ten-minute interview, without any need for computerised back up.

Another Immigration Officer who joined us in Group 13 for a relief spell was TJ Huss, who turned up from Gatwick one week. TJ was nicknamed by his colleagues "the colonel" for his military and authoritative manner. He had a thing about bogus colleges and immigration fraud in Brighton, and he had already set up a joint intelligence cell with Sussex Police from his base at Gatwick Airport.

The colonel's approach to the job was one that has stood the test of time, both at the border and in the visa offices around the world, for decades. Sort out the wheat from the chaff quickly, clear the chaff, then get after the wheat. The colonel would spend most of his working day on the telephone, loudly speaking a language that like-minded officers in the field would understand (and often offending Muriel in the process). His mission? To disrupt the organised crime rings that have riddled the immigration system ever since controls were built. To arrest and deport the fraudsters, and to catch the criminals that brought them here in the first place.

Of course, this approach did not sit neatly with the 80:3 casework formula described above. As soon as he arrived in group 13, the colonel set about hunting through his case files to identify culprits from the "Brighton student ring". Instead of processing their cases at his desk, he took the files down to Brighton police station, so a few "students" who had hoped to get an extension of stay at a non-existent college via a smile on their passport photo and a bogus attendance letter soon found themselves being detained and deported for illegal working. The colonel saw this as a great success and went on to hunt down the facilitators who had brought this hapless group to the country in the first place, to prevent further misery for others – and to bring the rich slave traders to justice.

In fact, the colonel was years ahead of his time. Going after the fat cats behind immigration fraud was always a good narrative for any incoming Minister. It was always an easier argument to win than the immigration numbers game, with a schizophrenic media quick to jump on the "porous borders" argument, but equally keen to stand up for any individual hapless illegal immigrant facing removal – especially if the person concerned has gained celebrity status. Decades later I went on to lead some of the biggest ever immigration investigations, putting some human smugglers away for a long time and appearing in regional and national media to praise my hard-working crime teams for their efforts in breaking up these gangs. This was tough, painstaking and dangerous work that deserved better recognition at the top of the Department than it got. At the same time, it was a political hot potato, with many illegal immigrants being portrayed as victims of circumstance rather than criminals in their own right.

The colonel faced the same dilemma. It is all well and good enhancing the Department's reputation with major busts like this, but it means nothing if it impacts badly upon case-working productivity performance along the way. Whilst the colonel was running around Brighton doing his bit for the community, his files were piling up around his desk in group 13. He had committed the cardinal sin of resorting to crates on the floor, full of files of the chaff, whilst he chased down the wheat.

This did not please the highly organised Muriel, who summoned him to a meeting with the Senior Executive Officer (SEO) the following Monday. This was high drama in Group 13. Being called to see the SEO was bad. It was like being called to the headmaster's office at school. We all awaited the outcome with bated breath.

The SEO at that time was Peter, who was a classic civil servant of his time. He had reached the exalted grade of SEO after many years of service. He did not need people like the colonel coming into his business and upsetting the status quo. Bloody IOs, who do they think they are?

Peter later gave me some words of wisdom before I set off on my Immigration Service career. He told me that there were two groups of IOs – the "drinkers" and the "non-drinkers". Only the latter were worth their salt – the former were a bunch of rogues and vagabonds who should never see the light of a promotion board. This made me chuckle in later years, as I sat in the Chief Inspector's office in Croydon drinking whisky and beer with the inner sanctum of the UK Immigration Service leadership team.

The colonel emerged from the SEO's office muttering expletives that ought not to be repeated here. Suffice it to say that this was ten times worse than Andy's cockney banter that had so offended Muriel. The colonel told them that he would "bloody show 'em", and he did. He started wading through his crates of files. By the end of the week he had cleared 240 cases – more than the normal weekly productivity rate of three Executive Officers. Needless to say, this did not get him off the hook. On the contrary, it caused even more problems for the hapless SEO, who then had to face questions from his Principal as to why the rest of his case working groups could not operate at the same pace. Peter did his worst and sent the colonel packing back to Gatwick.

I later heard that the colonel returned to the IS ranks as a conquering hero rather than under a cloud of failure. This experience was one I found telling in the years to come, as the whole future of the Immigration Service came into question because of its defiance of the philosophy imposed upon it by the case working and policy elite.

I spent two years working as an EO caseworker in Lunar House, between 1972 and 1974. After meeting up with Andy, the colonel and other IS colleagues, it soon became clear to me that I had made a big mistake by not joining the Immigration Service in the first place. The reality was that I would almost certainly be posted to Heathrow, which was expanding rapidly at the time. My chances of being posted away from London were very remote; any vacancies that did arise "in the sticks" were quickly snapped up by senior IOs from the South, looking to cash in on property prices and enjoy a better life elsewhere. Many of these officers originated from outside London – indeed the Scottish contingent was massive – and plenty relished the opportunity to disperse to ports closer to home, especially those with caring commitments back there. It was (and still is) the case that an Immigration Officer at a seaport or a smaller airport is a big fish in a small pond and often regarded as a pillar of the community. That does not apply in the vast arrivals halls at the major airports, where officers are seen more as small cogs in a much bigger wheel.

I also learned about the shift patterns. The Immigration Service made great play of the fact that they had to work shifts to cover the border. Most ports never sleep. Even when passenger arrivals stop in the dead of night there is work to be done, clearing up casework from the last arrival before the next one comes in. Immigration Officers (IOs) were already paid more than their "level" equivalents in the Home Office (EOs) by way of a "responsibility" uplift. Then they received a 16.5% allowance for "shift disturbance". On top of that – to cater for the social injustice of working at weekends – Immigration Officers received time and a half pay for Saturdays and double time for Sundays. Their salary scales were linked to the mainstream pay bands in the civil service, so they could expect to climb up the spine points with each year of service. The pay and allowances system in the Immigration Service sent the rest of the IND green with envy. It was quite possible for an IO with five years' service to take home as much as an SEO with 25 years' service. (I later wondered whether this formed part of the reason for Peter's vitriol towards the IS). The financial attraction of moving from the mainstream into the IS grades was a no-brainer, especially for a young lad like me, looking to get married and set foot on the housing ladder.

I applied to join the IS in 1973, but was turned down. I was never quite sure why that was. People didn't get feedback and appeals and grievances in those days. I just got a letter to say no. It might have been because I turned up late for the interview. More likely, they had read my file about my encounter with Captain Pugwash at London Bridge and decided that I needed a bit more time. Either way I often use this story as an example for young officers never to give up on their dream, even if they don't pass every Board along the way. I failed as many Boards as I passed on my way up the slippery pole, but I never let that deter me.

I was finally accepted into UKIS in the 1974 tranche, and received my posting notice to report to Heathrow Terminal 1 on 6 January 1975. By then I would have completed two years and three months as an EO. With hindsight, I am glad I did. It gave me a very useful insight into after-entry controls, something which was not readily apparent to Immigration Officers joining direct from outside the department.

The IOs on attachment to Croydon went out of their way to welcome me to the Immigration Service "family". There followed a significant number of sessions in a pub called the Alhambra opposite Lunar House (long since demolished), where lots of the IS allowances described above went on beer to wet the new IS baby's head. I have to say I thoroughly enjoyed the experience, although I did wonder if I was already starting to stray from the path advocated by my SEO and become an "IS drinker" after all. It certainly felt that way.

CHAPTER 3

Becoming an Immigration Officer on the Line, and First Refusals

There are many books which chronicle the history of migration to the UK, dating back to the Roman Empire when Caesar's fleet crossed the English Channel from the newly conquered Gaul and set up camp on the Thames. It is human nature to seek out pastures new. Some are motivated by money, some by greed, some by a sense of adventure, or a thirst for knowledge. Some have no choice – they simply must get away to have any chance of a decent life. Even the weather has become a factor, with millions of British citizens now owning property in Spain.

Equally, immigration control has always been an issue very close to the top of the political agenda. Immigrants – and especially asylum seekers – are often portrayed in the media as a drain on society and the fount of the nation's ills. This is the rhetoric of taxi drivers, who often joked that it was "all your fault then" when I told them what I did for a living. The immigration debate sometimes becomes dangerous and can fuel community tensions, which I saw first-hand on many an occasion. On the other hand, reticence can stifle debate about immigration policy for fear of drifting into racism (which is something completely different). For a full and thorough account of the history of immigration to the UK – and our attitudes towards it – I recommend "Bloody Foreigners" by Robert Winder.

In terms of controlling our borders, the most authoritative historical account is that of TWE Roche in "The Key in the Lock". Roche was himself an Immigration Officer, in the generation before mine. His book ends just as the vast jumbo jets have started to roll into Terminal 3 in the late 1960s. Roche describes the origins of the Immigration Service back to the Cinque Ports, and those who held the "keys to the kingdom" before air travel began. Much of this focus is around Dover as the original gateway to the UK. The Immigration "Branch" – later to become known as the Immigration "Service" – always had a strong spiritual home in Dover, where family dynasties have passed on the keys to the kingdom from generation to generation.

Roche's preface is particularly telling in seeking out the origins of the "Immigration Service culture" that became legendary. He says:

> "My special thanks go to all the rest of that great company of people who have been my colleagues in the Immigration Branch for more than a quarter of a century, who have moulded the very being of the Service to which I have been so proud to belong."

One of the sadder roles I undertook towards the end of my career was supporting bereaved families when officers who had given a lifetime service to the Immigration Service had passed away. I often sought anecdotes from former IS colleagues to assist me with individual eulogies that I delivered at funerals on behalf of the Department. In doing so, I learned of a world where the post-war civil service was built largely around young men who were drafted into London to work in the great Departments of State. Many of those young men were billeted in civil service "hostels", where great friendships were forged. This manifested itself in a world where professional and private lives became intertwined. Men would work together, play sport together and drink together.

It was from this cohort that much of the Immigration Service originated. Others joined after careers in the military, or in other services. This was exclusively a male domain – women did not enter the IS until the 1970s (although many had by then gained a strong foothold in the mainstream civil service).

There were major IS enclaves in place at the seaports. Southampton was a famous starting ground for some of the great legends of the Service, including Peter Tompkins (who went on to be the last "real" Chief Inspector), Colin Manchip (who made it to Deputy Chief and was often a great mentor to me), and John Caffrey (another Deputy Chief who followed Tompkins through the ranks in the eighties). Dover also expanded rapidly in the 60s and 70s as cross-Channel traffic increased, and many young men were posted there. Some went on to serve their entire career at the port. Then there was Heathrow, where Terry Farrage – another great IS leader who went on to become Director of Ports – grew up.

That is not to discount the significant enclaves of the Immigration Service that sprang up elsewhere. Much of the development of the Service followed the general trend of international passenger traffic, and the growth or decline of the major ports. For example, the port of London was once a very busy place for the Immigration Service. But as the big liners dropped away from the Thames, the Immigration Officers either moved elsewhere or turned their attention inward to enforcement (where I was later destined to play a significant role). Adelaide House on London Bridge – where I had my first interview - was once occupied by the Immigration Service, and the officers there had the dual role of patrolling the docks and undertaking enforcement visits in London. The Immigration Office at Becket House next to London Bridge station (which later went on to house some of the busiest local immigration teams in London) has its origins here. As the dual role of border control and inland enforcement became more enshrined into the ambit of the Immigration Service, so more "enforcement" offices sprung up in or around the major ports. This gave officers opportunities to broaden their careers by working both at the border and inland. It also had the useful side effect of breeding considerable experience in both disciplines.

I joined this unique brand of people in January 1975 and set off on a lifetime adventure that I could hardly have even dreamed about at the time.

Each new Immigration Officer was issued with their "kit" at the Immigration Service Headquarters (ISHQ) in Croydon, before travelling to their new duty station. I was allocated a large, solid briefcase with two keys, one which was to be retained in my locker at work and the other about my person. I was given a standard leather key wallet and chain for this purpose. The case number matched my warrant number – 1049. I was given a personal copy of the famous "suspect index" which was like a loose-leaf version of a telephone book, but with many spaces between the names and blank pages mixed in. This was my first taste of "watch lists" – something that would become very relevant to me in later life. I was also given my beloved warrant card – another topic that would become an issue in years to come.

Immigration Officers loved their warrant cards dearly. I was an Inspector at ISHQ in the early nineties when the "new warrant" was issued. This comprised a leather wallet containing a laminated card bearing the signature of the Chief Inspector (another practice that became sadly eroded with time) and a metal badge affixed to the front. The badge became such a symbol of the service that it was often mounted in a glass cover and presented to officers as a retirement gift, to sit proudly on their mantelshelves for evermore. Indeed, I know of one perched proudly on the mantelshelf of Mrs Lilly Green, mother of my late and dear friend Dave Green, who passed away in 2009. I delivered the eulogy at Dave's funeral in Streatham. Lilly invariably referred to the badge as a symbol of her only son's "other life".

Before I set off to Heathrow, I popped into the eighth floor to say goodbye to Muriel and the rest of my Group 13 colleagues in B1 Division. They included Dave – a CO who saw himself as a rock star with shoulder length hair, high heeled boots, and red bell-bottomed trousers – and John, a fellow QPR fan. I left Group 13 feeling as though I was departing the family home for a great new life adventure. I might even have detected a small tear in Muriel's eye as she wished me farewell.

I first reported for duty as an IO on 6 January 1975. I wore a suit and tie. There were no uniforms in those days – they were not brought in for IOs until 2008 (although Customs Officers were always uniformed). The IS had traditionally been a "plain-clothes" or "non-uniformed" organisation. Men were expected to wear jackets and ties (and usually did); women were still new to the job and wore what they liked. There was no "dress code" then, although this was introduced in the 1980s when a younger generation of officers started to push the boundaries a bit. I never quite understood this. I was always an advocate of uniforms, and I remember being a minority voice on the subject when it was discussed at IS Board level in the nineties. I certainly never understood why some officers felt that it was OK to act as keepers of the keys to the kingdom wearing scuffed boots and denims, or open-necked shirts.

"Right, you lot, you use this table when you are in this office. This is the bottom table, and it is for sprogs. You lot are sprogs.

When you get your knees brown, you might just get to sit at the middle table. After a few years you may even graduate to the top table. But know your place!"

This was Mike Moreton, the "training CIO" at Terminal 1. He was a tall, fair and handsome man who had previously served at the famous IS academy in Southampton. He also sported the famous "beer belly" that seemed to be part of the make-up of the IS constitution. I noted that Mike was particularly well spoken and seemed to be well educated, an observation that was enhanced when I later heard him switch to fluent Spanish.

Many Immigration Officers were also linguists in those days. The Department ran a series of "language tests" and offered "language courses" where there was a specific need (e.g. Greek or Turkish). The Department also paid language allowances, which varied depending upon the perceived difficulty of the language spoken. Standards were very high. I thought my French "A" level would be enough to get me through, but it wasn't. Although I scored 70% in the written form, I only achieved 46% in the oral, leaving me 4 points short of the overall 60% pass mark. Imagine my surprise, therefore, when I received a letter from HM Inspector David Hamilton congratulating me on my language exam passes and my particularly high mark in Spanish (something I had never spoken in my life). It turned out that they mixed up my results with another Anthony John Smith, an Immigration Officer at Terminal 2, who was less than impressed to see his allowances being paid to me. In fact, A J (John) Smith and I went on to become good friends, distinguishable only by our chosen first names (John and Tony) – or, as a last resort, by our National Insurance numbers. We were both known as "AJS" on the duty roster; we both served at Heathrow; and we both went on to work in Enforcement and Investigations together.

"Now you sprogs all need to be trained before I can let you loose on the control. I have a list here so listen carefully. Bob Dodd, Bob Tuff, Alan Woolston, Melanie Sales, Tony Smith…."

We all looked up. None of us had been introduced to one another – we had just been through a process of form filling to ensure the admin team had sufficient data to procure stamps, lockers, pigeon-holes and airport passes for us all.

"You lot are going to Harwich for training on March the third. Until then it is my job to find you something useful to do. The first thing is the SI. You will notice that your SI is way out of date. New SIs get printed in April. So, you have nine months' worth of entries to update before you can use yours. Here are the noting files." He pointed to some ring binders lying around on the tables, amongst the magazines, old newspapers, and dirty teacups. "Note that there are IL files and IL Gen files. The IL files contain the interport lists. Interport lists come out every day. It is your job to update your SI with additional IL entries before you go out on the control. When you are fully operational you will use your "yellow hour" at the start of your shift for this purpose. The IL Gen files contain interim instructions for you to read and digest – also during your yellow hour. Now I should tell you that updating the SI is not fun. Especially if you've been on leave, when it can be a pain in the arse. And for sprogs like you – with months to do – it is a balls ache of the first water."

I caught Bob Tuff's eye and we shared a snigger. This was language we understood. I wondered whether Mike Moreton came from the "drinking" or "non-drinking" fraternity described by Peter Pawsey. I suspected the former…

Like me, Bob was engaged and planned to marry later that year. He was a direct entrant – medium height and build, and very well turned out with sharp blue eyes and a good sense of humour. Bob became a good friend of mine in my early years – we played football together for Terminal 1 (Britannic) and both went on to serve at the Intelligence Unit at Harmondsworth before our paths separated.

Bob Dodd was another good friend who I met that day. He was my roommate at the Orwell Guest House in Harwich for seven weeks, during our training in March 1975. He also played for Britannic, but his greater skill lay in cricket, where he later represented Heathrow as a pace bowler.

One of my major recollections of those early days was the value placed upon staff who participated in sport – especially those that went on to represent their port or the Service in competition. One of the first approaches I had from a member of the top table was about sport. Tony Becks was a larger-than-life character who took it upon himself to interview the sprogs on behalf of the top table. We were all asked if we played football. Tuffy, Doddy and me all said yes and were promptly told that we were in the team to play against British Airways and the BAA ground at Harlington the following Tuesday. We were all quickly and miraculously switched onto early shifts for that day and told to bring our boots to work.

The Terminal 1 mafia had the early morning football shifts down to a fine art. The footballers were usually on the "B" shift – 7 am until 2 pm with a terminal meal break. The "C" and "D" shifts started later in the morning and ended up doing most of the work. The footballers were allowed to sit at the top table (even us sprogs) and were served breakfast, whilst the hapless C and D shifts rushed around covering all the fixed points and the arrivals. Although the shift did not end officially until 2 pm we were usually away before that, and off to Cranford Park or some other local football ground to start the match.

I was playing decent level Sunday football in those days and found myself playing centre half in my debut for Terminal 1 (known then as "Britannic FC"). We won 1 – 0. I scored the winner with a header from a corner and spent most of the rest of the game defending the lead. This did not go unnoticed by Tony Becks, and before I knew it, I got a phone call from an IO from Terminal 3 called Bob Mitchell describing himself in broad Glaswegian as skipper of "the fliers". Bob was also known as the "mad axeman" – it did not take me too long to work out why. The following Wednesday I became the sole Terminal 1 representative in the Heathrow IS team, known as "the fliers". They were a different league and mainly Scots, most of whom had played at a very decent level north of the border in their younger days. Playing with the likes of Ted O'Donnell, Fred Jennings, Chris Talman, Gerry Shields, and the Axeman himself helped me understand the hint of fear I sometimes saw in the eyes of those who lined up against the Scots in sport. Probably one of my more foolish errors of judgement in life was agreeing to accompany this lot to the England v Scotland game at Wembley, in the days when the "tartan army" took over Wembley stadium and most of London at the same time. A couple of the lads thought it would be great fun to identify me as "Unglish" as the crowd around us burned the flag of St George. I am probably only still here to tell the tale because Scotland won 1-0 that day!

Prowess in sport was extremely useful in those days. Officers spoke fondly of the "mafia" who controlled most of the shift patterns and work activities which could have a profound effect on working lives. Fortunately for me I possessed most of the qualities that soon endeared me to this crowd – although it later became clear to me that there was a lot more to the IS than this. In fact, this organisation was a family – a community of individuals that became lifelong friends rather than just work colleagues. At its height, the UK Immigration Service was the envy of the Civil Service, and the place where people wanted to be. It is ironic that this envy eventually became so powerful as to play a leading role in its downfall.

My Immigration Officer Training Course was an incredible experience. Having gone straight from school to the Home Office, I had missed out on the experience enjoyed by so many 18-21-year-olds at university. I had never really been away from home for any length of time before – or away from Marilyn, for that matter. It wasn't for long – only seven weeks – and I would be home at weekends. But for the first time, I tasted some of the

Immigration Service's spirit of adventure. I was pitched into a seaport with a crowd of other officers, holding between us the keys to the kingdom. In those few weeks we would learn, laugh, drink, work and play together. And I absolutely loved it.

The door to the kingdom at Harwich was represented by the passenger ferries that came in from Holland and Germany. The trainees would be put on the passport control under the watchful eye of a mentor. Ferries arrived at an ungodly hour in the morning. The aim was to get out of bed at the Orwell at 5 am, scrape the ice off the cars, drive down to the ferry port, and start the landing at 6 am. Some would go to "cars", others to "foots". Either way it was freezing, and we all wore overcoats. Car control was conducted through the open window of a small cabin out on the quayside, with gale force winds blowing in from the North Sea. It got quite crowded in there with the trainee, the mentor and the Special Branch officer.

The role of Special Branch at the border is another story. These were police officers from the local force but assigned specifically to the "Branch". Their interest was in criminality and security rather than immigration, so they did not handle passports at primary, although they would often ask us to hold the page open while they took down details of passengers.

We also had to learn about landing cards, which were completed by all foreign nationals entering the UK. These cards often needed to be copied and passed to Special Branch, or Box 500. We never learned what they did with them. This was another dilemma that haunted successive governments over the years. Who should capture what information from whom at the border; for what purpose; and who should they share it with, and why?

The ferry terminal was slightly more comfortable, but not much. These were draughty places where bleary-eyed passengers shuffled towards the control, frantically trying to extract passports from pockets and handbags. There were different lanes for "British" and "Foreign" passports. European Economic

Area passports went to "Foreign" in those days, before separate "EEA" lanes were created as EU influence over border controls expanded in later years (until Brexit, of course). Ultimately the "EEA" lanes and the "British" lanes merged into one – much to the chagrin of many older generation Brits who complained bitterly about it.

After we had "landed" the ferry – and assuming we were not on "embarks" for the outbound journey – we would retreat to the classroom for our daily programme of study. This involved several long afternoon sessions learning about Immigration Law. Unsurprisingly it was not unusual for students to doze off during these sessions – only to be quickly awakened by the booming voice of the Training Inspector.

These were heady days. There was not much to do in Harwich other than to head to the local hostelries. There was a police training facility there as well, and many local publicans made a living from the expenses of young immigration and police officers all competing to see who could drink the most beer. If there was such a thing as a "non-drinking" Immigration Officer (as described to me by Mr Pawsey) I did not have the pleasure of making their acquaintance in Harwich. Like many of the IS enclaves at the seaports, the Immigration Officers didn't just work together. They were part of the community. As such we were entertained at local folk clubs and working men's clubs as part of "the family". This is where I learned to live with hangovers. It was not unusual to be up drinking late into the night; but woe betide any officer who was not on the line in time for his early shift the next morning. We were in it together. And those breakfasts always tasted that much better!

Another aspect of the control that I learned at Harwich was the role of the Port Medical Inspector. Passengers came in all shapes, sizes, and conditions. Although it was never easy to spot those with physical illnesses, it was much more so with mental illnesses. The classic first two questions asked at passport control were "how long are you staying in the UK?" and "What is the purpose of your trip?". On one of my first shifts at Harwich I was faced by a middle-aged lady of perfectly normal appearance, who told me she was coming for three days to visit the Queen. Had this been part of a tourist group doing the rounds of the sights of London for a few days, this would not have been an unreasonable answer (Buckingham Palace was always a great attraction for tourists). But this was different. This lady told me she was personal friends with Her Majesty, and often took tea with her in the Royal Gardens. As the story developed, she also claimed to have a close relationship with several other members of the UK Royal Family; and indeed, with royalty all around the world.

Immigration Officers are empowered to refuse leave to enter the UK on medical grounds, but they are not qualified to judge medical condition in cases like this. Instead, they are required to serve the passenger with form IS81 (a notice requiring the person to submit to further examination) and then to "refer" them to the Port Medical Inspector (PMI). The hapless lady took great delight in repeating her story to the PMI at Harwich, who ultimately took the view that her entry to the United Kingdom was "not conducive to the public good" based upon her medical condition. He then signed a form port 30, which authorised me to "refuse leave to enter the United Kingdom" under the "Immigration Rules".

In those days, refusals and removals were inextricably linked. A form IS82 (notice of refusal of entry) was served on the passenger, and details of "removal directions" were added. At Harwich, this was invariably back to the Hook of Holland on the next available ferry (usually the one the passenger arrived on). A form IS83 (notice of removal directions) was served on the inbound carrier, notifying them that they were required to remove the passenger as directed by the Immigration Officer, and the passport was endorsed with an open date stamp with a cross marked through it, as a signal of refusal of entry.

The power to refuse leave to enter was vested by law in the Immigration Officer at the port of entry and it was usually enforced with due diligence. Unless they had a prior entry clearance, passengers had no right of appeal before removal and often found themselves back on the inbound vessel "before their feet had touched the ground", as many an old lag would say.

This was a power that became eroded over the years through the increased interference of the judiciary and the use of international instruments such as the 1951 Convention on Refugees, where the mere utterance of the word "asylum" at a port of entry placed forms IS82 and IS83 on hold – often for years – while others went on to argue the merits of the case. Although many asylum seekers had a good case to argue that they feared persecution if returned to their homeland, I never quite understood why this should apply to passengers arriving from "safe" third countries. At least, not until I rose through the ranks and learned about the huge national and international political factors involved in border controls – something which continues to haunt many world leaders to this very day.

Having completed my seven-week training course at Harwich, I was now a fully-fledged Immigration Officer and ready to take my place "on the line" at Terminal 1 Heathrow.

New trainees were allocated to a regular officer for "mentoring" for the first couple of weeks or so. This was where the true value of "experience" became clear to me. Heathrow was a completely different environment from Harwich. In those days Terminal 1 covered all British Airways flights to and from Europe. Rather than having just one or two main "arrivals" to deal with per day, flows on both inbound and outbound passengers were constant from around 6 am until 11 pm. Although perceived to be the quieter of the three Terminals, Terminal 1 received its fair share of casework in those days. Ironically, many of my early refusals were meted out to young Europeans on "economic" grounds. The onus upon passengers in those days was to "satisfy" the

Immigration Officer at the port of entry to the UK that they "were genuinely seeking entry for the prior of the visit as stated by them". In particular, leave to enter should be refused if there were grounds to suspect that the passenger intended to work or remain permanently in the UK. In those cases, an "entry clearance" (either a work permit, visa, or letter of consent) was required in advance.

Many inbound passengers came from countries that were not (yet) members of the new "European Community", and several were young people from southern European countries where the economic situation was significantly less favourable than that of the UK. Therefore, it was common practice for young unemployed people from places such as Spain, Greece, and Cyprus to come into Terminal 1 as "visitors" coming to see relatives in the UK – at least on the face of it – but with the true intention of coming to work. This turned into a game of "cat and mouse" with eagle-eyed Immigration Officers watching the inbound queues to see if they could identify the likely "duffers" (a colloquial term for passengers seeking entry by deception).

Some of my longer serving colleagues in those days had this down to a fine art. Whilst on the face of it a request by a passenger to enter for 2 weeks to visit his uncle in North London might seem reasonable – particularly when he was in possession of a return ticket and enough cash to last him for that time – this was often a "ploy" to gain entry as a visitor and then remain in London as an illegal worker for as long as possible. Which could be many years, given the lack of any meaningful immigration enforcement in those days. Many a story has been told by new entrants about the "hovering hand" of the mentor, where the entry stamp is about to be wielded, only to be intercepted at the last moment. Indeed, some tell of "inked hands" on mentors who sacrificed the backs of their palms to prevent a stamp coming down too soon on the passport page of a "duffer".

It was during this phase of my career that I learned a lot about the art of human deception and the willingness of people to tell lies in pursuit of their ambition. Passengers did not just practise this deception alone; it was often also backed up by their "sponsors" in the UK, and by a raft of forged documentation. This was where the true investigative skills of Immigration Officers came to the fore. Often entire life histories were fabricated to convince us that there was a genuine reason to go home after the visit; and it was far easier to believe it than to deny it.

One such case springs to mind as an example of the lengths to which some people will go. I was on duty at Heathrow when a young Uruguayan man arrived, having travelled all the way from South America via Madrid to visit his aunt and uncle in Scotland. His occupation – as specified by him on his landing card – was "ice cream salesman". Upon contacting his relatives in Scotland, I learned that they had recently opened an ice cream business in Perthshire and had been advertising locally for ice cream sellers, something that was certainly not skilled work and that could easily be filled by the local workforce. Yet both the passenger and the sponsor were adamant that only a short visit was intended, and that thereafter the passenger would return to Uruguay to sell ice cream. This was later belied by a baggage search revealing a letter of reference from the passenger's former employer in Montevideo wishing him good luck in the UK following the closure of his father's ice cream business there, and even a set of personalised ice cream scoops. This case – just one of many that I could recall from those early days – springs to mind because of the belligerence of the relatives who somehow managed to invoke the attention of their local MP and the Parliamentary Commissioner for Administration (ombudsman) to investigate whether I had exercised "maladministration" in refusing him entry and sending him back to Uruguay.

After about 12 months' investigation – where both the Chief Immigration Officer in the case (Paul Evans) and myself were subjected to far greater levels of interrogation than the passenger himself – the PCA grudgingly accepted that our decision was the correct one in law. Although we should not have been so hasty in issuing removal directions, so as to give his relatives in Scotland the chance to see him before he was sent home.

I later learned that "deferral of removal directions" became a classic ploy by immigration agents to buy time. The longer a person remained in the UK – even after refusal – the less likely they would ever be removed. If immigration control is to be effective it must be delivered instantly at the port of entry, or preferably before boarding. The longer the person remains the less likely removal becomes, as subsequent applications to stay on grounds of illness, newly developed relationships, human rights and asylum weave their way through the painstaking bureaucracy and associated appeals and judicial processes. One ex-immigration Officer turned agent once told me that he could guarantee a person's stay of removal for at least two years – if not indefinitely – by playing the right cards at the right time, regardless of the true merits of the case. I had to agree with him.

I also learned another lesson from this case – beware those with influence and power, who will challenge the rule of law to undermine immigration control in cases that come close to home. People are fickle – generally they want tough border controls, but only if it doesn't affect anyone close to their kin.

I kept a record of all my cases, as I found it helpful to know the outcome. Often an officer would "pick up a case" towards the end of a shift, then pass it on to somebody else to conclude. If it was a complicated case, it would be passed over to "casework" for follow up enquiries. This was often the case out of hours or at weekends when the Home Office was closed. Although the Immigration Service was largely autonomous in those days, some cases still had to be referred to headquarters (ISHQ) for a decision. All records were paper based, so where a previous immigration history was involved, it was necessary to consult the Home Office file. In these cases, the only decision to be made was whether to grant "temporary admission" – effectively allowing the passenger to leave the airport on specific terms and conditions – or to "detain".

Short term detention accommodation was available on the airport in the Queens Building Detention Suite (QBDS) for a maximum period of five days. Longer term accommodation was available across the Bath Road, in Harmondsworth Detention Centre. Where temporary admission was granted, the passport would be kept on file at the airport and the passenger would be required to reside at a specific address, and to return to the airport at a specified time and date for further examination.

Although refusal statistics were relevant in the performance management framework, they were not the only indicator. There was a reasonable expectation that a certain number of refusals per officer would accrue, and certainly, there were a fair number of "head-hunters" around who were looking to get a high score.

Christmas and New Year were always good shifts to get if you were a head-hunter. For some reason that I was never quite able to fathom, more "duffers" chose to chance their arm over the Christmas holiday period than at any other time of year. I remember one officer – a Welshman named Bob Morley – who determined to get a hat trick of refusals one Christmas Day. He achieved this with hours to spare, proudly marching into the office with a passport held aloft in one hand and a cigarette in the other. Where Bob fell short – as with many other officers of that era – was in his written work. The case notes were sparse and barely legible, making it much harder for casework officers to pick up the thread later in the day. I always prided myself upon my case file preparation, documenting the case as best I could for others to read. I think it was this more than anything else that got me noticed by the Inspectors, who spent a good deal of their time reviewing case files.

I suppose our primary purpose in those days was to protect the economy and the indigenous workforce from illegal foreign labour. The UK has never really welcomed unskilled workers, taking the view that for the most part we have enough of those of our own. Therefore, work permits went to those professions where there was perceived to be a shortage. One such area was skilled waiters, looking to come and work in Britain's booming catering industry. To get a work permit as a waiter, applicants had to satisfy the Department of Employment that they had the necessary skills and experience to take up the post offered by a UK employer. Work permits had to be obtained prior to travel, then presented to the Immigration Officer at the port of entry along with a valid passport.

Immigration Officers smelt a weakness in this system. It was easy enough to produce paper references from abroad to an official in the Department of Employment, but it was much harder to persuade an eagle-eyed Immigration Officer that they were genuine. We received a fair number of permit holders from Greece, Spain, and Italy in those days. Many were manual labourers who had fabricated evidence of their experience, often in collaboration with a local café owner back home. We developed an agreement with one of the restaurants in the Terminal whereby passengers with these permits were given a "trade test" by the manager to see if they knew how to set a table for a five-course meal. Many failed and were refused entry because they had employed material deception to secure the work permit in the first place. Because a work permit was a form of entry clearance, they were given a right of appeal before removal, meaning that the manager of the Terminal 1 restaurant ended up devoting a good deal of his time to providing witness statements on behalf of the Immigration Service.

I can recall many cases where passengers blatantly lied to my face to try to get around the immigration rules. Like anybody else, I started life in the Immigration Service with an open mind. I had assumed that when questioned by an officer upon arrival in another country, people would tend to be honest. And for the most part they were. But there were clearly many who were well practised in the art of deception, and would openly lie about all manner of things to get in. This was where the true skills of the job came in. Even as a global border security consultant – surrounded by biometric recognition systems, data analytics, blockchain and the like – I have yet to see any technology capable of determining intent. In those days an Immigration Officer spent a good deal of his working life trying to establish just that, and often succeeding.

In addition to immigration casework, there were other benefits of working at a major airport. A week rarely went by without a celebrity passing through our controls. In those days, we checked passengers inbound and outbound, so there was always a good chance of checking the passport of somebody famous. I can remember the late great Tommy Cooper coming up to my desk with his wife.

"'Scuse me – which way is the duty-free shop?" he asked.

He had a twinkle in his eye which almost demanded a witty response. I couldn't help myself. In a gruff voice, and with a shrug of the shoulders that was his trademark, I replied:

"Well, it might be this way – or there again it might be that way."

We both collapsed in fits of laughter, as did most of the other passengers in the line. One thing I discovered about most celebrities was that they always had time for a chat with us and were not at all aloof, as the media often portray them to be.

That is not to say that all passengers are friendly and compliant. On one occasion I was on the British desk facing quite a long queue when a passenger presented a photocard to me and demanded to be admitted. Now I hadn't seen such a card before, so I asked him politely to produce his passport. That was obviously what he had been hoping for. In a loud voice – so that the entire queue behind him could hear him, he said, "Now listen here young man. This card is an Olympic Accreditation Card for the 1976 Montreal Olympic Games. If you had bothered to read your instructions you would know that it confers international travel across borders without the need to produce a passport, but you obviously haven't. So just get on with it and let me through, would you?"

Whilst I racked my brains to try to remember whether I had seen any such instruction, I was saved by a wheelchair pusher who was behind him in the line, with an elderly lady on board. He leant forward as if to whisper to me – but in a voice loud enough for everyone else to hear, and – nodding at the man in question – said, "Bit of a dick, is he?"

"Well yes, I suppose he is really," replied the Special Branch officer at my shoulder.

The crowd behind the man roared with laughter and he promptly went as red as a beetroot, pulled his British passport from his pocket, and handed it over to me.

I later learned that the Olympic Accreditation card was not in fact a travel document in its own right and had to be presented alongside a valid national passport for those travelling on IOC business. So, I was right to stand up to him, even though it's not always easy under pressure.

Ironically some 30 years later I was to find myself leading the London 2012 Olympic Accreditation system. This memory served me well in making sure that instructions to the front line were clear and unambiguous, about what the card could and could not do for the holder's entitlement to enter.

I had some good times at Terminal 1 and made some lifelong friends. We worked hard and we played hard. We had fun, but we took our duties seriously. By the time I had completed four years there I knew it was time to move on – but I also knew that UKIS was the place I wanted to be.

During this period Marilyn and I were married on 16 August 1975, just eight months into my UKIS career, at St Luke's Church in Uxbridge Road, Shepherds Bush. The date had been arranged well in advance, mainly by our respective parents, who also took it upon themselves to arrange the reception.

Little did we know that our wedding date would clash with the QPR v Liverpool fixture that day, something that didn't please me or my mates, as it meant we would miss the game. The wedding took place at 4 pm, and the crowd came out just as we were having photographs taken outside the church. Although QPR won the match 2-0, the Liverpool fans were in good spirits and sang "Congratulations" to us as they passed by on their way to Shepherds Bush station. I was playing Sunday league football at the time and my manager, Geoff Burnhill, came over to tell me to make the most of it. This was the only time I would ever get acknowledged by the Kop!

I was (and still am) an avid QPR fan, and like all true Rangers fans I remember the 1975-76 season fondly. That was the closest we ever came to winning the league, with the great team of Bowles, Francis and so on. I even went to Norwich towards the end of the season for our last away fixture, where victory would have secured us the title. Sadly, we lost, then Liverpool beat Wolves 3-1 to pip us at the post.

We started our married life in a two-bed terraced house at Hayes in Middlesex, which cost us £9,500. We sold it two years later to a good friend and colleague from UKIS – Brian McAteer – for £12,400, and bought a three-bed semi in Windsor in 1978 for £67,500, at the height of the housing boom. This was to be our family home for the next eight years. Marilyn found work as a teacher in a local school, and I could get to Heathrow easily along the M4. Life seemed quite simple then. At least for a while.

One of the beauties of life in the Immigration Service in the seventies was the opportunity to "go on relief" to other ports of entry. My first relief stint came after about two years at Terminal 1 when I was allocated to the port of Sheerness for a month. The Isle of Sheppey in Kent was not the most attractive location for a posting – particularly in the bleak midwinter – but life at Sheerness port was never without incident.

One of the great benefits of relief was the capacity to earn "allowances". In those days officers were paid a reasonably generous rate of "night subsistence"; and were invited to spend it on accommodation of their choosing. No need for receipts or any of that nonsense. Sheerness was not blessed with many five-star hotels, but even if it had been, I doubt that many Immigration Officers would have stayed there. Most officers chose to find the cheapest accommodation they could, preferring to pocket their subsistence for other uses. I recall one officer sleeping on the office floor so that he could buy a new washing machine when he got home after his relief spell was over.

To cater for relief officers, a small community of landladies cropped up around the port, offering cheap bed and breakfast to young officers like me. I was fortunate to stay with Mrs Barker – known affectionately as "Ma" Barker – who was famous for cooking the most magnificent English breakfast. As with Harwich and many of the other UK seaports, the passenger ferry always arrived early in the morning, usually before dawn. It took us about two hours to clear the inbound ferry, then, assuming we had not picked up any "duffers", we would have an hour's break before we started the embarkation. This was more than enough time to nip back to the digs, where Ma Barker would have a huge English breakfast and a pot of hot tea waiting for us. I have been fortunate enough to travel the world and I have dined in some of the very best restaurants and hotels, but I cannot remember anything as mouth-watering as Ma Barker's breakfasts.

It was during my first stint at Sheerness that I first experienced the infamous "rope ladder". Before the days of e-manifests and advanced passenger information, the only way to clear cargo ships entering UK waters was to board them. In many cases these ships did not come to the dockside but remained anchored in the harbour, and the window for visiting them did not always fall at a convenient time of day, or during pleasant weather conditions.

I will never forget boarding a small customs launch in the middle of the night with colleagues from HM Customs and Special Branch to visit my first ship, anchored off the coast of Sheerness. It was customary to carry the Immigration Officer's official bag – carrying the famous "suspect index" and an assortment of landing stamps and general instructions – over the shoulder, fastened with a leather strap. As we approached the vessel a crew member would throw a rope ladder over the side and we would have to grab it, hang on for dear life, and steadily climb up the side of the hull to the deck. The return journey was equally perilous, particularly in choppy waters.

I remember that the "rope ladder" experience was often put forward as a reason not to admit ladies into the service, particularly by the "old guard". In fact, as women entered the service in later years and joined UKIS arrest teams they soon proved themselves to be just as agile and adaptable – if not more so – than some of their male counterparts.

My other noteworthy spell of relief was a wonderful three weeks at Plymouth docks in the summer of 1978. This was the year of the Argentine World Cup, Ally's army, Dutch total football, Kempes, Ardiles, and all that. The weather was superb too. What a summer that was.

The office at Plymouth in those days was at the end of a jetty, and a good 15 minutes' walk from the main town. As such it was prone to a significant battering from the sea, and there were huge metal shutters that had to be pulled down at night or during adverse weather conditions. The Immigration Officers who were based permanently at Plymouth had a great many years' experience behind them. Postings to places such as these were based mainly on seniority and they were seen as a great prize by many, often more so than promotion. Indeed, when I look back over my career, I often wondered what might have happened if I had chosen that route. I would never have achieved as much career wise, but the stress levels would certainly have been much reduced. I rarely saw an unhappy officer in ports like these, something I could not say about many of my colleagues at the larger ports of entry.

The "drinking culture" I had been warned about in UKIS was alive and kicking in Plymouth. Given the remote location of the office, it was customary for officers either to spend more time at the ferry port itself or – more likely – in the local hostelry. The local team soon realised that they could see inbound ferries from miles away from a viewing area in a pub at the top of Plymouth Hoe. They could track the vessel as it approached the harbour, so much so that they could tell (within seconds) the point at which it was time to drain their glasses, jump in the office car and head down to do the landing.

It was during my sojourn in Plymouth in 1978 that I undertook my first venture into inland enforcement work. Whilst on early duty in the office one day, I happened upon a small pile of Home Office files gathering dust in the safe. Much to the surprise (and amusement) of the regulars I took it upon myself to look at these. I remember asking first, only to be told that these were "local enquiries" sent down from IS Headquarters, which the local team would get around to someday when they weren't "too busy".

Of course, unlike them – despite their years of experience in the job – I knew these files well from my time in Lunar House. Where a caseworker had some doubts about an application and wanted a "home visit" it was customary to refer the case either to the "Aliens Branch" of the Metropolitan police, or, if the applicant lived outside London, to the local immigration office. It then fell to the Divisional Enquiries Officer of the nearest police station (if in London) or to the local Immigration Officer from the nearest port of entry (if outside London) to conduct the visit. Most of these visits were "marriage cases", where the aim of the visit was to check co-habitation between the parties (marriages of convenience have long been a tool to circumvent immigration rules).

Although inland visits in London were conducted solely by the police in those days (something which was about to change, as we will see in the next chapter), visits outside London were conducted jointly by an Immigration Officer and a police officer. In the case of Plymouth this would be a task for the local Special Branch officer.

During a quiet period, I went to the local SB office to suggest they might want to come out with me to an address somewhere to the North of Plymouth to check whether an Iranian man was still living with his British wife, whom he had married some 18 months previously. Leave to remain had been granted for the customary 12-month probationary period and it was now time to grant indefinite leave to remain if the marriage was still subsisting. A local officer named Fernley, with a very strong West Country accent, agreed to do so – provided I could arrange transport. Since the office car was being used as a taxi service between the pub, the ferry port and the office, the only option was to use my private car.

So off we went, with me driving and Fernley in the front seat. He was an experienced officer from the Devon and Cornwall constabulary – very well versed in the local landscape, and with a keen eye for any criminality in the area. As we headed out across town, I came up behind a lorry load of timber, which was rather precariously stacked, in front of me.

"'Ere does that bloody load look safe to you?" said Fernley, in his gruff West Country burr.

"No not really," I said.

"Me neither – pull him over."

So there I was pulling over a hapless trucker in Plymouth in my Mark 2 Ford Cortina so the local constabulary could detain him for "carrying an unsafe load". Fernley contacted the local highway police who turned out in force, creating lane closures and associated mayhem on the roads around Plymouth.

Having satisfied ourselves that this incident was under control, we continued our journey and found the happily married couple at home. They excitedly told us about their future together over a cup of tea, leaving me in no doubt that if ever there was a genuine marriage, then this was it. The applicant was a keen medical student who aspired to go on and serve the people of Plymouth as a surgeon. As we went to leave, he asked me (politely) why it had taken six months for this visit to take place. I didn't have the heart to tell him that it was probably because the local UKIS team in Plymouth were too busy eating and drinking in a local hostelry to get around to it.

I have happy memories of my time on relief as an IO back in those days. I thoroughly enjoyed the work, the company and the lifestyle. Immigration Officers in those communities were highly respected figures – alongside magistrates and police officers – and the job was a good one.

It still is, in some ports. One of the last things I did in the job – after 41 years' service – was to go up to Hull for an early shift out on the docks there. It is hard to understand the camaraderie that exists in these ports unless you have been a part of it. These officers work hard, often in harsh locations and inclement weather, to keep our borders safe and secure. It is a shame they do not always get the recognition they deserve, for what they do.

CHAPTER 4

THE BIRTH OF IMMIGRATION
ENFORCEMENT: THE IMMIGRATION
SERVICE INTELLIGENCE
AND INVESTIGATIONS UNIT,
HARMONDSWORTH

About seven years after my initial entry into the Immigration &
Nationality Department, I undertook my first venture into the
world of Immigration Enforcement.

At the time, UKIS was not well known for immigration
enforcement work. Their job was either to stop people at the
border, or, for the more senior and experienced officers, to travel
abroad as visa officers, interviewing applicants in far-flung places
such as Delhi and Dhaka (as we shall see later). Once somebody
was in the country, they were left largely to their own devices.

This began to change with the emerging concept of "illegal
entry". An illegal entrant was defined in section 33 of the
Immigration Act 1971 as someone who "unlawfully enters or
seeks to enter in breach of a deportation order or the immigration
laws". The definition has changed with various amendments

over the years, but at the time it meant people who had either been deported and had managed to get back in somehow, or people who had entered without first getting the permission of an Immigration Officer. In that sense, the powers to detain and remove an "illegal entrant" – as set out in Schedule 2 to the Act – were broadly like those that applied to passengers. Immigration Officers were empowered to arrest (without warrant) and detain illegal entrants and to remove them summarily from the country. There was no need to charge the person with a criminal offence, or to go to court to invoke the criminal justice system. These powers were very significant. Indeed, they have been the subject of huge political and judicial scrutiny ever since.

On the face of it, this did not seem an unreasonable power for Immigration Officers based at the ports. If a passenger were to dive off a ship and swim ashore, thus avoiding passport control at the ferry terminal altogether, why should he get a better deal than the person who presents himself to an immigration officer and is refused leave to enter? If a person tries to leave an airport by circumventing the passport controls and is intercepted at the perimeter fence, why should he not be detained and removed in the same way as a passenger who presents at passport control without the right documents?

The problem, of course, was that the concept of illegal entry was not just applied to those who had just arrived – known colloquially as those with "wet feet". It was more likely that illegals would not surface until some time after arrival – often many years after. They usually managed to survive in the community either with the help and support of friends and relatives ("harbourers") or by being exploited by unscrupulous employers. At some point, sooner or later, they would come to the attention of the authorities, either because they had been arrested by the police for some other matter or because somebody had chosen to inform on them, usually by writing anonymously to the Home Office.

As the numbers of "illegals" in the UK began to grow, so governments came under pressure to develop some kind of reactive force to deal with them. Most of the powers conferred in Schedule 2 to the immigration Act 1971 (such as to detain without trial, and to set removal directions) were only available to Immigration Officers and not to police officers. On the other hand, although Immigration Officers had statutory powers of arrest, they were not trained in their use and were not encouraged to use them. Also, somebody needed to start to do something with all the denunciatory letters and other forms of intelligence that were beginning to pile up in the Department. Not to mention the popular press, who were quite willing to print stories about the ever-increasing number of "illegals" entering and staying in the UK to discredit the government of the day.

The UKIS Intelligence and Investigations Unit (IU) was born in a small office in the Queens Building at Heathrow, in the early 1970s. One of its founders was Peter Tompkins, then an Inspector at Terminal 1, who went on to become the last "real" Chief Inspector of the UK Immigration Service. In the days before computers, intelligence was built around index cards containing various items of interest including names, addresses, passport numbers, suspect establishments and so on. In that respect it resembled the collators' offices that used to exist in police stations around the country before the advent of electronic records. As the index grew, it became too big to keep on the airport. It moved across the Bath Road to an old Ministry of Defence estate, which also housed other immigration facilities including a training unit, an appeals court, and the immigration detention centre. Although there were a small number of permanent Immigration Officers based there, the IU soon became a regular temporary posting for relief streams from Heathrow. Particularly during the quieter winter months at the airport when traffic was down. This was where my inland enforcement experience began.

My first memory of the IU was an attachment to the "Joint Overstayers Exercise" (JOE) at Harmondsworth, in 1979. I was selected for this alongside a small team of Immigration Officers across the three Heathrow terminals that existed at that time. Colleagues included Roy Kirkwood (from Terminal 1, like me); John Hughes and Henry Rooney (both Scotsmen who had originally worked in Dover and transferred to Heathrow Terminal 2 together); Billy "bad boy" Mulholland (another Scotsman from Terminal 3, who went on to become my great friend and partner in the JOE team); and Nigel Freer and Wendy Boden (which turned into the office romance, and subsequently one of many lifelong marriages formed from within the Service).

The origins of the JOE exercise go back to my experiences of my time as an EO in Lunar House. The UK has always struggled to build an "entry/exit" system – something which ultimately ended the career of my good friend and colleague Dave Roberts in later life. Dave fell victim to the infamous grilling of the Home Affairs Select Committee when, in a brief unguarded moment, he confessed to the chairman that he "hadn't the faintest idea" how many people were remaining illegally in the UK. He was of course right – nobody did. But an appearance before the HASC was more about political correctness and protecting the government of the day than being brutally honest. Dave was unnecessarily and unfairly vilified in the media in the following few days, with editors unmercifully running headlines that the Head of Immigration Enforcement in the UK "hadn't the faintest idea" how many illegals he was looking for. The whole thing became a political row, and, as is often the case these days, somebody had to take the blame. But more of that later.

In the 1970s the Immigration & Nationality Department built something called the "traffic index", which housed all the landing and embarkation cards collected from the ports of entry. Where somebody had been admitted on a "controlled" landing (ie, other than a visit stamp, where cards were not retained other than for statistics), the (white) landing card was flagged in traffic index in alphabetical order to await the arrival of the corresponding (yellow) embarkation card. Assuming the two cards matched all was well, and we could safely assume the person had complied with their conditions of entry and left the country.

Traffic index was a great source of employment for CAs in Lunar House. They were each allocated their own set of cabinets, which they guarded jealously. Many an Immigration Officer got his comeuppance if he had the audacity to do a search without asking permission. I know, I was one of them.

Anyway, the system worked in such a way that if, after a few weeks' grace, a yellow card did not turn up, then the white card was extracted from the traffic index, placed on a Home Office file, and sent to a case working group for action. Many of these came to me in my time in Group 13. My options were threefold. First, to send the file back to Traffic Index to see if the yellow card had turned up yet. Second, to assume embarkation on the grounds that the person had probably gone back anyway, and the yellow card had got lost or something. Third, to refer the file for a home visit. These files – known as "No Trace Embarkation" (NTE) files – were a great way of boosting your file clearance rate without achieving very much at all.

As indicated in the previous chapter, files sent out for home visits in London were sent to the "Aliens Registration Office" (ARO) – otherwise known as G11 Branch – of the Metropolitan Police. From there they were sent on to "Divisional Enquiries Officers" (DEOs) in the local police stations, for a home visit to the last known address. Invariably, some months later, the file would return from ARO with the DEOs report indicating that there was nobody at home when he called, or the person was not known at that address, or something similar.

With one or two notable exceptions, the DEOs were not really in the market for finding overstayers. They were usually senior beat officers approaching the ends of their careers and looking forward to retirement and a nice pension. The easy route was to call at the given address, ask a few polite enquiries of the householder (assuming anyone answered the door), and return the file with the subject either not known at the address or known to have moved on to an unknown location.

The function of the JOE team was to bring Immigration Officers into this process to work alongside the police in undertaking these enquiries. It was felt that IOs would be better equipped than PCs to make these enquiries (given their ability to identify "duffers"), but PCs still needed to be present to effect any arrests that may ensue.

I was allocated to F Division – Fulham, Hammersmith, and Shepherds Bush – which suited me perfectly. There I was patrolling the very streets I used to walk as a teenager, looking for illegal immigrants with the local constabulary.

It was here that I learned very quickly that asking people for passports in their homes is an entirely different proposition from doing it in the controlled environment of an airport. On my first visit to the notorious White City Estate, I happened upon a couple of Rastafarians who made it very clear – in no uncertain terms – what they thought of me, and the job I was doing. I eventually managed to get sight of their South African passports, which showed they had valid leave to remain in the UK as students, but their respect for authority was zero. I wondered how immigration enforcement worked in South Africa, and whether this kind of aggression was tolerated by the police there. The DEO accompanying me did nothing other than frown at me, look at his boots, and nod towards the door. But in any case, there was no sign of the person we were looking for, so we had no option but to beat a hasty retreat and apologise for disturbing them. After several visits like this we soon got to learn why the DEOs returned the reports they did. It is far easier to accept an account on the doorstep that closed the file than to provoke a row with the occupant. Community tensions in London were high at the time, and immigration enquiries like these would only serve to fan the flames.

But IOs being what we were, we were not going to leave it there. We were pretty sure that there were plenty of overstayers out there – we just weren't looking in the right places. So we took it upon ourselves to adopt a similar number of "denunciatory letters" for visits, and to compare the results to those we were getting from Home Office files.

The results were astonishing. Of 100 Home Office file referrals, only 6 were found. Even then they required follow up enquiries to trace them. By contrast of 100 denunciations, we found 160 offenders – more than 100%, because some visits yielded multiple offenders in the same location. If our mission was to find overstayers and illegal workers, then this was like shooting fish in a barrel.

Here I learned a couple of lessons about immigration enforcement, which probably saved the Home Office Immigration enforcement teams a lot of wasted time and effort in later years. Firstly, don't assume that overstayers will be at the address given on their landing card, or on the Home Office file. They won't. And secondly the UK had – and still has – a vast community of illegal entrants, overstayers and illegal workers living and working in its communities, and intelligence will lead us to the places where they are most likely to be found, should we wish to act upon it.

In fact, it has never been difficult to find immigration offenders in the UK in my experience. But it has become much harder to remove them from the country, especially if they are determined to stay. This is a problem that has become steadily worse over the years with the growth in asylum and human rights claims, and something that haunts immigration enforcement to this day. When I found myself leading immigration enforcement operations across London and South East London decades later, I made sure that we only took on cases where (a) we were satisfied that the intelligence was good and (b) that there was a realistic possibility of removal. Because – at the end of the day – what was the point of deploying scarce resources to detect and arrest immigration offenders simply to "close files"? If legislation and public consent demanded firm immigration controls, then we needed a system which enabled us to arrest and remove illegal immigrants. This policy has been consistently supported by governments of all colours during my 40-plus years in office, and since. Yet despite the tough rhetoric of incoming governments, removals have declined to the point where the whole existence of immigration enforcement has been brought into question. But more of that later.

Meanwhile, the spectacular success of the immigration enforcement JOE team in tracing overstayers in London did not go unnoticed. Our Chief Immigration Officer was Brian Smith, who took great delight in recording the "stats" the moment we got back to the office. Brian was a kind man, much more so than many gave him credit for. During this period, I managed to break my leg (or at least have it broken or me) during a particularly vicious Sunday league game. I found myself in plaster for about 18 weeks, and off work as a consequence. The boredom drove me to distraction, so Brian kindly arranged to pick me up from home on his way into work, load me into the back of his estate car (crutches and all) and help me into the office, where at least I could help with reports and background research before I was fit to go out on ops again. I remember that during this time there was a "major operation" in the West End, where Brian arranged for me to attend and work in the control room helping to collate results. This was another example of the UKIS culture – we looked after one another.

The main lesson we learned from the JOE exercise was that there were indeed many overstayers living and working illegally in London. Amongst them were some illegal entrants who had evaded border control altogether, but the vast majority had come in as short-term visitors or students and then simply stayed on. Many had changed their names and disposed of their passports to conceal this fact. The only way to get to the truth was to conduct a thorough interview about mode of entry to the UK, initiate a property search for any documents, and check the given names against Home Office records.

The most common defence for an overstayer was to say that they had lodged their passport with the Home Office to seek an extension. This was sometimes backed up by a "receipt" from the Home Office, acknowledging the receipt of a passport on a specific date. These "receipts" were easily forged, copied and circulated widely around the illegal community in West London as a first line of defence to be shown when challenged by a police officer or an Immigration Officer about lawful status. Under the terms of the Variation of Leave Order (VOLO) 1972, any application lodged "in time" (i.e., before the expiry of previous leave) was automatically extended until 14 days after the Home Office decided on the case. So we spent a huge amount of time telephoning the Home Office from police stations to see if there was a record or not. Of course, we all knew that the Home Office filing system was far from perfect. It was based on a nominal index and many of the names could be spelt in different ways. This was before the introduction of the Police and Criminal Evidence Act 1984 (PACE), so it was quite possible that a suspected offender could be detained in a police cell for two or three days whilst we continued to search the halls and corridors of Lunar House for his file or his landing card.

There was no "administrative" solution to removing overstayers in those days. Our only recourse was to either release the individual and write a report to the Home Office to say that they had been found, so that deportation proceedings could be initiated, or to prosecute them for "knowingly overstaying leave", contrary to Section 24 of the Immigration Act 1971. It was not possible to simply serve them with an administrative detention order, as we could with illegal entrants. By using the prosecution route, we could at least keep tabs upon the individual to allow the Department to start proceedings – usually by getting a remand for seven days in custody to enable a Notice of Liability to Deportation (IM3) to take effect.

The sudden explosion of section 24 prosecution cases hit the West London Magistrates Court like a tornado. Magistrates who were used to dishing out fines to drunks and thieves were suddenly faced with foreigners who (allegedly) had failed to observe their conditions of entry to the UK. Magistrates had received little or no training in the complexities of immigration law. When weighed against other offenders rolling through their courts, most saw this as no more than a minor administrative offence. I sat through many a court hearing where convicted immigration offenders were told "not to do it again" and released with a conditional discharge or a small fine. On many occasions we were admonished by court clerks and defending counsel for "wasting court time". Despite our requests, very few convicted immigration offenders were recommended for deportation by the court. And because overstaying was not a "continuing offence", many of the overstayers we prosecuted were back working at the same establishment where we had arrested them the previous week, but this time with impunity, at least until such time as the Deportation Groups at Lunar House could get through the administrative paperwork to enable the Home Secretary to sign a deportation order, which could take months. By that time, they had duly scarpered.

Despite these frustrations, the JOE exercise served its purpose. We were able to prove beyond doubt that there was a significant and growing cohort of overstayers and illegal workers in London, and that by and large the powers available to law enforcement agencies to arrest and deport them were woefully inadequate. The difference between administrative removal (for illegal entrants) and deportation (for overstayers and illegal workers) was stark.

The case for a new concept of "unlawful presence" and a more efficient route to removal for overstayers and illegal workers had been made, although it would take a few more years before this would finally be enacted in primary legislation. So, if the UK Immigration Service were to continue to extend its footprint into inland enforcement work, how would it do so in the meantime?

One of the rising stars in Immigration Enforcement in those days was Colin Manchip. Colin differed from many of his peers in that he had an extraordinary intellect for the business, and a keen legal mind. This prompted several initiatives in the Home Office to extend the concept of illegal entry beyond those who had "wet feet". Through a series of landmark judgements in the 1980s, the Home Office successfully persuaded the courts that a person who had entered the UK as an imposter (using the passport of another) was also an illegal entrant under the terms of the Immigration Act – having "entered in breach of the immigration laws". This concept was later extended still further to those who had entered "by deception" – by telling lies to the Immigration Officer on arrival to gain entry. Other versions emerged, including "NELEs" (No Evidence of Lawful Entry) and "entry without leave" (where people had entered from the Republic of Ireland and had unwittingly failed to benefit from the provision of the "Entry via the Republic of Ireland" Order 1972). Indeed, I recall one specific case I dealt with myself – an Algerian called Ahmed Bouzagu, who had been arrested by Marylebone police on suspicion of theft. I discovered that he had overstayed his leave to remain in the UK and then travelled to Ireland and back. There are no physical immigration controls between Ireland and the UK, so Mr Bouzagu could not have known he needed to get leave to enter on his way back. But the fact that he did not seek it was enough to persuade the court that he was an illegal entrant. Although the fact that he had also contracted a marriage of convenience – and had been arrested in Harrods for handbag dipping – did not go unnoticed by the court.

These judgements led us to draw up a series of "categories" of illegal entrant, sometimes labelled by mode of entry (e.g., clandestine) and sometimes by the name of the stated case judgement upon which the decision was taken (e.g., Khawaja). These categories were recorded – alongside the individual's name and case reference – on a whiteboard in the casework office. They also enabled us to turn a great many "overstayers" into "illegal entrants"; thereby facilitating enforcement and removal action against them.

Of course, Immigration Officers being Immigration Officers, the categorisation system was open to widespread fun and games as new tranches came through. During one major operation I can remember a case where the offender was found quite by chance in the street, when officers stopped to ask him directions. This was technically a breach of process. We were under strict instructions to only question people if we had a "named offender" we were looking for, something Mr Manchip was quite keen about. However, this individual committed the cardinal sin of "having it away on his toes" when confronted by a police officer and an Immigration Officer – probably a bit of a giveaway in terms of raising grounds for suspicion about his immigration status.

Anyway, this individual ended up being arrested and detained as an illegal entrant, having entered the country on a falsified passport. He was not somebody we were looking for – he just happened to be in the wrong place at the wrong time. The names of all illegals arrested in the course of the operation were listed on a whiteboard in the casework office, which included a column to describe the relevant "category" of illegal entrant they were (e.g., clandestine, imposter, deception). In this case, instead of writing "deception" some wag had written "street type" under category on the casework whiteboard. I never saw a colleague move so quickly to erase the offending entry, upon hearing Mr Manchip's footsteps approaching.

Ultimately, the solution would be to create a new concept

of "unlawful presence" to remove the distinction between illegal entrants and overstayers. But in the meantime, it was commonplace for Immigration Officers to try to turn the latter into the former to facilitate removal. This was usually achieved through an admission that the offender had intended all along to come to the UK to work, and had deceived the visa officer or the Immigration Officer by falsely claiming to be a visitor.

Many of the criticisms focused upon immigration enforcement in those days – and even today to a lesser extent – were that we were randomly trawling through London businesses and properties checking people's identity and immigration status. The most famous criticism levelled at us at the time was that we were "fishing" – in other words conducting enforcement raids without having undertaken sufficient background checks and research to justify the visit in the first place. In fact, despite the odd example of "chance encounter" described above, most enforcement visits were carefully researched before authority to visit was granted.

As at the ports, some Immigration Officers had higher arrest rates than others. Some were prolific at locating offenders and were rarely seen in the office, spending most of their time out on field visits with the police. Others with a smaller returns rate were regarded as paper pushers who would spend most of their time in the office conducting "research" and writing on files, and very little time out on the ground. Obviously, there were various shades in the middle – but terms such as "deep sea trawlers" at one end of the spectrum and "pilot lights" (who never went out) at the other end were commonplace.

My temporary attachment to the IS Intelligence and Investigations Unit soon became permanent, and it lasted for five years. They were wonderful times with wonderful people. There I met colleagues who would become lifelong friends – something that epitomised UKIS and set it apart from other parts of the Home Office.

My daughter Sharon came into the world at Heatherwood Hospital in Ascot in 1979, and my eldest son Mark followed in 1981. Having worked as a primary school teacher before the children were born, Marilyn decided to stay at home to a become full-time mother – at least until they both reached school age. This was fine by me, but it did place a greater burden upon me to bring in sufficient income to cover the mortgage, family expenses and the like. This became a vicious circle – overtime was unlimited in those days, and weekend working attracted premium payments. As with many Immigration Officers of that era, I found myself working longer and longer hours and spending more and more time with my "work" family. This was fine for maintaining the family budget, but less so for maintaining a solid marriage and a close family connection at home. I didn't realise it at the time, but with hindsight I can see now that the cracks in our relationship started to form in those days. Little did I know that they would lead to earthquakes in later years.

CHAPTER 5

WORKING ABROAD – ENTRY CLEARANCE OFFICER BANGLADESH

The primary pillar of immigration control – and probably the most important – is the entry clearance operation. Otherwise termed "pre-entry" or "visa" work, this is a process where some people must apply for permission to enter the UK before they travel.

Like most countries of the world, the UK has a "visa list". Nationals of countries that are on the list must get a visa to come to the UK, even if only a visit is intended. This means lodging an application abroad, via the nearest British Embassy or High Commission. If successful, the applicant is granted a "visa", which takes the form of a vignette affixed to their passport. Airlines have access to the visa list and are trained to spot and stop visa nationals trying to board flights to the UK without a visa.

The concept of visa controls and their various forms has fuelled the development of the "multiple borders strategy" – something I helped to develop in later life, and now give lectures about in various parts of the world. Without going into too much technical detail, the concept is simple. If you stop non-compliant people before they travel, then you don't have to go to the trouble of doing so when they land – or better still once they are in your country. Meanwhile if you go through all the bureaucracy and risk assessments before travel, then you don't have to do it all over again on arrival. At least so long as you have the confidence in the effectiveness of your visa operation in the first place, which (alas) has seldom been the case in the UK. Or elsewhere for that matter. Indeed, one of the major contributory factors to the 9/11 attacks in the United States was a failure in the US visa system to identify security risks – something we shall explore later.

One of the traditional ways to split responsibilities at government level is to draw a line between those functions of state conducted at home, and those conducted abroad. In the US, they are the responsibilities of the Department for the Homeland and the Department of State. In the UK security services, it is MI5 and MI6, and in Whitehall, it is the Home Office and the Foreign & Commonwealth Office. Therefore, in general terms, it was the Foreign & Commonwealth Office (rather than the Home Office) that managed the UK visa operation, although ultimately the Home Office retained overall responsibility for immigration and border control.

Some visa cases used to be referred to the UK Immigration and Nationality Department for a decision, whereas others were decided locally. I remember dealing with some of these when I was an EO in Lunar House, back in those early days. They would have a slip of paper entitled "visa case" affixed to the top of the file with a pin, so they would stand out in the pile of files queued up on the EO's desk. Within the file was a copy of an application form and copies of supporting documents – although not the original passport of course, because the applicants had yet to travel.

The main reason why visa cases were referred home was to facilitate enquiries in the UK. Before the age of the internet, papers were transmitted by diplomatic bags between posts abroad and Whitehall. So, for example, a visa officer in India might receive an application for a visit visa to stay with a sponsor in the UK. Rather than try to contact each sponsor directly, the visa officer would refer the case to London so that follow-up enquiries could be made. Often this would be by correspondence between the Home Office and the sponsor, although in some cases an interview would be required. This was another area of "in country" work that soon became the domain of the UK Immigration Service. Once the enquiry had been made, a report would be submitted to assist the decision maker. Thereafter the applicant would either receive his visa – duly affixed to his passport – or receive the dreaded endorsement "Entry Clearance Applied For" which was our signal that a visa had been refused.

As immigration controls extended after the implementation of the Immigration Act 1971, so did the volume of fraud. It became commonplace to see immigration agents springing up outside our High Commissions and Embassies in some parts of the world, offering services in fraudulent documents such as sponsorship letters, leave of absence letters from non-existent employers, fake bank statements / references and the like to convince visa officers that applicants were only going to the UK for a short visit. At the same time significant fraud emerged in settlement applications where dependent children were added to applications to join a "father" who was settled in the UK, when in truth they were not related as claimed. This was before the days of DNA testing, so there was no way of determining the validity of these relationships without lengthy interviews with "family members" involving the compilation of extended family trees. Sometimes even a "village visit" would be needed, to interview friends and neighbours. Some of this work did not lend itself well to officers from the Diplomatic Service. It demanded investigations by officers better equipped to undertake it, namely the UK Immigration Service.

CHANGING BORDERS: A KINGDOM UNLOCKED

Overseas postings for Immigration Officers were seen to provide the third dimension needed for advancement in the Service, the others being "on-entry" work at the border, and "after-entry" work in enforcement. So, the piece missing from my own portfolio at that time was an overseas posting. Something I knew I needed to fix if I was to achieve promotion to Chief Immigration Officer.

In those days, Immigration Officers were only posted to countries of "high immigration". These were, by definition, not the most attractive places in the world to live and work. There were essentially two options: "long term ECO" and "Short term ECO". A long-term posting was usually for three years and offered "accompanied rates". This meant that the Department would provide travel and accommodation not just for the officer, but also for his or her immediate family. A short-term posting meant that officers would be paid on a subsistence basis for up to six months, but would not be offered accompanied rates.

Towards the end of my posting to the Intelligence Unit I received a call from Colin Manchip, who was by now an Assistant Chief Inspector in the Immigration Service.

"Hi Tony, it's Colin Manchip here. I've got a proposition for you, but I need a quick reply. Can you go to Bangladesh for six months?"

"Hi Colin – when?" I replied, struggling to come to terms with the thought of such a thing. The furthest afield I had travelled before then was to Tunisia on holiday, where I had the screaming shits for most of the fortnight we were there. And I hated curry.

"Well, we need you out there right away really. Peter Hayes, one of their long-term ECOs, has been medically evacuated back home and their casework is piling up."

"Er – well – the wife's not here at the moment and obviously I need to talk to her about it. Is there any chance of somewhere else, at some other time?" I didn't know much about life in Bangladesh, but I imagined that of all the postings in the world this must be one of the worst. And God only knows what Marilyn would have to say about it.

"No sorry Tony, it's this one or nothing. I have only been offered one slot for Enforcement. You are one of the best IOs I have, which is why I thought of you first. But if you can't do it, I'll find someone else."

"OK I understand – let me speak to the wife and I'll call you back."

I put the phone down, sat down and gazed at the wall. Now what? This was going to be one of those days in my life which would be a defining moment. Not just from a career point of view, but from a personal point of view. I had made my bed – 31 years old, married with two kids, living in semi-detached suburbia. Things were fine. Marilyn was happy; she had made her life here with me, and her friends and family were nearby. Bangladesh was on the other side of the world. We had hardly been apart for more than a few days since we had married. And here I was being asked by my boss to leave her and the kids behind for six months, to go and live in some godforsaken country where I would hate the food and probably end up getting quite ill. And for what purpose? So that I could come back and have a better shot at promotion.

But then I thought back to my interview as a teenager at London Bridge. I had (eventually) chosen the life of an Immigration Officer. I knew that this was never going to be a boring nine to five job, and that there were always going to be new challenges around every corner. And the fact was, I loved it. I loved the job, the culture, and the people. If I turned this down, I would end up back on the line at Heathrow, always wondering what might have been. Surely there was a way through this?

Marilyn was inconsolable when I told her. "How can you even think such a thing? Your life is here with me and your children. Don't be so ridiculous. Ring him now and tell him you're not going."

I tried all kinds of things to reason with her, even suggesting that she could come with me (and bring the kids) at my expense. She wasn't working, and the kids were pre-school age. We could even have a nice holiday in the Far East on the way home. We could rent the house out to recoup some of the money. And my prospects of promotion when I got back would be significantly enhanced.

All of this fell on deaf ears. This reaction – for the first time – gave me pause to think about our relationship. The easy option would be to ring Colin, say thanks but no thanks, and put it all behind me. But then what? Would this mean I would never be able to live and work abroad? Would I end up living in semi-detached suburbia forever? I had my own life to live, and my own dreams to realise. In the end there was only one answer. I had to go for it – and hang the consequences. I rang Colin and told him I would go. Marilyn gave me the silent treatment for the next few days, but the die was cast. As to our future together, only time would tell. And it did.

Meanwhile news of my imminent posting to Bangladesh caused great joy and amusement in my other family – UKIS. I was well known in the flyers football team as being the only team member who didn't like a curry after the game. My diet was quintessentially English – pie and chips, bangers and mash, and so on.

I had no idea what clothes to take with me. I took counsel from Bob Owen, a colleague who had served in Dhaka himself. His main advice was not to take socks – according to him, nobody in the High Commission ever wore them. Imagine my surprise then, when on my first day in the office I found myself being the only person wearing open toed sandals and no socks! Another great source of amusement to the lads.

The day of my departure was obviously a traumatic one. Saying goodbye to Marilyn and the kids was a very emotional experience. How do you tell such small children that Daddy is going away for six months? We agreed that once we said our goodbyes Marilyn would take them out. My brother Mike took me to the airport. I had a scotch to stiffen my nerves en route (I don't know why, as I don't even like scotch) but as soon as I got to Heathrow the mood changed completely. The flyers decided to gather "en masse" in the bar at Terminal 3 to see me off. Then the late shift turned up airside to have a few more with me before I boarded. By the time I got on board the BA flight to Dhaka, I was legless. I was in business class, which meant I was served champagne and smoked salmon on board – which required me to use the paper bag much sooner than I had expected. I crashed somewhere over Portugal, and woke up again with a thumping headache and hangover somewhere over Bombay.

Another piece of helpful advice from Bob Owen was to wear a suit on the flight, as it would be very likely that the "old man" (High Commissioner) would be at the airport to meet me. In fact, a couple of colleagues turned up in shorts and T-shirts: Tony Mercer (an old mate of mine from UKIS) and Paul Williams (one of the Entry Clearance Managers). They whisked me straight off to a barbecue, where a party was already in full swing. Many of my new colleagues expressed some surprise that this new ECO had turned up in a suit and no socks looking decidedly the worse for wear, and stood in the corner sipping water whilst everyone else was partying.

And so, the adventure began. The first thing was sorting out my accommodation. Tony Mercer put me up at his place for the first few nights. He was on a long-term posting with his wife (Viv) and two small boys, Justin and Gareth. As such he had a nice big detached villa with servants. As a short termer I was not automatically entitled to such luxury, but fortunately for me Peter Hayes' house was empty, so I was able to stay there to begin with. This was also a luxury four-bed villa, and my first task when I got there was to interview the queue of potential "servants" waiting outside the house looking for work. That was how it worked. A pool of local workers watched movements in the diplomatic quarter of Gulshan and Banani. They knew full well that as soon as a house was vacated a new occupant would arrive soon, and that this was their chance to secure employment. Most of the houses were equipped with servants' quarters, which meant that not only did they earn a reasonable wage, but also they had somewhere reasonable to live (at least by local standards).

There were different opinions on how many servants should be engaged, and for what purpose. Depending upon grade, the cost of servants was met by the Foreign Office. Not so however for short-term postings, where servants were paid for directly by officers from their subsistence allowance. Some of the diplomatic wives were happy to perform some domestic duties themselves – especially where they were not working. This would usually involve catering for the regular house and dinner parties that were a key part of the social scene in the Foreign and Commonwealth Office. However, I was alone, and cooking had never been my strong point. I plumped for a cook, a cleaner and a security guard who doubled up as a gardener. I didn't go too far behind the scenes in the kitchen, but I was a very good customer of the local commissariat, where you could buy a decent range of imported UK foods.

My house was a couple of miles away from the office. The most common form of transport to and from work was by tuk-tuk, although rickshaws and taxis were also available. The working week was Sunday through Thursday, from 0730 to 1430 every day. I soon got into this routine and the local social scene that surrounded it.

From a work point of view, most of the casework involved applications for family reunification from wives and children seeking to join husbands/fathers in the UK. Prior to the introduction of controls in the 1971 Act, a great many young men had travelled from the Sylhet region of Bangladesh to work in mainly manual jobs in various parts of the UK, including

Yorkshire, the Midlands, and the East End of London. They had subsequently acquired British citizenship and travelled back to Sylhet every year or two to see family. During some of these prolonged trips home, they might marry or remarry and conceive children. Then at some point – usually to enhance the prospects of their children – they would apply for their relatives to join them in the UK. These sponsors were known locally as "Londonis".

One of the major immigration abuses of the day was the concept of "bogus children". This would arise when a Londoni applied to bring many children from his local village to the UK with him, some of whom did not belong to him. To achieve this, the sponsor would need to set up a complex web of deception with his family and those around him, to ensure they were all singing from the same hymn sheet when interviewed about their family connections. Birth and marriage records in the villages of Sylhet were few and far between, and easily altered upon payment of a small fee. The only way to get to the bottom of these cases was to complete a full family tree from each of the applicants – or at least those old enough to be interviewed – and look for any discrepancies.

This type of painstaking investigative work was ideally suited to the UK Immigration Service. Before long, an extensive library of family trees and local history had been built in the British High Commission, enabling us to cross-reference different applications from the various villages and districts of Sylhet. In this way we were able to locate evidence given by previous applicants as to the number and parentage of children declared in the past, and cross-match this with new applications.

It was not unusual for sponsors to "adopt" teenage boys from other families in the village as their own, as a way of securing passage to the UK. Often these would be sons of other members of the extended family. This was difficult and time-consuming work, often involving a game of cat and mouse between the UK sponsor and the Entry Clearance Officer.

When I got to Dhaka, I was told that it was our policy to refuse the entire application if we believed any of the children to be bogus. It was standard practice to call the sponsor and his entire "family" into the room before commencing the interview and to instruct the interpreter to tell the sponsor that if any of the "dependants" were not really his then now was the time to say so. Anything less could lead to a refusal of the entire family. In most cases the family would shuffle out into the waiting room for a discussion, then come back in ten minutes later with a slightly smaller group.

We would be allocated a set number of cases per day, usually three settlement cases and maybe a couple of visit cases. For the settlement cases there were three options: grant, refuse, or defer. The visitor cases were usually either grant or refuse, and the vast majority were refused on the grounds that it was simply not credible for the average Bengali to spend something like two years' salary on a short visit to see a family member in the East End of London, or in Lancashire or Yorkshire. Some of these refusals were contested by relatives in the UK, often with the support of local MPs eager to attract the immigrant vote. I always found it interesting that MPs and others making representations in these cases were never held to account if the applicant failed to comply with their entry conditions. Or how their pronouncements on the need for firm immigration controls in the UK contradicted their behaviours in the constituency on individual cases. But I guess that's politics for you.

One of the major failings of the UK visa operation in later years was the quest for efficiency savings. It became customary to increase the daily interview rate in overseas missions, thus denying officers the necessary time or resources to properly assess applications. It is very easy to accept what an applicant says, take their documents at face value, and grant a visa. It is much harder to probe in more detail, to conduct more rigorous background research, and to mount a refusal. Middle managers were encouraged to get more and more cases cleared every day, and hang the consequences if the applicant subsequently overstayed or claimed asylum in the UK. This cannot be reflective of an effective immigration system yet sadly it is something that UKVI continued to countenance, despite the protestations of the UK Border Force or Immigration Enforcement who were left to pick up the pieces.

In those days back in Dhaka we were under no illusions that we had been brought in from the UK Immigration Service not just to fuel the supply of legitimate migration to the UK, but more to tackle the very significant number of fraudulent applications that were being submitted – often with the help of unscrupulous agents – on a daily basis.

Communication with folks back home was either by letter or by audio tape, which went out every week on the diplomatic bag. I got into the habit of sending a tape to Marilyn every week and getting a letter back the following week.

I soon got caught up in the social scene in Dhaka. Because work finished at 2.30 pm it was customary to have a couple of beers in the office, and then head down to the British High Commission club for the rest of the day. I became a member of the legendary "MFA" – the Magic Fridge Association – so called because it had a habit of "magically" refilling itself with cold cans of beer on a regular basis. I also joined the famous "Hash House Harriers", a cross country running group which invariably ended up in some paddy field somewhere with a bunch of wet and muddy Englishmen standing in a circle singing rugby songs and drinking beer in the sunset. We played football on Saturdays, and volleyball on Mondays. There was a poker school on Thursdays, and a regular round of parties at weekends.

Not long after my arrival there I was notified that I was to house share with another new arrival, Kevin Lynch. Kevin was from an FCO background rather than a UKIS one, although his whole culture and behaviour suggested otherwise. Like me, Kevin liked his sport and his beer. We soon teamed up together and became known as "Smiffy and Lynchy" – we even had our own house party, which ended up as a bit of a riot. Looking back, this was the first time in my life when I had been left to my own devices, with nobody else depending upon me. The freedom was infectious. Kevin ended up spending his entire career in the Foreign Office, and his book *The Road to Deal Pier* and the many stories therein was one of the main influencing factors in my decision to write this one.

My boss in Dhaka in those days was Dave Barrell. I was destined to work for Dave in later years too. He was a lovely man – an affable Brummie, with a down to earth, almost cavalier approach to the job. Dave was there with his wife Hazel. As an Entry Clearance Manager, he was entitled to an even bigger villa and more servants than the rest of us. He enjoyed the camaraderie of UKIS and was very generous in hosting house parties, which were legendary in Dhaka at the time.

About halfway through my posting Dave called me into his office for an interim performance appraisal. He was very complimentary, telling me not just how well I was doing in the workplace but how well I had settled into life in Dhaka. He told me that he had a couple of long-term postings coming up and that if I was interested, he would offer one of them to me. I wouldn't even need to go back to the UK – I could just send for the wife and kids and stay on.

I saw this as a fascinating prospect. Marilyn wasn't working, and Sharon and Mark were still pre-school age. Even when they were old enough to start school, there was an excellent American school in Dhaka which catered for the younger F&CO kids. We could rent the house out in Windsor – getting the mortgage paid for three years – and travel the world during my mid-term leave, visiting places I could only have dreamt about visiting in my younger days.

I sent a message back to Marilyn but, as I expected, she had severe reservations about it. I suggested that she should bring the kids out on holiday for the last few weeks of my posting, so she could look at the lifestyle and talk to some of the other mums out there before deciding. We could also have a holiday in Thailand, Malaysia and Singapore. She was much more taken with the idea of the holiday than the idea of coming to Dhaka, but in the end she agreed. I picked her up at the airport and drove her to the house in Gulshan, where the servants were waiting with garlands for her. I also hired a nanny – Amina – who spoke very little English but was perfect for looking after the kids.

As I feared, Marilyn did not take well to life in Dhaka. Unlike the other wives she could not work during the day, so she found herself very lonely whilst I was at work. And she certainly did not fit in neatly with my social scene. She began to resent my ongoing involvement in the hash, the football, the volleyball, or anything else that didn't involve her. In the end she couldn't wait to get away from the place, swearing black and blue that she would never contemplate the idea of spending three years there.

Again, I got that sinking feeling that I was being held back from realising a dream. This time there was no way out. I could get away with a six-month posting, but three years was out of the question without her support. I resigned myself to coming back to the UK and to Heathrow.

CHAPTER 6

BACK TO HEATHROW, AND BACK ON THE LINE

By now, I had my sights firmly set on promotion to Chief Immigration Officer. I had racked up 12 years' service and had achieved a full house in terms of immigration work: pre-entry, on-entry, after-entry, and enforcement. Upon my return to Heathrow, I wanted to go to the busiest terminal with the broadest range of casework, which was Terminal 3. In those days, all the long-haul flights from around the world landed at Terminal 3, whereas the other two terminals handled mainly European flights.

I had to return to Terminal 1 briefly before I could transfer to Terminal 3, but the place had changed beyond recognition. Many of my friends and colleagues who had served there with me in the 70s had moved on. A few had been promoted, but most had moved out to the provinces. I found myself surrounded by a younger crowd, including a significant intake of young women as UKIS lurched towards becoming an equal opportunities employer. As stated elsewhere, I personally had no difficulty with this. Many of the female officers were better and brighter than their male counterparts, although obviously few had made it into managerial roles, simply because of the length of time it took to become ready for promotion in those days. Meanwhile the mainstream Civil Service was moving much more quickly, with many more women being promoted into HEO or SEO roles than to CIO or HMI roles. Therefore, it was easy to see why many viewed UKIS as a misogynistic organisation. Apart from a few notable exceptions, I don't think it was. The absence of females in the upper ranks of the service was more due to the nature of progression and history than anything else.

Terminal 3 was indeed tougher. The work was more intense, with a much larger secondary examination and casework area. It was not unusual to pick up two or even three cases per shift. The workforce was larger, with officers split into three separate "rooms" – Red, Blue, and Green. I found myself in the "Green Room" with the non-smokers. Here officers had a pigeon-hole for their post and files, and a locker for personal stuff including landing stamps. The warnings index had by now moved onto a shared system, where you booked a copy out upon start of your shift and booked it back in again at the end of it. Timekeeping was monitored by the CIOs, who would stand by the "stamping on" book with one eye on the queue of officers stamping on and another on their pocket watch. Some CIOs took this responsibility more seriously than others. I remember one in particular whose catchphrase became "Why you late?" This gave rise to his nickname of 'Blakey' from the character in "On the Buses", a popular ITV sitcom of the time.

One of the biggest problems for management at Terminal 3 was matching the shift patterns to the flight schedules. The airlines had a habit of "bunching" flight arrivals in the early morning, starting from about 0430 onwards. This meant a lot of work for the night shift and increasing demands for earlier starts, which were fiercely opposed by the unions. In the end we agreed the famous "S" shift, which meant starting at 0545. There was limited public transport to Heathrow at that time in the morning, so the Department agreed to pay for taxi fares to bring officers in. The additional agreement was to allow both a terminal meal break at 1300 and a half hour "breakfast break" which was staggered between 7 am and 8 am. This was fine for the S shift, but not so great for the night shift, who often found themselves having to work through until 0830 or even 0900 whilst their S shift colleagues slipped away for breakfast.

Although it was hard to get to sleep the night before an S shift, the benefits of getting away by 1 pm were considerable – especially for the football team who might be kicking off at 2.30 pm.

One of my best memories of that time was returning to the football field. Having fully recovered from my broken leg I was ready to play again and soon found myself back in "The Flyers". I was by now one of the older players. Many of the "old guard" had hung up their boots, so my role was more player/manager. But a new generation of players had now joined up, some of whom were playing at a good standard elsewhere. We played in the Hanwell and District League on Wednesday afternoons and our home pitch was the civil service sports ground at Duke's Meadow in Chiswick.

Having learned lessons from my own experiences as a new entrant and footballer a decade earlier, I took on the role of interviewing new arrivals whom I could add to the Immigration FC squad. One such player was a young Scottish lad called Phil Hunt. Phil was a Civil Service first team player and I managed to get him released from his training course to play in a big match for us. Phil was indeed a great player, but like many of the Scottish contingent of the day he had a wild streak and was easily led astray on match days. I can remember him turning up late for one game very much the worse for wear and without any kit, yet still coming on in his jeans, trainers, and pulling on a spare team jersey to win the match for us. We played an annual "interport" tournament every year at Chiswick – usually won by Dover teams. As a Terminal 1 player I was never victorious, but I did pick up a winner's medal with Terminal Three.

We also used to play the Dutch Border Force (known as the Marechausee) every year. The match location would alternate between London and Amsterdam and invariably the home team would win the trophy, mainly because of the difficulties in getting our best players to go across to Amsterdam for a few days. However, the Dutch managed to buck the trend and beat us on our own turf, which meant they had won twice on the trot. The agreement had always been that any winning team for three years on the bounce would keep the trophy permanently, so it fell to me as captain of the Flyers to get a squad to Amsterdam that would be capable of beating the Dutch on their own ground for the first time in ten years.

This was never going to be easy. The Marechausee was a uniformed disciplined force not unlike the military, with their own barracks and fitness requirements. We were a rag bag of Immigration Officers – with a couple of customs guys thrown in – whose best form of training had always been in the bar after the game. On this occasion my co-manager in the Flyers was Barry (Badger) Jeavons, a great defender and a big Hammers fan. Upon arrival at Schiphol Airport, we were treated to a grand reception by our Dutch friends and Barry and I were taken into a side room to meet the referee, discuss the rules of the game and the location of the pitch, and even examine the match ball for the game the next day. These guys clearly meant business and their skipper, Jakob, had clearly staked his reputation on beating us and winning the trophy outright.

Whilst Barry and I tried to work out our best line up for the big game, Jakob and his mates were lining up minibuses to take our lads down to the red-light district for a big night out. Jakob came over to us at around 9 pm to say that he and his boys were retiring to bed early, but he would leave some officers with us if we wanted to stay for another drink.

I tried to round up my guys to do the same thing, only to get a chorus of boos (led by Phil) and shouts that the night was still young. If the tactics were to wear us down with a heavy night before the game, they worked. My managerial skills failed me completely, as my squad dispersed into the various downtown bars. All I could hope would be that they would turn up on time for the big game the next day.

Sure enough, they didn't. We started with nine men and we were 2-0 down by half time. Needless to say, Phil Hunt had gone AWOL. He turned up still drunk from the night before, came on and promptly threw up on the side of the pitch. I figured that it was time to concede that the trophy would be lost to the Dutch for good.

Then somehow, something changed. I still don't know what it was. Maybe the British bulldog spirit came out in us. Suddenly we were shouting at each other, encouraging each other, and playing some decent stuff. We scored. Jakob was becoming increasingly animated. Then we equalized. I thought I was dreaming. Phil was playing out of his skin. Not only that, but so were the rest of us. Greg Watts picked up the ball on the half-way line, shimmied past two Dutch players, and hit a shot from 30 yards. On any other day this would have screamed over the crossbar – but not today. He hit the top corner of the net with five minutes to go. The Dutch were beaten, we could see it and feel it. We won 3-2 and brought the trophy back to Heathrow, against all the odds. Greg went on to be a good friend, and we still talk about that goal to this day.

We also played against some legends in the Hanwell and District Wednesday league – and a few hooligans too. I remember the Market Traders in particular, where many former professionals from Brentford and QPR would turn out - Peter Gelson, Eddie Reeve and Terry Hurlock amongst others. For me, the highlight of it all was playing against the legendary Stan Bowles. Stan was my hero, and here I was lining up against him on a Wednesday afternoon. A lot has been said and written about Stan – some by himself. He was indeed a compulsive gambler – he was in the bar after the match with a pack of cards inviting us for a game of poker. But in my limited experience of him he was a gentleman too and he had the sweetest left foot to ever grace a football pitch. Sadly, Stan suffered from dementia in later life, but still turned out on the pitch from time to time to wave to his adoring fans at Loftus Road before QPR games.

I met a few professional footballers over the years, including the late, great George Best. I never had the honour of playing football with George, but he did turn out for the odd charity game at Loftus Road after he retired. George had a bar in Marylebone, and I popped in there with a police colleague from Paddington after work one day. George was very welcoming, but completely legless. He tried to sign a poster of himself for my son Mark (who was a junior at Corinthian Casuals at the time), but the result was no more than a squiggle which could not be deciphered by the reader. When we met again, I recounted this story to George, who apologised profusely and promptly signed a new poster stating very clearly "To Mark, good luck with your football at Corinthian Casuals. With best regards, George Best." He didn't need to do that – he didn't really know me at all. It was just in his nature.

A few professional footballers used to call in on George after training, including Peter Reid. Peter was playing for QPR at the time and nearly fell off his bar stool when I told him I was a Rangers fan. I had to pull out my season ticket to prove it. I had been trying to get Mark into the mascot scheme for a while without any luck. Peter quickly took this on board and gave me Sheila Marston's private number (Sheila was a secretary at the club at the time). She was great and arranged for Mark to turn out as mascot for QPR against Norwich later in the season and gave us six complimentary tickets to take the family to the game. As I said before, I ran into a fair few celebrities over the years, and for the most part they were always warm-hearted and generous to me.

I quite enjoyed my brief spell at Terminal 3, but I had to admit I had become jaded by returning to the front line after all my previous experiences. I wanted promotion, and I had deliberately moved to the busiest port in the country to maximise my chances of getting it. This finally paid off towards the end of 1985 when I got a call after my CIO Board from my old mate Dave Wilson – himself a CIO at the time – to tell me the letters were out. I agreed to let him open it for me and I was delighted to hear that I had passed the promotion board to Chief Immigration Officer that year, some 13 years after entering the Civil Service as an EO and over 10 years after becoming an Immigration Officer. My climb up the slippery pole of promotion had begun. Little could I have imagined at that time where it would end.

CHAPTER 7

PROMOTION TO CHIEF IMMIGRATION OFFICER AND BACK TO ENFORCEMENT: ISIS HOUSE, LONDON

Accompanying my notification of promotion letter was a form asking me to list my three preferences for posting in the higher grade. An area that I thought was ripe for development – and close to my heart – was Immigration Enforcement. The two main enforcement offices in London were the Intelligence Unit at Harmondsworth – where I had already spent many happy years as an Immigration Officer – and Isis House in Southwark Street, London. These were my first two choices, with Heathrow third.

I had no great desire to move out of London. Many of my colleagues were keen to do so – particularly to Dover, which was also expanding rapidly at the time. There are some very nice communities along the coastline between Dover and Deal, and under the "Crown transfer" system the government was prepared to pay significant relocation fees to facilitate transfers between the regions. This, coupled with the ongoing allowances attached to CIO grade work, meant that newly promoted CIOs from Heathrow could move up from a three-bedroomed semi in the Thames Valley to a four-bedroomed detached on the Kent coast with little financial penalty. I did take Marilyn down to Dover one weekend to look around. Whilst she was impressed at the idea of a bigger house, she was less impressed at the idea of moving to Kent. Her view was that it was a shame that I hadn't done rather better in my career – or chosen another "more normal" one – so that we could upgrade to a detached house in Windsor.

Once again, I found myself on the horns of a dilemma. I wanted to try to maximise my income to meet up with Marilyn's expectations, but at the same time, I couldn't move away from London altogether. Of course, the sad thing was that had we taken up Dave Barrell's offer of a long-term posting in Dhaka we would have made enough money to buy a bigger house when we came back anyway. But there we were, no point crying over spilt milk. Life goes on, and all that.

In the end I went for the option which (I thought) would give us the best of both worlds. I applied for a posting to Isis House and – because of the difficulties in commuting to Southwark from our home in Windsor (which seem quite frivolous nowadays) – I was able to secure a "Crown transfer" to my new location. This was on the proviso that my new home would be significantly closer to my new station in London than my current home.

We spent a good deal of time looking at houses in various parts of South West London within easy commuting distance of Waterloo and London Bridge. What we hadn't anticipated was that house prices in that area were rising much more quickly than they were in Windsor. In the end, we couldn't get much more for our money than we already had. But the die was cast. We plumped for a detached chalet home in Malden Manor, just around the corner from the station. This was perfect for commuting to Waterloo, although the house itself still fell short of Marilyn's expectations. The previous owner was a bit of a DIY buff, although not very good at it. He had built a small outdoor swimming pool in the garden, but the kitchen was in an odd place and the garden backed directly onto Malden Manor station. Once we moved in, Marilyn made it very clear that it had fallen short of her expectations. She was happy in Windsor, and this was all my fault (again). It had got to the point where I just couldn't seem to do anything right. I couldn't help recalling the words of Captain Pugwash ringing in my ears – "It takes a certain type of wife to put up with the lifestyle of an IO".

Back then, newly promoted CIOs went through a series of training and development courses to prepare us for "management" and to broaden our horizons to the more contentious areas of immigration control, such as immigration appeals and casework. This applied to all of us, whether we were destined for a posting to a port or an enforcement office.

I attended my residential CIO course in a small hotel in Hastings. Promotion to CIO was quite a big deal in those days – we had all developed a considerable depth and breadth of knowledge in the business over many years' service as Immigration Officers, and there weren't so many of us compared with today's numbers. I can remember a few of my peer group on that course – John O'Shaughnessy, Peter Wheelhouse and Alastair MacDonald. John was a lovely guy and a keen Pompey (Portsmouth FC) fan, who went on to spend most of his career in the regions. Peter and Alastair also remained in UKIS and (like me) went on to higher things within the Service over the years. In those days there was little or no expectation that you would ever leave the Service. The only question would be whether you had the ambition to take an even more exalted grade in Her Majesty's Inspectorate of Immigration.

My most vivid memory of that course was a presentation by Terry Farrage, who was himself an Immigration Inspector in Dover at the time. Terry came to talk to us about some of the management issues he was facing there. This coincided with a period when UKIS was going through a huge transformation through the intake of a very large number of young women. Many of these had been posted to Dover, away from their friends and family. Terry described in detail how this had changed the office there beyond all recognition. Personal relationships quickly developed between male and female officers who worked on shifts and socialised together within a relatively small community. Extra-marital affairs, marriage breakdowns and even brawls in the streets between officers involved in love triangles became rife. This certainly wasn't something I had seen or expected when I joined up, but it was indeed a phenomenon that a great many officers faced in some point in their career, including yours truly. But more of that later.

In addition to the CIOs course, we all had to spend a few weeks on relief to the Immigration Appeals Section, at Harmondsworth. CIOs were responsible for presenting cases to independent adjudicators when an appeal had been lodged against an immigration decision. This might be the refusal of a settlement visa, or permission to remain, or (in the case of entry clearance holders) a decision to refuse leave to enter at the border.

The "courtrooms" were in a building on the same site as the Intelligence Unit, at Harmondsworth near Heathrow. The adjudicator would sit on a raised platform, confronted by the appellant's representative on the one side and the Home Office Presenting Officer on the other side. Appellants were usually represented by the UK Immigration Advisory Service (UKIAS). We weren't given much training about rules of evidence or court proceedings during these attachments, although we usually had a "mentor" at our shoulder when we were presenting cases.

I can remember presenting one case about the refusal of a visitor visa where the visa officer was not satisfied that only a visit was intended. The sponsor was a relative who had himself entered the UK as a visitor some years previously and had then overstayed before gaining settlement by virtue of marriage to a person settled here. This sponsor was produced as the witness in this case and guaranteed on oath that the appellant was only coming for a visit and would go back afterwards. The Immigration Officer (rightly in my view) had used this as a reason to doubt the credibility of the sponsor – but when I raised it in court, I was subjected to a torrent of abuse from both the witness and UKIAS that this was irrelevant. Such was the level of abuse that even the adjudicator was intimidated by this and turned on me to challenge the relevance of my question.

The appeal was allowed, and I can still remember both the representative and the sponsor following me out of court and hurling abuse at me for being a racist Immigration Officer, spitting venom along the way. This was my first encounter with a legally appointed "representative" who clearly bore a personal grudge against anyone involved in immigration law enforcement. It had nothing to do with the case in question – they had already won that. This was personal.

I subsequently discovered that it was quite common for presenting officers to be abused in this way – it was part and parcel of the job. The answer was to roll with the punches, do your job, and get out of there. Even to this day I often face abuse on social media for standing up for firm border controls by those with political motivations not to have any – but I have never let that deter me.

The third component of my CIO training – and probably the most memorable – was my attachment to ISHQ Passenger Casework Section (PCS) in Croydon. This unit dealt with cases where representations had been lodged by Members of Parliament to challenge decisions to refuse entry. This was another way to defer removal – persuade the constituency MP to "make representations" to the Home Office when passengers destined for their constituency were refused entry at the border.

This usually prompted a deferral of removal directions whilst a letter was drafted on behalf of the Secretary of State and sent to the MP. Ports were not empowered to do this themselves. They had to submit a case report to ISHQ, who would then prepare the response to the MP accordingly.

It was around this time that I first worked work closely with "the Chief Inspector" – Peter Tomkins, who was later to become the last "real" Chief Inspector of the Immigration Service.

One character who stands out above all others in my mind in those days was Michael Durose, an Assistant Chief Inspector at ISHQ. Michael was unlike most Immigration Officers of his era – highly articulate, extremely well spoken, and an absolute master of prose. Indeed, he was much more aligned to the mainstream Civil Service than the Immigration Service. Small wonder that Peter Tompkins put Michael in charge of passenger casework. Michael's strength was in his drafting. As Assistant Chief Inspector of passenger casework, he prided himself on the "red pen".

Draft replies to MP representations were prepared in long hand by us newly promoted CIOs who were doing our "porridge" at ISHQ before going back into operational roles the ports and enforcement offices around the country. We didn't even have typewriters then, let alone PCs. Drafts were submitted in double spacing, in anticipation of the Durose red pen. If you were lucky, your draft would come back with various "red pen" amendments, which you then sent off for typing and despatch. The less fortunate would see Mr Durose wander into the office and throw a file on their desk with the immortal words "Have another stab at that one". The final cut would be a summons into his office, to sit on a very low chair looking up at him whilst he told you what a poor effort this was, and how you really needed to learn how to write properly.

This was water off a duck's back for quite a few CIOs, who saw it as no more than a test they had to go through. But others were mortally wounded by it, and I saw some emerge from his room in tears. It was a form of bullying, although I don't think Michael ever saw or intended it so. It's just the way he was. I was to return to ISHQ and the Passenger Casework Section myself in later life, although I never believed at the time that I would end up taking over Mr Durose's post myself. Indeed, I purchased a good supply of red pens, specifically for the purpose.

After completing my training, the day finally arrived in March 1986 when I would start my official duties as a Chief Immigration Officer at Isis House in London.

Isis House was an odd triangular building on the corner of Lavington Street and Southwark Street, often described as a kind of upright stick of Toblerone. The grand offices in Adelaide House on London Bridge had become too expensive for the likes of Home Office Estates and UKIS had now acquired something much less expensive, and on the less favoured side of the river.

When I got there, I found myself being part of an eight-man CIO team managing a workforce of about 50 IOs and reporting to one Immigration Inspector. The office was configured so that the CIOs each shared the "end office" on each floor, with the Inspector occupying the "end office" on the top floor. The officers were divided into "Sectors", which were aligned to the District boundaries of the Metropolitan Police. Apart from one early and one late "Docks Officer" duty, the work was entirely devoted to inland enforcement and investigations. For some reason, the Sectors ranged from 4-7; I never did quite understand what happened to 1-3, but I suspect this was the code used for those Police Districts to the west which were covered by my former colleagues from the Intelligence and Investigations Unit at Harmondsworth.

I was a bit surprised to discover that my first duty as a CIO at Isis House was scheduled for a Sunday. I knew this was a shift-working post, and that weekend working would form part of it, but I thought I might be given a few days of office training before

I went on the operational duty list. In fact, when I got there, I discovered that the first Sunday in every month was reserved for "CIO meetings". This involved a gathering in the Inspector's office for a couple of hours in the morning, followed by another gathering in the Rose and Crown in Union Street afterwards. The official justification for doing this on a Sunday was because it was quieter then, and we had more time available for strategic discussions. Of course, it had absolutely nothing to do with the fact that we were paid double time for Sunday working. This was something that would have sent the National Audit Office into a frenzy if they had known about it at the time.

The Inspector was an affable giant of a man called Kelvin Crocombe. Like many of his generation of Inspectors, Kelvin was closely aligned to the Chief Inspector. So much so that Kelvin met Peter religiously after work every Friday night, to find out the latest gossip (sorry – developments) from the top of the office. This would form the basis of the agenda for the CIOs' meeting on Sunday. Kelvin would try his best to recount some of the conversation that had taken place in the pub in Croydon with the Chief the previous Friday, before they had got too pissed and fallen off their bar stools.

As a new CIO, it was inevitable that I was going to be given the short straw by the others. That meant taking responsibility for tasks such as office accommodation, car parking, telecommunications and all the other boring administrative functions that nobody else wanted to do.

However, the one silver lining in all this was the advent of the 'car phone'. The first iteration of these new-fangled devices came with a battery the size of a briefcase. They were too heavy to carry about the person, but they could be carried (and charged) in official vehicles. This was a great boost to our communications system in the field. We had previously had to rely upon the consent of a householder to phone through for enquiries and references or to drive round looking for a red telephone box whilst some hapless immigrant sat in the back of the car, waiting verification of the fact that his passport was indeed at the Home Office along with an application to extend his stay in the UK.

One of my tasks was to run a pilot for the use of these new portable phones in Immigration Enforcement and to write an evaluation for Kelvin.

Now Kelvin had a great many qualities, but technical awareness was not one of them. I will never forget being called into his office one day to go through the report.

"Now then young Tony, I have been reading this report of yours about these portable telephones, and I think it's very good. So good that I am going to send it to the Chief Inspector".

He paused and looked at me, as if to say that this was a real honour for me to have my report sent on to the Chief.

"OK, thanks" I said, feeling a bit bemused. I was expecting some critical feedback about the report, or maybe some questions about it at least. The report was always going to end up with the Chief. After all, it formed part of an evaluation that had been commissioned by ISHQ in the first place.

"Anyway, I am going to send it to the Chief with a covering note from me and I want you to help me draft it".

He wrote his notes in longhand using a blue fountain pen, and I could see he had started to write something but hadn't got very far with it. It read:

"HM Chief Inspector

Please see this report from Tony Smith, CIO at Isis House, about the use of mobile portable telephone devices for Immigration Enforcement operations in London.

It is a very good report; and I am convinced…."

Whereupon he looked at me over his reading glasses and said, "What am I convinced about?"

I was assigned to manage Sector 5 with Bob Perks – another great man, with a fantastic sense of humour. Like many CIOs of the time Bob was way too intelligent for this line of work, and he held a healthy cynicism for the government and the judiciary, and those that occupied key positions in it. We spent many hours discussing the way High Court judges were interfering in the immigration process, and their various comments and interpretations of immigration law. This gave us some pretty good clues about their political views on immigration policy, rather than the forensic examination of the facts and legislation that we should expect from an independent judiciary. At one point we were barred from conducting operations altogether, while judges contemplated whether we had any powers under the Immigration Act to examine people away from a Port of Entry at all.

The interference of the judiciary, and the use of judicial processes, have been a major barrier to effective immigration controls in the UK for a great many years now. As case working CIOs, we saw only too often the tactical intervention of lawyers at the last moment to stave off removal through the application of "leave to move for a judicial review" of the decision – even though the case had already been subject to independent appeals and reviews along the way. Although various governments have tried to streamline this process over the years, it remains a significant barrier to proper and effective immigration controls in the UK.

Although Bob and I were on the same sector, we didn't share an office. Instead, I found myself co-located on the second floor with the two Sector 4 CIOs, Jim Edgecombe and Terry Duffy. As the most senior CIOs there, these two held the reins of power there at that time. They were like chalk and cheese. Terry was a great thinker and writer, who took great pride in going into detail about the intricacies of a case but was much less inclined to make a decision. Jim, on the other hand, relied much more on his instinct and was always looking at what lay around the corner. He drove a classic black taxi – which he often used for official purposes – and he had a great sense of humour too. I can remember being told by Jim in those early days that it would be difficult to schedule me early duties on Sundays, because he always covered early duty officer and Terry covered early casework. The fact that he was the CIO Duty List compiler, and that double time was payable for Sunday working, had nothing to do with it of course.

I can remember Jim driving me down to Stratford one morning, to look at the site where the new London City Airport was to be built. The proposed runway was no more than a huge jetty in the old East London docks, surrounded by water. Jim was caught short during this trip, and I will never forget the sight of him urinating on the weeds that protruded from the proposed runway which was to be used by short-haul business flights in later years.

Sector 6 was run by Geoff Vignes and Steve Wood. Geoff was an enforcement stalwart and something of a legend in terms of operational activity. He worked with the famous Sergeant Tony Hughes in Deptford, where immigration enforcement operations were rife. It was commonly the case that we were more active in those areas where we had enthusiastic support from nominated police officers than where we did not. Although we had powers of arrest, we were not trained to use them in those days, so we were entirely in the hands of the local cops in terms of what we could or could not do.

I remember chasing a Nigerian through the streets of Deptford with Tony Hughes. We didn't have any arrest training and we were not supposed to chase runners, but we did it anyway. Having caught the offender, we escorted him back to his flat in Deptford only to find he wasn't an offender after all. He had been given leave to enter for one month, exactly 30 days previously. He promised us faithfully that he would leave the country the next day. So it became a question of whether we believed him or not.

Upon further interview he told us that he was in the import/export business and was buying carburettors from breakers' yards in South London to take back to Lagos. When asked to produce evidence of this he dragged a suitcase out from under his bed which was packed with second-hand carburettors.

"So, what do you think Sarge. Is he going back?" I asked.

Sergeant Hughes shrugged. "Yeah, he's going back", he replied.

"What makes you think that?"

"Because he wouldn't have that bloody lot with him if he wasn't!"

Geoff Vignes was one of the original pioneers of Immigration Enforcement, who sadly fell victim to the bottle. Although the office had a drinking culture, most of us left it in the pub; but Geoff brought it into the office with him. It became the norm to see him with a fag in one hand and a glass of scotch in the other, sometimes on an early shift. I later learned of his passing well before his time, due to liver failure.

The last CIO team – sector 7 – comprised Peter Gibbs and Ian Carter. Both were extremely capable, but both sadly suffered from ill health, particularly Ian. He was a very tall man – about 6 feet 7 inches – and a diabetic. Unfortunately, Ian was a bit of a loner and he also liked a drink. He too was taken before his time, but he was a very kind man. I remember spending some time with him in the Rose and Crown. He was a great music fan and loved the "oldies", especially the Everly Brothers. He once copied an entire cassette of theirs for me, and when I hear an Everly Brothers track I still think of him to this day.

That was the thing about Isis House. Like many other places where I worked in UKIS, we were family. We worked and played together, and lasting bonds were formed. I count some of those days there as the finest in my life and remember them fondly.

Another big turning point in my career was the arrival of Dave Barrell as my new boss, after Kelvin retired. Dave had returned from Dhaka and successfully applied for promotion to Inspector. He too was very close to Peter Tompkins at that time, and very much a forward thinker. He was also prepared to take risks to advance the business, and to challenge some of the policy thinking in the corridors of power to attack and disrupt organised immigration crime.

This was very welcome to us. Although we had extended our influence and capability to trace and remove immigration offenders in greater numbers, we were not involved in the investigation of immigration crime. We had become frustrated at our lack of capability to investigate and prosecute the facilitators and the organised crime gangs who were making lots of money from the proceeds of it. This was very much in the domain of the criminal investigation department of the Metropolitan Police, but not something that rated very high on their agenda.

As our intelligence systems developed, we started to notice trends in specific areas of immigration abuse. The fact that we were able to expose these to the public – and achieve significant changes in the way we resourced and tackled immigration crime – was due largely to the efforts of Dave Barrell. Although like most things in life, it required a great deal of courage and innovation to achieve it. Fortunately for us, Dave had bucketloads of both.

The first area we looked at was the phenomenon of bogus educational establishments – later known lovingly by the popular press as "dodgy colleges". We discovered that we were arresting more and more "students" as illegal workers who had either been given leave to remain – or applied for leave to remain – at the "London School of International Business" (LSIB). A pattern soon emerged to suggest that these "students" were not attending college at all. Instead, they were paying an "enrolment fee" to the LSIB in return for a letter of enrolment and a confirmation of good attendance, to support applications to remain in the UK. This was making the proprietor of the LSIB, a certain Frederick Wolfgang Rosner, a very rich man. When we took our suspicions to the police, we were told that there was insufficient evidence to mount a prosecution and that any witness evidence would be unreliable because it came from conspirators who were using Rosner's services simply to stay in the country illegally.

Undeterred, Dave saw this as an opportunity to bring UKIS into the world of investigating serious immigration crime, and he saw me as one of the key people to support him in this mission. Between us, we set up a team to investigate the college with a view to securing the necessary evidence. This meant circulating a note to all caseworkers in Lunar House to send us all applications to remain based on studies at the LSIB.

The sheer scale of the operation was frightening. It soon became clear that literally hundreds of "students" were getting leave to remain in the UK on the basis of enrolment at what was, in effect, a non-existent college. Covert visits to the premises showed that Rosner was employing some of the "students" himself to undertake the registrations and issue the enrolment letters. After a lot of painstaking work, we were able to persuade the police that we now had sufficient evidence to raid the premises, arrest Rosner and seize his assets.

On the day of the operation, we found the evidence we were seeking. This was clearly a bogus college, and a major organised immigration crime racket. We amassed a huge amount of evidence against Rosner, who was subsequently convicted of a conspiracy to defraud the Secretary of State for the Home Department, and sent to prison. Not content to stop there, Dave courted publicity for the operation (much to the chagrin of the Home Office Press Office) and appeared on national TV that evening discussing the operation and the likely extent of immigration abuse in London. I vividly remember standing in the Rose and Crown with him watching him on the television news and seeing him answer his phone shortly afterwards, with a summons to report to the Home Office immediately. Dave just shrugged, said in his broad Brummie accent that he seemed to have upset someone up there, and bought another pint!

At this stage in my journey, it is worth mentioning a very

pretty young blonde who turned up in the pub that day. She was from the Overstayers Tracing & Investigations Section (OTIS) at the Home Office. Her name was Jill Arnfield, and she had the biggest blue eyes I had ever seen. What's more, she seemed to be thoroughly enjoying the UKIS culture – so much so that she wanted to become an Immigration Officer. But more of that later.

Actually, it was the popular media of the day that drove operational policy in the field of immigration abuse. Dave Barrell's foray into Fleet Street was frowned upon by the Home Office elite, but in those days newspapers such as the *News of The World* wielded great power. They were always on the lookout for the next big scam they could "uncover" – and their "investigations" often took the form of exposing immigration rackets. In addition to the colleges scam – where it had by now become clear that a lot of people had been making a lot of money to set up "fake colleges" to facilitate leave to remain applications – other rackets soon emerged. These ranged from smuggling illegals in the backs of lorries to passport factories and fake marriage rackets. However, it was the practice of such "undercover reporters" to infiltrate the underworld to gather their "evidence" for the "dossier" they would end up passing to the police about an hour before their headline went to print. This was often outside the codes of practice required under the Police and Criminal Evidence Act (PACE), meaning it was often inadmissible in court.

Dave took a slightly different view to the police, who would often decline to follow up on such grounds alone. He felt that the disruption caused to the organised gangs by a press exposé of their activities made them fair game for immigration enforcement officers, and he encouraged us to work with undercover reporters rather than against them.

I vividly remember two such characters, who have long since passed on. They were Gerry Brown and Chris Blythe, both undercover reporters with the *News of the World* back in the 1980s. Gerry was the older and wiser of the two and - having made a living out of such work for a long time -he knew exactly where to look for the juicy stories. One such place was amongst the vagrant community in Clapton Park, who spent most of their lives drinking themselves into an early grave and looking for ways to make money to pay for their next can of Spitfire.

Poor Chris was stationed in Clapton Park for a few weeks, posing as a tramp. Now it is fair to say that both Chris and Gerry were quite capable of fulfilling such a role – not just in appearance, but also in their capacity to absorb copious amounts of alcohol. Anyway, once Chris became a "trusted" member of the community he was approached by an Irishman called "Tommy Connolly" to enter into an arranged marriage with "a black girl" for the sum of £300. This included the provision of a suit and a wedding ring for the big day – all designed so that the "wedding photos" could be sent to the Home Office as evidence of the marriage. The girls concerned were invariably young Ghanaian ladies who had overstayed their leave to enter the UK, and were seeking a route to settlement in the UK based on a marriage to a person settled here.

Of course, there was never any intention of the marriage subsisting, or even being consummated. To be fair I don't think poor old Tommy or his mates would be up to the task, even if it had been offered to them. The arrangement was quite simply to turn up at the registry office, take the pictures and the money, and then disappear. Unless of course the hapless groom was required at some later date to attend the Home Office for a "marriage interview"; whereupon a search party was sent out into Clapton Park and surrounding areas in the hope that the groom was still alive and kicking.

Chris Blythe was a good candidate for such a wedding. He made it his business to find out just how this scam worked, how much money was involved, and who the mastermind was behind it all. Not only that, but he also carried a concealed tape recorder about his person to gather evidence along the way. On this occasion the reporters passed their "dossier" to us before they went to print. This gave us time to research some of the cases involved.

As with the London School of International Business, a pattern soon emerged. I was appointed as senior investigating officer for "Operation Goldring", which went on for three years and probably merits a book of its own. We asked Home Office caseworkers to refer any files to us where they had received an application to remain based on marriage from that part of London, and where the parties were Ghanaian females and white men of British or Irish extraction. It wasn't long before we started to amass a huge pile of files, all bearing photographs of the happy couple, with the groom usually wearing an ill-fitting suit and holding a can of Special Brew. It turned out that there were potentially 300 cases fitting this description, and a visit to the local registrars revealed many more in the pipeline.

One common thread across the files was the involvement of one Dr Ohene-Djan, an "immigration adviser". After lengthy consultation with Scotland Yard, we were able to build a strong case against Ohene-Djan and his gang for "conspiracy to defraud the Secretary of State for the Home Department". A subsequent raid on his property revealed large amounts of cash and several wedding suits of different shapes and sizes, along with a significant number of Ghanaian passports belonging to female overstayers. Of course, for the *News of the World*, this story had it all – sex, money, and scandal. But for us, the road to Crown Court was a long and rocky one. We had three days of legal argument on whether Chris Blythe's tapes were admissible, and several hours of sometimes hilarious evidence from the defendants about how this was just a marriage bureau helping people to find love.

Our case was not helped by the fact that poor old Tommy had drunk himself to death by the time the case came to court, and the good Doctor Ohene-Djan suddenly became so ill that we wondered if we could ever secure a conviction. In the end he and his co-defendants were convicted, but prison sentences were suspended on grounds of ill health. However, our job was done. The ring was dismantled, and the abuse stopped – at least in that case. Hence, I later learned that in many cases crime does pay – and often the best tactic available to law enforcement is to disrupt it rather than prosecute.

Of course, another way to tackle abuse of the immigration laws was to change the policy. As my career progressed, it became clear to me that neither the UK Immigration Service – nor the UK Border Agency for that matter – would ever have enough resources to raid all the dodgy colleges and dodgy marriages out there. Better to introduce a sponsorship system, placing greater obligations upon the beneficiaries of such services to ensure compliance. This led to a huge row between the government departments responsible for law enforcement (who wanted to clamp down on abuse) and those responsible for education (who saw serious financial benefits in bringing overseas students to the UK). I also remember several arguments between church and state, with the church fiercely defending the sanctity of marriage, to the extent that the racketeers turned to dodgy vicars to ply their trade as we tightened the rules on registry office weddings.

Another area that continued to attract our attention – and still does, in many respects – was illegal working. Picking up on the lessons of the JOE teams, I continued to advocate intelligence-led operations into those employment sectors most likely to be hiring illegal workers. These were invariably the cleaning companies, catering companies and construction industries where work was readily available to unskilled workers for low pay rates.

One area I helped to develop was the "upper tier" enforcement operation. As time went by, we began to finesse rules of engagement into immigration enforcement work. This meant introducing a "grading system" for enforcement "visits" (which was the politically correct term for "raids"). One or two potential offenders would be a "lower tier visit", which could be authorised by a Chief Immigration Officer. Between three and eight potential offenders would be termed a "middle tier visit", which could be authorised by an Immigration Inspector. Anything more than that was an "upper tier operation" which required the authority of the Chief Inspector, and Ministers would be informed.

Organising an "upper tier operation" took quite a bit of work. Having dabbled in this area in my JOE days – and having by now inherited the role of "Training CIO" – I took it upon myself to build a training pack on how to run such a thing. This included a lot of guidance about how to set up a governance structure and control room; what papers to prepare; how to conduct briefings; and so on. The operation we chose to build our training package around was "Operation Tanker" – so named because it related to a raid upon the entire cleaning company of the Shell building in Waterloo. In the end we effected 64 arrests that day – a haul which still stands as one of the highest in living memory. And all captured on film by the UKIS video training unit.

The raid was so high profile that it sent the powers that be into a high panic when the story started to appear on the national TV news. I remember overseeing the control room at City Road police station when an army of TV reporters turned up outside looking for someone to interview. After referring the matter to my then Inspector – a lovely man called Tony McCormack – I was advised to do it as the "man on the spot". I later learned that this was the only time a certain Deputy Chief Inspector physically ran along the corridors of the Home Office demanding to know where I was and what I was doing. "Get Tony Smith away from those cameras now! Where the hell is he?" To which my control room co-ordinator replied, in truly UKIS fashion, "Sorry guvnor, I think he's in make up at the moment".

Looking back on my career, I think that those heady days

as a CIO at Isis House were amongst the best. We had a great team spirit. We worked hard and laughed, cried, and drank together. Without doubt, we changed the face of immigration enforcement work in the UK. It wasn't always plain sailing and like any pioneers we took a wrong turning here and there, but we achieved a great deal, and for the most part we took a keen interest in our work.

I can remember doing a great deal of research into the immigration service codes of practice under PACE and delivering training courses at Ashridge College in Kent with my dear departed friend Jimmy Green. Jimmy was a lively, affable Scotsman with a twinkle in his eye and a great sense of humour. I was his Cockney alter ego. He was the training CIO at the Intelligence Unit, and I was the training CIO at Isis House. These were then the two biggest immigration enforcement offices in the land, covering the whole of London and most of the south-east of England between us. Our training sessions became legendary, and we became known affectionately as "Saint and Greavesy" after the popular football pundit duo of that era. I remember racing Jimmy round the square at Ashridge at midnight, in a take from the movie "Chariots of Fire". We had some great times there, but we worked hard too, and our efforts had not gone completely unnoticed by the powers above. Although I didn't know it at the time, my career was about to take another turn.

CHAPTER 8

JOINING HER MAJESTY'S
INSPECTORATE OF IMMIGRATION

The role of "Her Majesty's Inspector of UK Immigration" was first created under the Aliens Act of 1905, following a Royal Commission of Immigration. The role was augmented to Chief Inspector after the First World War. The incumbent of both posts was Sir William Haldane Porter, a lawyer from Belfast who had graduated from Queens College Belfast and Lincoln College Oxford.

Under the Aliens Act of 1919, the Chief Inspector was enabled to "control alien entry and departure" to and from the United Kingdom. Haldane Porter set about building the "Immigration Branch", and he remained in post until 1930. A series of Chief Inspectors succeeded him over the years, as the Immigration Branch expanded and transformed to become the UK Immigration Service.

These Immigration Inspectors went on to form a body of men (remember there were no women in the job before the 1970s) who between them set up and managed immigration controls at ports of entry across the country. It now fell into place – the person who interviewed a young fresh-faced Tony Smith for the Immigration Service in 1972 was a member of this illustrious breed of Inspectors.

I had met the previous "Chief" (Dick Richards) once before when he had visited Heathrow. But prior to my attachment to ISHQ I had only met the current Chief, Peter Tompkins, once or twice. His office was based in Lunar House in Croydon at Immigration Service Headquarters (ISHQ). He was an affable man, always approachable and keen to speak to any officers who appeared at ISHQ from the front line. His career path had taken him through the ranks – Immigration Officer, Chief Immigration Officer, HM Inspector, Assistant Chief Inspector, Deputy Chief Inspector, Chief.

Obviously, there were people above the Chief Inspector in the Home Office hierarchy – up to and including the Permanent Secretary – but to us they were invisible. The Chief was the Chief, and that was that. There was a pecking order for the top job, and inevitably when the time was right one of the DCIs would take over. But the thought that anyone who hadn't come up through the ranks could ever become Chief was inconceivable to us, just as the post of Chief Constable could never go to anyone other than a copper.

One thing I recall about Peter Tomkins was his remarkable memory. He could almost recount word for word every piece of advice I had given him the previous week, in detail. So much so that I found myself re-briefing myself before each encounter with him, to be consistent. Like so many of the UKIS hierarchy in those days, Peter also liked a drink. It was not unusual for him to host a drinks meeting in his office on a Friday evening, to which all the members of the Service who had the unfortunate privilege of having been posted to ISHQ were invited. This was frowned upon by many of the senior civil servants in the wider Home Office, to the extent that a Home Office notice to staff came out forbidding any drinking of alcohol in the office other than in the office bar on the 19th floor, during meal breaks. Undeterred, Peter's disciples made sure that despite this order, there was always an ongoing supply of bottles in ISHQ, which was deemed necessary for "hospitality" purposes.

Colin Manchip was someone I had earmarked to be the next Chief, after Peter. He knew me from my days at Terminal 1, where he was an Inspector, and he had by now become Assistant Chief Inspector (ACI) for Enforcement and my Head of Division.

In those days you were marked annually both for performance and for suitability for promotion. The performance levels ranged from box 1 to box 5 as follows: 1 "Outstanding" 2 "Above Average" 3 "Satisfactory", 4 "Needs development in some areas" 5 "Needs significant development". In the promotion box you were either "Exceptionally Fitted", "Fitted", or "Not Fitted" for promotion to the next grade.

The expectation was that you would start out as a box 4 NF, with the aim of getting up to box 3 NF as soon as possible. Once that milestone was achieved, you were pretty safe and unlikely to face any disciplinary proceedings (unless you managed to screw up badly enough to attract the wrath of senior officers). From there your ambition – if you still had any – was to progress to Box 2 (which might attract a small bonus) and to a "Fitted" marking, which indicated that you were considered at least capable of performing the tasks at the higher grade, subject to training and development. A Box 1 was reserved only for those perceived to be performing at an exceptionally high level, when compared with the broader peer group. "Exceptionally Fitted" was reserved for those who could slip seamlessly into the higher grade with minimal training or development.

To be fair, promotion to HMI was not for everybody. With shift disturbance allowance, weekend premium payments and overtime a CIO could make a very good living in those days – so why jeopardise that? Added to which promotion to HMI would always mean an initial posting into a "non-shift working" post in ISHQ, at a significant financial loss. This was a crossroads for me and for many other CIOs of that era, but by now I had the confidence to know that not only could I do a good job at the higher grade - but I would also most likely relish the challenge too.

Most of my peer group at the time were receiving either a 3 NF or a 2 F marking, depending mainly upon the extent of their ambition. By contrast, after a few years in post and some spectacular successes in the role, I was awarded a 1 F marking. Which meant that I was an "exceptional" CIO, and that I was "fitted" for promotion – but not "exceptionally fitted" for it. This was extremely unusual.

Colin was my countersigning officer at the time, and he set out the reasoning behind this marking very clearly in his feedback on my performance report. *"Mr Smith is an exceptional CIO who clearly has significant potential. Although he perhaps lacks the outward poise that would be necessary to perform well at higher levels in the organisation"*.

Although we laughed about it in later life, Colin was right. There was a big difference between the behaviours required and expected at the front line in middle management roles, and those expected in the upper echelons of the Home Office. There was a bridge to cross, and it wasn't an easy one, particularly for someone like me, having come from a working-class background and with a very clear view of right and wrong, fairness, and respect for the rule of law. There was a political awareness required in the world of immigration enforcement – something that I struggled to balance throughout my career.

After passing a promotion board I was appointed as one of Her Majesty's Inspectors of Immigration in the class of 1990, at the age of 37.

Now in those days HMIs were in shorter supply than they are nowadays, and they were split between "shift working" and "non-shift working" posts. This led to a complex creation of postings, managed entirely by the Chief Inspector himself. Having secured promotion, I was invited to put forward my three preferences for posting. Given my penchant for enforcement work, I put down the Intelligence Unit as first choice, Isis House as second choice and Heathrow as third choice.

In the end I found myself back in Lunar House where it had all begun, but this time as an Immigration Inspector in ISHQ, and with an annual pay packet that dropped from £28k to £18k overnight.

It was then that I received the famous "Tompkins letter". These were meted out to all newly promoted HMIs at that time. Invariably they indicated that your "permanent posting" would be to one of your operational choices, but that in the interim you would be posted on "detached duty" to ISHQ in Croydon, for a period of no more than three years. This was significant, because at that time the Home Office would pay "detached duty terms" for a maximum of three years. This meant that at least you could claim excess travelling time and expenses from your permanent station, to take the sting out of the pay drop.

In my case, this backfired on two fronts. Firstly, I was living in Worcester Park. Croydon was no further away from my home than my "permanent" station in Southwark. And secondly, the Chief didn't keep accurate records of what he had promised to whom. So, although my letter told me I was in first position for the next HMI post at the IU, the fact was that another newbie who had been promoted shortly before me had received the same promise!

This put an even greater strain on my marriage. Marilyn liked the good things in life, but we had to tighten our belts significantly with this "promotion". Things hadn't been great between us for some time, and once again I found myself spending more time with my UKIS "family" than my real one. Changes introduced to the secondary school system in the London Borough of

Kingston at that time didn't help. One of the few saving graces of the transfer from Windsor to Worcester Park was the education system, and the hope that both Sharon and Mark would make it to Tiffin's Grammar school in Kingston. However, around that time the law changed regarding admission to grammar schools. Although under the old rules both my kids would have sailed through the eleven plus and into grammar school, they now found themselves competing with the brightest and the best from across the land for school places. Marilyn's solution to this was to spend money we didn't really have on expensive private schools for the kids, and to complain endlessly that if only I had done better in my career, we could have moved up the road to a new estate that had been built in Worcester Park. This did nothing for my self-esteem, whereas in the workplace I felt considerably more valued and respected.

Life as an Inspector in Immigration Service Headquarters was certainly different. This really was the "Civil Service" rather than the "Immigration Service" and a far cry from chasing round London playing cops and robbers with overstayers or searching people's bags in the midnight hour at the airport. I soon learned that the main role of ISHQ was to bridge the gap between the bureaucrats in the Home Office and the officers in the field.

This was around the time that asylum applicants started to appear in ever increasing volumes at the border. Under the 1951 Convention, asylum cases could not be decided summarily by Immigration Officers at the border and had to be referred inland to a separate decision maker. This in turn led to a massive duplication of effort. Ports would be responsible for logging the case, conducting a "screening interview", sending a report to ISHQ and then invariably granting temporary admission to the applicant pending a full asylum interview later.

Word soon got round that the asylum system was a great way to get into the UK – at least temporarily – pending an interview. Even after that there were a range of opportunities available to spin the process out, fuelled by an ever-increasing army of immigration lawyers. Further representations, fresh applications, MPs representations, appeals and judicial reviews were all used to prolong an applicant's stay in the country, as mountains of paper built up both in casework offices at the ports and in ISHQ.

Meanwhile, decision making became more complicated as people realised that they could also thwart removal by making representations via their MP, or by lodging an application to remain on grounds of "Human Rights" – most commonly under Article 8 (right to family life). As Immigration Officers, we were increasingly vilified by lobby groups for not accepting these applications at face value and granting leave to enter. If someone says they have fallen in love and established a genuine relationship with a person settled here, who were we to say they hadn't? We were qualified to do so because many of us had seen life at the operational end of the spectrum, where gangs were making lots of money by setting up marriages of convenience; or where heartbroken spouses were later contacting us requesting deportation action against their partner, who had done a bunk the moment his or her permit to stay landed on the doorstep.

After being thrust back into Lunar House as a non-shift working inspector, I soon realised that my new line manager was to be Michael Durose, the master of the red pen. Michael was the Assistant Chief Inspector for Passenger Casework at ISHQ at the time. And he was still marking CIO's drafts with a vengeance – as well as overseeing instructions to the ports of entry on matters of immigration policy and practice.

I got to know Michael well during this period. He was coming to the end of his career by then, but he still retained a keen interest in his work, and particularly the written word. It was clear from the start that I would have to work hard to get his respect and also gain the respect of some of the long-term CIOs that were there at that time.

One lasting memory I have of working with Michael Durose

was working on the instruction to abolish the re-entry visa. The great policy makers of the Home Office and the Foreign Office had convinced Ministers that requiring foreign nationals with extant leave to remain in the UK to get a re-entry visa every time they travelled abroad was a complete waste of time. Which it probably was.

The challenge for us was turning this into an operational instruction to ports. This file came to me to draft this, and after three returns from Michael telling me to "have another stab" I decided to seek an audience with him to discuss it. When the time came to do so, I sat in front of him, took out my notebook, and started to interview him.

"What are you doing?"

"I want to ask you some questions about this instruction on re-entry visas" I said.

"Yes, I know but why are you taking notes?"

"Well, I am going to write down what you say Michael. Then I might get it right next time."

For the first time I spotted a gap in his defences. He obviously wasn't used to being interviewed – especially by somebody lower than himself in the food chain. Without further ado he cut short our conversation and asked me to come back again the following Monday.

The weekend came and went, and I duly reported to his office on Monday as agreed. This time he had his own notes, which he started to read out to me.

"Michael, what do you have there?" I asked.

"It's some notes about the format of the instruction on the abolition of the re-entry visa" he replied.

"Oh great" I said, without thinking, and picking up the paper from under his nose. "I can use these now. It will save me taking notes of my own".

Michael went scarlet with embarrassment as I looked at the paper before me. Yes, these were notes about the format of the instruction, written in his classic red pen – on the reverse side of the order paper from the Sunday service at his local church! He had obviously got bored during the Sunday morning sermon and had taken it upon himself to sketch this out in church. I had to smile – and I think he saw the funny side as well.

That marked a turning point in our relationship, so much so that Michael asked me for some 360-degree feedback on his own performance later that year, and seemed to take a lot of it on board in changing his behaviour towards newly promoted CIOs after that. His retirement was quite sad. He insisted that he didn't want a party or any speeches, but we arranged one for him anyway. I am sure that if you looked closely enough you could spot a tear in his eye as he departed ISHQ for the last time.

Meanwhile, internal politics at the Home Office continued to abound. There had always been an uneasy tension between the UK Immigration Service (as the operational arm of immigration and border control) and the UK Immigration and Nationality Department (as the lead policy and case working arm of the business). The independent role of "Chief Inspector of Immigration" never sat neatly with the Home Office hierarchy and Peter's attempt to keep UKIS as an arm's length operational agency within the Home Office was beginning to lose momentum. Upon his retirement in 1990, the Home Office decided that the time had come to abolish the post of "Chief Inspector of the Immigration Service" altogether. His job – previously set at SCS Grade 4 level – was split into two "Director" (Grade 5) Posts – IS (Ports) and IS (Enforcement). Likewise, the terms that had previously applied to the upper echelons of UKIS (Assistant Chief Inspector, and Deputy Chief Inspector) were replaced with "Assistant Director" and "Deputy Director" and broadly aligned with Home Office Grades 7 and 6 respectively. These grades have survived to this day. Below that, HMI, CIO, and IO grades remained broadly aligned to SEO, HEO and EO grades

– although the pay gap between them remained stark due to overtime, shift premiums and the like.

The post of "Chief Inspector of Immigration" was retained as a nominal title only and added to the portfolio of the "Director General" of the Immigration and Nationality Department. Peter Tompkins was to be the last "real" Chief Inspector of the Immigration Service. The beginning of the end of the UK Immigration Service was nigh.

During this period Kate Collins, a former Immigration Officer from Terminal 2 and subsequent Home Office "fast streamer", was appointed as Director of Immigration Service (Ports). Kate brought in John De Llanos (known affectionately to us as "Dilly") as her Deputy Director from Heathrow, where he had been serving as ACI for some years before that.

Dilly was the complete opposite to Kate. She knew the Civil Service ways of working very well and was capable of managing Senior Civil Servants and Ministers with great skill. Dilly was old school UKIS. He had risen through the ranks and knew the UKIS culture very well.

Upon his arrival, Dilly pulled us all into his office and told us in no uncertain terms about how this was going to work.

"Right listen up you lot. Kate is the mandarinette, and she is the boss. She will be dealing with the Ministers and the Permanent Secretaries and all the other mandarins and mandarinettes around here. She will be looking upwards. I am here to keep an eye on you lot. I will be looking downwards. If you need me for anything my door will be open. Now go and get on with it."

I liked Dilly a lot. He was very smart – much smarter than some gave him credit for. He had a great sense of humour and he helped me out a lot during those times. He even managed to get me a small pay rise – nothing like the amount I had lost by taking promotion to a non-shift working HMI post, but a help. When I thanked him, he just told me to stop complaining about money and spend less bloody time in the pub if I was short of cash.

Of course, although I was an Inspector at ISHQ and not in the field, I was still a member of the "Inspectorate". The Immigration Service Inspectorate in those days was much smaller than it is now. As such, we were a senior management group comprising of shift working and non-shift working Inspectors managing ports, borders, and enforcement operations across the UK.

In London and the bigger ports and enforcement offices, it was standard practice to have Immigration Inspectors on site. In some places, such as the North East, Inspectors oversaw both port and enforcement work. These became known as "hybrid" ports – known affectionately as "the land of hybridity."

I really liked the idea of hybridity. It preserved the link between port work and inland work and led to a more interesting job pattern, and it delivered a lot of efficiencies too. For example, an immigration officer could easily be deployed to land a ferry in the morning and then conduct an enforcement visit in the afternoon. Having CIOs and HMIs covering both disciplines was also helpful for job diversity and career patterns. In some regions it was also feasible to conduct after-entry interviews for marriage or asylum applications.

Because the organisation was still relatively small, it was not difficult to get the Inspectors to come together on a regular basis for a conference. These events usually took place at or near one of the main airports, and they became legendary in their day.

One HMI's conference that stands out above all others was held at the Russ Hill hotel near Gatwick. These invariably involved an overnight stay and – in the best traditions of the UK Immigration Service – a very significant amount of alcohol being consumed after dinner.

We were always up for a sing-song in UKIS, and we had our share of talented musicians (and less talented singers) in our midst. It was not unusual for a UKIS band to pipe up out of the blue, with people like Brian Malone and Brian Parks on guitar and Tony McCormack on the piano. I fell into the latter category of singers, frequently called upon to sing a few Chas & Dave numbers and invariably in the wrong key.

Another character of the day was a short and rotund Scotsman with a great sense of humour, Gerry Maguire. Gerry's famous party piece was singing 'Sixteen Tons' by Tennessee Ernie Ford, together with a significant amount of arm waving and foot stamping. With a bellyful of Scotch whisky on board, Gerry took it upon himself to deliver his rendition of 'Sixteen Tons' from on top of the piano in the Russ Hill hotel lobby. All was fine until we heard a massive crack as the glass top to the piano gave way under his weight. This had us all rolling about laughing until well into the night.

The first session of the conference the next morning saw a lot of bleary-eyed Inspectors diving for the water bottles at the side of the room at the first opportunity, prompting the chairman to suggest he might ask the hotel management to turn on the sprinkler system to rehydrate us! This was only bettered by the sight of a hotel waiter coming in mid-conference looking for a Mr Gerry Maguire, armed with an envelope on a silver platter. This turned out to be the repair bill for the piano he had broken the night before – prompting more howls of laughter across the room.

This is just one of many stories I could tell about life as an Inspector in the UK Immigration Service in the nineties. We had a great camaraderie and sense of team spirit between us, and a huge amount of respect for each other. They were indeed happy days.

One of the other jobs in my portfolio as an Inspector at ISHQ was to manage international liaison work. This was my first foray into international borders, often attending meetings with representatives from other control agencies from around the world to discuss matters of mutual interest. Indeed, it was the International Air Transportation Association (IATA) and the Control Agencies Working Group (CAWG) that developed the

Carriers Liability framework. This involved delivering training to airline agents on immigration fraud and forgery detection, in order to stop the ever-increasing flows of "inadequately documented arrivals" that were turning up at airports around the world. The standard practice used was to show a forged passport to get on board the aircraft and then to destroy it or hand it off to another en route.

I can remember conducting "sweeps" at Heathrow during the night shift and regularly finding 30-40 people huddled in the transit lounge who spoke no English (other than the word "asylum") and had no passports. Smugglers had instructed them to do this, and had often provided them with fake passports as part of the package. They knew very well that if we didn't know who they were or where they came from, then it would be nigh on impossible for us to return them whence they came. They were right of course. That's why we introduced the Carriers Liability Act and pre-boarding checks at source and transit airports around the world, and installed CCTV on piers and in gate lounges. It was a constant game of "cat and mouse" between the human smugglers and us – one that continues to haunt us to this day.

One day, Dilly called me in to his office.

"So young Smith I have been speaking to the mandarinette about you, and she seems to quite like you. So do I, for that matter," he growled.

I looked at him, wondering what was coming next. Dilly wasn't renowned for handing out positive feedback to his Inspectors.

"Well, we've had a call from the Americans, and they want us to send someone over there for a few weeks. Don't know why. Sounds like you don't have to do too much either – just eat their burgers and look interested. Are you OK with that?"

I nearly fell off my chair. I had never been to the States, but I had always dreamed of going. Financially this was out of our reach for a holiday. Yet here I was being offered the trip of a lifetime at government expense! I couldn't say yes quick enough.

You can guess the reaction I got when I told Marilyn. This was Bangladesh all over again.

"What about me? What about your children? We can't afford to go to America, and you are just going swanning off on your own again. If you had a proper job, then you could afford to take us to Disneyland just like Dave and Linda, but we are stuck here again on our own whilst you have all the fun," she said.

So off I went again trying to get a deal to bring them over for part of the trip, rather than focusing upon the benefits this would bring me in learning about how they manage their borders in the USA. There was clearly a pattern emerging here.

It turned out that I had been selected to participate in the mid-level managers' exchange programme, which had been set up under the auspices of the Four Country Conference (FCC). This was a programme where a middle manager with potential for future leadership in each country would visit one of the Four Countries (Australia, Canada, UK, US) in turn, to observe border operations and compare notes.

This was an unbelievable experience for me, and something I will never forget. I flew to Washington DC, where we spent the first couple of days at the old Immigration and Naturalisation Service (INS) building on "I" street. There I met with Larry Weinig, our US host from US Immigration and Naturalisation Service (INS); Gary Blachford, an intelligence and enforcement manager from Citizen and Immigration Canada (CIC); and Diane Bilow from the Australian Department of Immigration and Multicultural Affairs (DIMIA). We got on like a house on fire – particularly Gary and I, who remained good friends for many years thereafter. I can remember being taken into a bar in DC by Gary on our first night where he introduced me to "Moosehead" Canadian beer – so much so that between us we managed to demolish an entire crate of the stuff.

We travelled to Arlington Virginia to look at their immigration processing centre, before flying across the country to El Paso, Texas where we went out on operations on the Mexican border with the US Border Patrol. I kept a log of the trip and wrote at the time:

> *Without any doubt, the highlight of the trip for me was accompanying the US Border Patrol on operations. It is impossible to describe the situation on the US/Mexico border realistically – you have to go there and see it. I stood on the banks of the Rio Grande and saw for myself how migrants gathered in an attempt to get across.*
>
> *The border patrol apprehended over a million illegal entrants in 1990. Nobody knew how many got through. The supervising officer – Jim Olech – was philosophical about the whole operation. "Most get caught 3 or 4 times then get in", he said. "Our job is simply to slow down illegal entry – we can't stop it."*

Words that would no doubt ring in the ears of a certain US President 25 years later, who promised to build a wall to do the job for them.

Our tour took us to the Bridge of Americas at El Paso, where we were escorted by Joe Salazar, the local supervisor there at the time. I heard that Joe retired on 1 November 1991, after 50 years' service with the INS at the El Paso Border. He passed away the following year. The US Immigration Service was his whole life. Very much like my predecessors in the UK Immigration Service.

We then went to Florida to visit the theme parks, where we learned about the specific visa and immigration programmes deployed there – particularly in the country pavilions in the Epcot Centre.

We also visited the Krome detention centre in the Everglades. Naively, I asked the Supervising Officer there if they had many escapes. She laughed and said "nobody escapes from here, man.

We're in swampland, surrounded by alligators. If anyone gets out, they're screaming to get back in again an hour later!"

The INS reserved their New York detention facility for the most dangerous detainees. This was located on the fourth floor of a Central Office block. I wrote at the time:

> *Bars and grills have been installed on the 4th floor of an office block in downtown New York City, which now houses some of the meanest villains in America, all awaiting deportation. Here we saw convicted murderers, rapists and bank robbers staring out at us through reinforced glass under the watchful eye of INS guards. I don't know how the other occupants of that office block feel about their co-tenants on the 4th floor. I never thought I would say this – but give me Lunar House anytime.*

The tour ended with a visit to the famous Ellis Island museum, where I observed a familiar INS catchphrase – "A century of service to a nation of immigrants – 1891-1991". The Immigration Act of 1891 was where it all began, and Ellis Island proudly records the fact that it was the primary staging post for the millions of immigrants that travelled from Europe on the great steamships of the early 1900s.

I was so taken by the entire experience that I wrote a lengthy report of my visit and lessons learned (completely unprompted) together with photographs, which I presented to Dilly and Kate upon my return to Croydon. That report still sits proudly on by bookcase, alongside a multitude of other memorabilia from that trip.

I did manage to cobble together the funds to bring Marilyn and the kids over to Florida, where they got to stay at the luxury Disney hotel, courtesy of US government rates.

If I wasn't already in love with international border management before that trip, I certainly was when I got back.

This was an unbelievable experience. I made some great friends from border agencies in other countries with similar interests to my own and learned a huge amount about the challenges of managing borders in different countries. Something that I was destined to return to in later life.

CHAPTER 9

BACK TO IMMIGRATION ENFORCEMENT, COMMUNITY TENSIONS, AND IMMIGRATION ARREST TEAMS

With the Tompkins letter now burning a hole in my inbox, it was time for me to return to operations after nearly three years at ISHQ.

UKIS had by now substantially extended its footprint into immigration enforcement, particularly in London. Isis House had crammed more and more Immigration Officers into their tiny office in Southwark Street – so much so that Home Office Estates recognised the time had come to find larger premises in the London Bridge area. Ultimately, they settled upon Becket House, a stone's throw from London Bridge station. At the same time, they decided that a third Inspector post was needed there – and that door had my name on it.

Things had not gone well for immigration enforcement in London during my absence. At 07.40 am on 28 July 1993, three police officers from the Metropolitan Police Service's Aliens

Deportation Group accompanied by an immigration officer from Becket House raided an address in North London in order to arrest and detain a Jamaican overstayer, Joy Gardner, and her five-year-old son. As police officers used increasing force to restrain her, Mrs Gardner suffered respiratory failure and died in hospital three days later. This was a watershed moment for immigration enforcement operations and led to significant community tensions for years afterwards. In May 1995, the three police officers stood trial for manslaughter; one was acquitted and two were found not guilty. But immigration enforcement would never be the same.

I returned to Isis House in 1994 in the midst of this, where the entire operation was under review. It was clear that immigration enforcement would need to secure community consent in the future, and this would be a long and difficult road to travel.

I worked at Isis House for a brief spell before the office move, and I can remember being appalled at the state of the place. One of my responsibilities as the new Inspector there was training, so I decided to attend a course for new entrants for a day just to see how it was being delivered. Imagine my surprise when I was told that due to office overcrowding, training courses were now being held in a room above the Red Lion pub around the corner. Even more shocking was the fact that some of the "trainers" chose to deliver their classes with a pint of beer in one hand and a cigarette in the other.

Don't get me wrong – I enjoyed spending time in the local after work with the best of them. Life at home had now become miserable, and this was my other family after all. But I knew enough about the business by now to be able to draw the line between socialising and working. I concluded that part of my management role at Isis House would be to clean up the operation there and help to turn immigration enforcement into a much more professional organisation than it had become. This meant not only better training, but a culture change. Fortunately for me, this was a view shared by the UKIS management hierarchy. They decided to bring in a newly promoted Assistant Director to Becket House to help them to deliver this change. That person was David Wilson.

I had known Dave Wilson personally for many years, going back to my Heathrow days. He wasn't everybody's cup of tea, although I always got along fine with him. He wasn't a great socialiser – probably not least because he was teetotal – but he was a fine sportsman. I remember picking him regularly to play striker in the Heathrow flyers. Even though he wasn't much of a team player, he was always likely to pop up from nowhere and score the winning goal for us. Rather than celebrate in the bar afterwards Dave would stand looking out of the window with an orange juice in his hand, waiting for Malcolm Paul (who car shared with him) to finish his half of shandy so they could go home. After they left, most of the rest of the team proceeded to get drunk and tell me that I should drop him the following week, even though he was our top goal scorer. But I took no notice, and we went on to win many games that would otherwise have been lost without him. I never really understood why Dave was so miserable all the time. I assumed that he had an unhappy marriage – but he wasn't the only one. He did go on to marry a UKIS girl like so many of us, but even that didn't cheer him up.

Anyway, Dave rated me quite highly, so I was pleased with his appointment as my new boss. There were two other Inspectors at Becket House with me – Dave Ellis and Tony McCormack. Dave Ellis moved out to join the Dover crew living in Deal, and Dave Roberts took over. Ironically both Dave Roberts and I were destined to go on to bigger and greater things, whereas Tony McCormack (who ended his career as an Inspector) was probably the most gifted of us all. Tony kept a very strong sense of realism and a healthy cynicism for the work, which pegged him at that level, but he was truly a great man and a great leader. Something I remarked to his son and daughter when I braved the "Beast from the East" to attend his funeral in 2018. Indeed, Tony helped me a lot through a very difficult time in my own life in those days. But that was him all over, always putting others before himself.

I mentioned earlier how the introduction of women into the Immigration Service had a massive effect upon the organisation. Like the men, many of them fully embraced the UKIS culture and wanted to be a part of it. That meant not just working together but socialising together as well. Places like Heathrow, Gatwick and Dover turned into a kind of UKIS version of "Love Island" as marriages broke down, new loves were found, and affairs were the talk of the office.

I was not exempt from this and was flattered to receive a good deal of attention from some of these ladies myself. Although I always tried to keep my home life and my work life separate, it didn't take a genius to work out that Marilyn and I were together in name only, primarily for the sake of the kids.

Just before I returned to Becket House I was invited by a couple of mates, Nev Johnson and Ken Simpson, to go to the funeral of Andy Stevens. I didn't know Andy very well, but he was a larger-than-life character who often held court in his local pub after a shift at Terminal 4. Sadly, Andy died young from a heart attack, and such was his popularity that we hired a coach from Heathrow to go to his funeral in Bath. This was typical UKIS behaviour – we were after all a big family rather than just workmates, and we often buried our dead together.

Heathrow was a bit of a journey for me on public transport, so I chose to drive over to Terminal 4 and pick up the coach from there. With hindsight I should have known better – as soon as we pulled out onto the M4 the wine and beer broke out, followed shortly by the usual sing-song. The coach was packed, and I couldn't help noticing a stunning blonde sitting near the front with her mates. She had the biggest blue eyes I had ever seen in my life, and I nearly fell off my seat when she smiled and said hello to me.

After a very moving service at a church in Bath we adjourned to the local hostelry where, I was even more surprised when she came over to talk to me. Then I realised that this was Jill Arnfield – the very same young lady who had helped us with the college investigations during my spell as a CIO at Isis House. She had cut her hair short and had recently returned from a short-term posting in Lagos, and she was now an immigration officer at Terminal Four. Small world.

We chatted for a while, and I soon learned that we had a lot in common. Like me, Jill had joined the Home Office in Lunar House before moving into the Immigration Service. Like me, she had been posted to Heathrow. And like me, she had completed a short-term ECO posting. What's more, she was now interested in moving into Enforcement. We went our separate ways, but as we left the bus at Heathrow, she asked me to join the rest of the gang for a drink before I headed home. I didn't really want a drink as I was driving, but I did stay and chat to her for a little longer. As I left, she asked me if I knew of any opportunities coming up for Immigration Officers in London Enforcement. I promised to get back to her on that one. Little did I know at that time where this would take us.

Marilyn and I finally split up in 1994 and went our separate ways, after 19 years of marriage. Looking back, I have some good memories of our time together, but we married very young and simply drifted apart as the years went by. I moved into a flat in Sutton with a friend, so I could stay close to the children.

Getting back to work, things were moving on rapidly in immigration enforcement. A main bone of contention was our relationship with the police, particularly in London. The Met had been working hard on community engagement during this time, trying to rebuild in the wake of the Joy Gardner tragedy. I found myself increasingly being asked to stand in front of community groups to justify why immigration enforcement operations should be allowed in this area or that area. Whilst the police were generally supportive, it gradually became clear that they were no longer prepared to support immigration raids (or visits, which was the more politically correct term for them). Although immigration officers always had the power of arrest, we had not been arrest-trained and had seldom used it. Some borough commanders started to take the view that we ought to handle our own arrests from now on, and this led to the creation of the "Immigration Enforcement Arrest Teams".

Now I have to say at this point that I was never an arrest team fan, maybe because I was old school UKIS. The arrangements I had been brought up on back in the JOE days always worked well for me. The true value of an Immigration Enforcement Officer was their ability to determine the immigration status of an individual quickly and easily. Chasing runners, applying handcuffs and restraining people was best left to the police, who were well equipped to deal with that. Although it was highly sensitive, particularly in immigration cases. Bringing in arrest training and then recruiting officers directly into immigration enforcement with no experience of interviewing passengers or immigrants at the border seemed to me to be a retrograde step. In effect, we were creating our own immigration police force, armed with batons, handcuffs, and the like, to go into highly volatile communities in a politically sensitive area.

I spent a lot of time as an Inspector at Becket House working with the Metropolitan Police on community relations. Tensions were running high, particularly in some parts of London. This is where I learned stakeholder engagement the hard way. I sat in several meetings in town halls with senior police officers and faced up to significant attacks from community groups as to my motives for enforcing immigration laws in London. Unlike the police, I did not have a public protection role to offer. Our mandate was to locate people living and working in communities illegally, and to require them to leave the country in accordance with the law of the land, and as directed by Ministers. Many community groups saw me as a representative of a racist organisation, whose officers would not be welcomed into the area to perform such a role. This was to become a perennial problem for immigration enforcement – up to and including the "Windrush" scandal, which still reverberates through the Home Office to this day.

That said, the government continued to advocate "firm but fair" immigration policies and showed no signs of discouraging active immigration enforcement operations, either in London or anywhere else. In fact, I cannot recall any single government that I ever worked for in over 40 years' service that ever advocated an open-door immigration policy, or the abolition of enforcement. Pressure remained upon us to investigate allegations of illegal immigration and to arrest and remove immigration offenders. At the same time, applications for asylum and judicial review continued to increase, leading to more case work backlogs in the Home Office. If there was ever a difficult policy area to navigate in the whole of Whitehall, this was it.

CHAPTER 10

Promotion to Assistant Director, the Asylum Influx, and a new UKIS Leadership Team

As time passed, some of my peer group in the Inspectorate were looking for their next promotion. Tony Mercer (who joined Lunar House around the same time as me, and hosted me briefly in Bangladesh), Peter Wheelhouse (who served with me at Terminal 1) and Dave Roberts (an HMI with me at Becket House) were all getting promoted to Assistant Director level, and it was made clear to me by my own managers that I now had the potential to follow suit.

My turn came in 1996, when I successfully applied for promotion to Assistant Director, Immigration Service (Ports) Directorate. I was posted back to ISHQ in Croydon in order to take charge of Passenger Casework Section (PCS) and the Asylum Liaison Unit (ALU). Ironically, this was the post once occupied by Michael Durose, so I took it upon myself to procure some red pens just for the occasion. By now a new management team had been installed in the Ports Directorate. Terry Farrage had succeeded Kate Collins as Director, with Vic Hogg coming in as his Deputy.

This was another crossroads in my career. The jump from HM Inspector to Assistant Director was not for everyone either. Just like the jump from CIO to non-shift working Inspector, the financial loss was considerable. Inspector was the highest grade to still attract shift disturbance allowance, premium payments for weekend working and overtime; by and large these were not available at AD level. Although the basic pay was of course higher, and eventually this would overtake the allowances at HMI grade.

I have lost count of the number of people who have told me that they could have been promoted to Inspector or AD if they wanted it, but just weren't prepared to take the financial hit. Some may have been right. Others just had delusions of grandeur, and their own self-importance in their specific role in their specific area. There had been attempts to reconcile the pay gap between the shift-working HMIs and the non-shift-working HMIs, but this could only be achieved by "sharing the pot" across the board. This was something the shift-working HMIs were not prepared to do – especially those who had already "done their porridge" in a non-shift working post and were now reaping the benefits. This was rather short sighted, as they were only storing up problems for the future by "blocking posts" for those coming up behind them, something I didn't want to do. So, I was happy to go for promotion and see where my career would go next.

My appointment as Assistant Director at ISHQ coincided with the arrival of Jack Straw as Home Secretary in the Blair government, and the creation of a new "Asylum Directorate" in the Home Office. In 1996 we received 37,000 asylum applications, rising to 41,000 in 1997 and 46,000 in 1998. Many of these applications were made at the border and many arrived by Eurostar at Waterloo International. I found this ironic, because during my previous spell at ISHQ I had argued long and hard that we should extend the Carriers Liability Act to Eurostar under the Channel Tunnel Act, to prevent people boarding without proper documents. I was shouted down by more senior colleagues, prompted by the business and tourism lobby who claimed that illegal entrants would not use the Eurostar route, because it would be the reserve of business people and genuine tourists.

I had heard this argument before when I was a CIO in charge of the new London City Airport, a role that led me to the first of my two conversations with Her Majesty the Queen. I was invited to the official opening of the London City Airport (or Stolport, as it was first known) where Her Majesty asked me about the immigration controls there. I told her that we had already refused three people in the first week of operations there, for trying to enter the country on false passports. The fact is that immigrants who are desperate to get into the UK will use any route and any opportunity they can to breach our controls. So it turned out at London City Airport, and at Waterloo International some years later.

The inexorable rise in asylum casework was taking its toll on the beleaguered Home Office, both in the Asylum Directorate and at the UK Border. To cope, the Asylum Liaison Unit took on a life of its own. Based in Croydon, it was the role of the ALU to act as the bridge between the ports of entry and the Asylum Casework Directorate. Remember, this was still in the days before technology arrived – either at the Border or at the Home Office. This meant that massive amounts of paper built up both at the ports and in the Home Office, as cases progressed slowly through the asylum system.

Despite the pressures placed upon us, one of the great things I remember about ISHQ in those days was the leadership team and especially its leader, Terry Farrage. Terry was one of the all-time greats of the Immigration Service, who had served at both Heathrow and Dover on his rise up the slippery pole. Terry was ably supported by Vic Hogg, who became my line manager. Vic always made it clear that unlike most of us he wasn't from a UKIS background. When asked how he had managed to fit in so well, he simply said that he just went to the pub with us a few times, and before he knew it, he had become an honorary member!

Some people subscribed to the view that you couldn't ever call yourself "UKIS" unless you had worked there all your life. I didn't take that view. I had a great working relationship with people from different departments and agencies who came in and out of the organisation over the years. Indeed, I count myself lucky to have so many friends and former colleagues scattered far across Whitehall and beyond. I found Vic to be a true friend and a gentleman, and the perfect foil for Terry.

It took me 25 years to make it to Assistant Director (Grade 7 level). Nobody could accuse me of not "getting my knees brown" first. It makes me smile these days when I see new recruits with aspirations to reach Grade 7 level within five years of joining the Home Office. What I lacked in academic qualifications was more than compensated by depth and breadth of knowledge and experience, as was the case with many of my contemporaries of that era.

However, I did feel that I needed to prove (at least to myself if not to others) that I had the capacity for higher education if I wanted it. I therefore embarked on a 4-year part time course of study with the Institute of Legal Executives, specialising in Criminal Law and Practice, European Law, and Immigration Law. It was hard work on top of my day job, but I was proud to graduate in 1998 with a distinction in Immigration Law. This is quite a well-kept secret but something I am very proud of, and I admit I did occasionally confess to it when challenged by immigration lawyers about my competence to manage complex immigration casework.

The role of AD for the ALU and PCS was ideal for me. It took me close to policy and away from operations for a while, and I learned a lot in that time. I also felt empowered as a representative not just of UKIS, but also of the Home Office and the UK Government more widely.

One area that I inherited in this post was the management of the Common Travel Area (CTA) between the UK, Ireland, and the Channel Islands. I was the lead official for the Home Office in this area, and spent many happy days working with my counterparts in the Department of Justice in Dublin to ensure that freedom of movement between Ireland and the UK was preserved, and that the external CTA perimeter was as safe and secure as we could make it.

The CTA probably deserves a book of its own. Little did I know that some years later I would be invited to join an expert panel to a Parliamentary Commission on Alternative Arrangements for the Irish Border, post Brexit. Despite all the political argument and posturing, the most effective borders are those where the practitioners on either side are allowed the freedom to collaborate with each other. Something that was sadly lacking in the Brexit process.

Although it wasn't everybody's cup of tea, I was also very happy working in Croydon. Yes, it was scruffy in parts, but Lunar House (and its neighbour Apollo House) hold happy memories for me. I enjoyed working with the "generalists" in the Immigration and Nationality Department just as much as with the "specialists" in UKIS. Indeed, many IND staff were specialists in their own right (eg asylum, casework, finance, HR, technology and so on). The best leadership teams were built around a mix of people from different backgrounds with different skills and experiences – a lesson I would learn later as I entered the Senior Civil Service.

Another landmark event in my life occurred during this period. Vic came into my office in Croydon one day to say that we would be receiving a secondee from the Canadian Government and we needed to find a role for him in ISHQ. Apparently one of our senior civil servants had heard this guy speaking at an international event and thought it would be a good idea to inject some international experience into UKIS at our level. I therefore carved out some policy files that required attention and found an office adjacent to mine, to welcome our new AD from Canada.

His name was Brian Grant. Brian had previously served in the enforcement branch of Citizenship & Immigration Canada. We discovered there was an exchange programme between the UK and Canadian governments which allowed this type of secondment, and Brian was keen to come to London for 2-3 years to broaden his experience. Although having moved from the lovely city of Ottawa to Croydon, I am not sure his posting quite lived up to his expectations.

So why was this event such a landmark for me, personally? Because it was the beginning of the next chapter of my life…

CHAPTER 11

BACK TO HEATHROW AND HEAD OF LAD 1 DISTRICT INCLUDING MIDLANDS AND NORTH-WEST PORTS, AND CANADA BECKONS

Being an AD in the Terry Farrage/Vic Hogg leadership era was a great honour, and I was very proud to be part of that team. We worked well together, and I thoroughly enjoyed our "away days" to Dover where we would hold quarterly strategic management meetings. In fact, these took place over two days with an overnight stop, which enabled us to build upon our working relationships over drinks and dinner, as well as in the boardroom.

That said, there were clearly two camps in the team. This came down to "operational" and "non-operational" posts. Four of us were in non-operational posts, and the other four were operational. The four operational ADs were in fact in charge of all UKIS operations at ports of entry across the UK – and as such were based out at the ports. Dave Roberts was the AD for the South East ports; he was based in Dover. Dave Bawden was the AD for Gatwick, but also in charge of South West and

Scotland/Northern Ireland ports. The other two posts were at Heathrow: London Airports Districts (LAD) 1 & 2. LAD 1 covered Heathrow Terminals 1 and 2, as well as Midlands and the North West ports; LAD 2 covered Heathrow Terminals 3 and 4 (Terminal 5 was not built then) as well as North East and East Coast ports.

Terry Farrage was always one for looking after his own, especially those that had served him well in the less popular posts in ISHQ. Therefore, when the LAD 1 post became vacant upon the departure of Colin Passey in 1998, I was invited on level transfer to take over.

This was a great honour for me. Firstly, it took me back to my spiritual home at Heathrow, where I had started out as a young Immigration Officer some 25 years earlier. Secondly, it gave me responsibility for ports in the Midlands (including Birmingham Airport and East Midlands Airport) and the North West (including Manchester Airport and Liverpool Docks).

My reception upon return to Heathrow was mixed. For the most part, the Immigration Officers and the Chief Immigration Officers were pleased to see me back there as their leader. The Inspectors were less enthused. Some of them were senior to myself (in terms of years served rather than grade) and I think they resented the fact that I had been promoted beyond them. One or two told me in no uncertain terms that they could be sitting in my seat if they wanted to, but they weren't prepared to go for promotion because of the financial loss (allowances, premium payment, shift disturbance and so on). I found myself beating the M25 traffic to get into work before the early shift Inspector turned up; and sometimes working late into the evening and beyond the time the late shift Inspector went home.

Around this time, Terry Farrage announced his departure, and a new Director for IS (Ports) was appointed. His name was Peter Higgins, and he came from a Customs background with little or no knowledge of the UKIS culture. Peter decided to take on the shift-working Inspectorate in a way that nobody had before. He found it outrageous that officers of such a rank could be allowed to "cruise" at this level simply to preserve their pay and conditions. Previous proposals to share allowances between shift working and non-shift working posts came back with a bang. This was the beginning of the end of shift disturbance and weekend premium payments for UKIS operational grades. The move toward Annual Hours Working (AHW) had begun.

My fonder memories of the LAD 1 post were actually in the regions outside Heathrow. It made more sense to me to take a road trip to the Midlands and the North West once a month, often over a weekend. Following my breakup with Marilyn, I found myself spending even more time with my "UKIS" family. Jill Arnfield had by now moved into Immigration Enforcement and had herself split up with her boyfriend, and we began seeing more of one another at work related events. Our relationship developed to a point where we began living together at her house in Sutton, so she would often come with me on my trips to the North. This would give us the opportunity to call in and see her parents in Lichfield along the way and spend some quality time in the Peak District as well. One of our favourite places was Buxton in the high peak, where we spend many happy hours exploring the area together.

The Inspectors in the Midlands and the North West were also very kind to me. As was often the case in the smaller ports they took a keen interest in the job, as did most of their staff. I always enjoyed visiting the front line, and never missed the opportunity to spend some time working alongside them. This was where the true strength of UKIS could be found.

It was during my time at LAD 1 that an opportunity came up that would change my life forever. Some of us had questioned the fact that Brian Grant's secondment to UKIS was supposed to be part of an exchange programme. So why had none of us been given the opportunity to work in Canada for a while? I had also by now attended the four-country conference in the USA representing the UK, and I had met a few guys from Canada Immigration.

Anyway, agreement was reached that there would be a competition for UKIS Grade 7s to apply to go to Canada for a 2-3-year secondment. Some of the guys weren't interested because of family reasons or one thing or another, and the field was whittled down to a short list of three. One of them was me.

I went through the interview with Kate Collins and Jonathan Potts, who was Head of HR at that time. I was sitting in my office at Heathrow when Kate called me. "Congratulations Tony, the Canada job is yours if you want it."

My dream had come true. A long-term overseas posting at last. This time there was no need for second thoughts, no sinking feeling in the pit of my stomach worrying about what others might say. Marilyn and I were divorced – she had found a new husband. Sharon and Mark were old enough to come and see me if they wanted to. And Jill had been behind me all the way.

I rang Jill and she was as excited as I was. She would be able to take a career break and come with me – something we had always talked about doing.

"Thank you, Kate, I would be delighted to accept," I said.

So that was that. The beginning of the next phase of my career was about to take off. Even then I could never have dreamt where it would end.

Mum and Dad on their wedding day – 20 March 1952.
I came along about 18 months later.

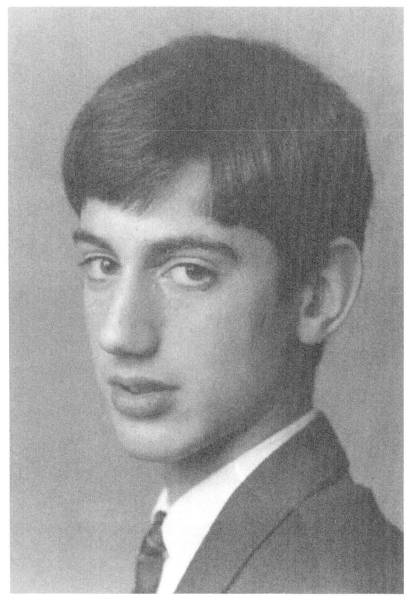

Me in my school uniform – St Clement Danes Grammar School,
Shepherds Bush – 1965.

Visiting the El Paso Office, US Border Patrol, a 4-country middle management exchange programme, 1991.

My wedding to Jill Arnfield – 15 October 1999.

Reviewing forgery factory seizures in 2004 from Operation Maxim, with Assistant Commissioner Tariq Ghafur, Metropolitan Police.

Senior Responsible Owner and Gold Commander, UK Border Agency
Olympic Programme, London 2012.

Director General, UK Border Force, 2012-2013

Delivering mince pies to the Border Force early shift, Christmas Day 2012, Gatwick Airport.

Olympic expert knowledge transfer delegation to Rio, Brazil, with Assistant Commissioner Chris Allison, Chairman of Metropolitan Police Olympic Security Gold Group, 2013.

The author outside Horseguards Parade on Remembrance Day, 2012

Retirement day with presentation from the Rt Hon Theresa May MP,
Home Secretary, 2013.

Receiving the Order of Commander of the British Empire (CBE) for services to Border Security during the London 2012 Olympics from Her Majesty Queen Elizabeth II, Windsor Castle, 2013.

Showing off my CBE medal with Mum, Dad and Jill, Windsor Castle, 2013.

HOME SECRETARY
2 Marsham Street, London SW1P 4DF
www.homeoffice.gov.uk

Dear Tony,

Thank you for your significant contribution to the smooth-running and security of the UK border during your 40 years of public service.

Your commitment to our border security has been exemplary and your knowledge and experience have not only been invaluable to Border Force, but has been recognised around the world. Delivering a secure and well-run border during the Olympics and Paralympics was a high point in a worthy career.

You have truly been a fine example of a dedicated public servant

With best wishes for your retirement

Theresa May.

Retirement thank-you letter, Theresa May, Home Secretary, 2013.

TONY SMITH CBE

10 DOWNING STREET
LONDON SW1A 2AA

THE PRIME MINISTER

8 March 2013

Dear Tony,

I wanted to take this opportunity to offer my personal thanks on the occasion of your retirement.

I am grateful to you for your leadership of the UK Border Force over the past five months, and understand that interestingly you retire as Interim Director General having served at all grades in the UK Immigration Service.

From leading the development of local immigration teams across London and the South East, to ensuring the smooth running of the UK Border Agency's London 2012 Olympic and Paralympic Programme, I have no doubt that all you have achieved will serve as a fitting legacy to your long and distinguished career.

I hope that you will be able to spend many happy and relaxing days with your family and although I can imagine it might be difficult at the moment, that you are able to cheer on your team at Loftus Road!

Please accept my best wishes for a long and enjoyable retirement.

Yours,

David

Mr Tony Smith CBE

Retirement thank-you letter from the Rt Hon David Cameron MP, Prime Minister, 10 Downing Street, 2013.

PART TWO

NORTH AMERICA AND BEYOND – 2000-2013

11 SEPTEMBER 2012

As I was sorting through my papers in my office in Marsham Street, the phone rang.

"Tony, it's the Home Sec's office. She wants to see you. Apparently, it's personal."

Uh-oh. This was not good news. I knew Theresa May well. I was at the Home Office when she arrived there, and I had briefed her regularly over the past couple of years on our readiness for the London 2012 Olympics. What could she possibly want?

I walked along to the third floor and knocked on the door of her office. I was astonished on entering to find the Home Secretary alone.

"Hi Tony, thanks for popping in. Cup of tea?"

I had to pinch myself to ensure I wasn't dreaming. It was virtually unheard of for a senior civil servant to meet a Home Secretary without some third party in the room – let alone over a cup of tea.

"Tell me Tony, how serious are you about retirement?" Before I could reply, she went on, "Look, I know you have done your time here and we really are very grateful for everything you have done. But the problem is I haven't been able to find anyone suitable to take over as Director General of the Border Force. And my boss over the road at Number Ten wants a name now. I would really like you to do it. What do you say?"

CHAPTER 12

DIRECTOR OF PORTS AND BORDERS, OTTAWA, CANADA

News of my posting to Canada spread fast, and my personal life moved along just as quickly. I decided to propose to Jill on one of those long trips to the North West, at one of our favourite beauty spots. The stepping stones at Dovedale in Derbyshire were one such place. We often stopped there along the way, to stroll along the stream and across the steps to marvel at the amazing scenery around us. I bought an engagement ring and smuggled it into a pair of socks as we set out.

We had by now bought a place together in South Sutton, a big old four-bedroom semi that needed a fair bit of work. Canada gave us the opportunity to rent the place out for three years, and hopefully raise some cash for much needed renovations.

Jill had no idea that I planned to propose and didn't even expect us to stop at Dovedale at all. "I thought you had meetings to get to in Manchester?" she said. "No need to stop now, we can always go some other time."

Not to be deterred, I drove into the car park at Dovedale, and we set out towards the stepping stones. Sadly for me, there was a huge party of schoolchildren there at the time, so the chances of me going down on one knee by the stones went up in smoke. So I led an increasingly bemused Jill up the steep slopes trying to find a quiet spot somewhere, whilst she looked at her watch and asked me what on earth was going on.

Finally, I found a spot, went down on one knee, and popped the question. "I love you and I know we will be really happy together – will you marry me?"

She burst into tears. "I never thought you would ask me that. I love you too – of course I will!"

We were married at Wallington Methodist Church on 15 October 1999. Jill was 34 and I was 45. Many said the age gap was too big, and it wouldn't last. Sure, we have had our ups and downs over the years, and there were times when I did wonder. But for the most part we have been very happy together. Neither of us was particularly religious, but my mum was, and we enjoyed the value of the church in the community regardless of the denomination. Sometimes they let themselves down a bit with the "holier than thou" stuff – I remember a particularly difficult encounter with a pastor at a church in Sutton over the fact that I was a divorcee – but in general terms they are nice people offering comfort to many people in times of need.

We didn't waste much time cracking on, as they say these days. By the time we were ready to go to Canada in the spring of 2000, Jill was four months pregnant. Moving to Ottawa under the Canada/UK exchange programme was a much bigger challenge than we thought. Given that I would be working for them (not us) I did not have any of the diplomatic privileges that normally came with overseas postings. We had to apply for work permits and find ourselves somewhere to live. No diplomatic house with servants at the ready this time.

Jill went out there ahead of me and had great fun house hunting. She found a lovely place to rent in Riverside South.

The only drawback was that in general terms homes for rent in Ottawa are let unfurnished. This prompted some frantic exchanges between myself and ISHQ about how I could get some furniture over there – our house in Sutton had already been rented out as furnished. In the end Jill and I moved into a lovely three-bedroomed home in Ottawa with just a sofa bed between us.

Fortunately for me the folks back at ISHQ were very understanding – especially my old mate Peter Graham, who managed to secure a budget for me to purchase some furniture whilst I was there. This threw the Home Office Accounts Branch into chaos. There was no accounting code for this sort of thing. They just kept sending me more and more money, which I had to find a way of returning to them once the cap was reached! In the end we bought some furniture in Ottawa which was technically the property of Her Majesty's government, with a promise that we would either pass it on to my successor (if there was one) or sell it and return the proceeds to the Department.

Upon arrival in Ottawa in April 2000 the first thing I noticed was big lumps of ice dotted around the place. Winters were brutal there with snow and ice on the ground well into spring – we had arrived just in the middle of the great thaw. There were still days where the temperature fell below zero, and it took me a while to get the hang of this. I remember setting out to work one morning and being unable to get up the hill to the bus stop because of the icy pavements. And my ears were burning with the cold. I am sure a few hardy Canadians spotted this English guy trying to get along without the right footwear or headwear in the winter, sprawling around on the icy pavements like Bambi on ice.

I was given the post of Director of Ports of Entry in the Enforcement Branch of Citizenship and Immigration Canada. This placed me rather higher up the pecking order than I had expected. I was effectively Head of Ports and Borders in CIC, a role that was a Grade 5 post back home. Although to be fair

I didn't have line management responsibility for all the officers at the ports, as that was managed by Regional Directors in the various provinces. Nonetheless it was a pretty powerful position for an "outsider", and one that would test my leadership skills to the full.

The odd thing about the Canadian border at that time – and others such as Australia – was that Customs Officers were on the primary line at the border, with Immigration Officers in secondary. This was the opposite way round to the UK, and such a thought would make many a UK Immigration Officer shudder. Customs controls at UK Ports of Entry were conducted in red and green channels after baggage collection; only those who had something to declare or those who were selected for an examination were seen by a Customs Officer. Indeed, I can recall many occasions when there were no UK Customs Officers to be seen at the UK Border at all, especially at the airports. So imagine my surprise when I discovered that the first person to examine you on arrival at the Canadian Border was a Customs Officer; and – unless you were an immigrant – the main line of questioning was about the goods you had with you and what you had purchased abroad rather than the purpose and duration of your visit to Canada.

Canada Customs Officers in those days only had limited training in immigration law or forgery detection – a major source of concern to many of the Canadian Immigration Officers, who could only stand by and watch as a stream of potential "duffers" were stamped into the country upon payment of ten dollars tax for some item they had purchased along the way. Although to be fair the vast majority of travellers crossing the Canada Border are either Canadians or Americans; third-country nationals were rarely seen at the land borders, and only at the major international airports such as Toronto, Montreal, or Vancouver. Nonetheless, this was a very different set up from the one I had been used to for the previous 25 years.

I was also dismayed to discover that many of the more talented and experienced officers from Canada Immigration had retired the year before I got there. This was following something called "Program Review" – which was government speak for clearing out a lot of public servants to save money. I saw similar exercises in the UK in later life, although we called it "ventilation", which was the UK government's term for the same thing. Many of my UKIS colleagues took early retirement when the offer came along. You could hardly blame them – the financial pay-off was reasonable, and many of them had become tired and jaded by constant changes in the management structures and degradation of their powers and authorities. But the downside to the Department was devastating – much-needed experience and expertise evaporated at a time when it was most needed.

One such person who had taken early retirement shortly before I got to Canada was Eunice Bartolucci. I had met Eunice some years earlier when I hosted the four country middle managers' exchange programme in the UK. She was the Canadian delegate. We had kept in touch over the years and Eunice had previously been in charge of the CIC transportation company liability section, which fell within my new command. This was where airlines would be fined for bringing improperly documented passengers to Canada. We had a similar system under the Carriers Liability Act in the UK, although the Canadian system was rather more sophisticated than ours and involved agreeing a Memorandum of Understanding with each individual airline based upon their track record. There was also a good deal of litigation involved when disputes arose. The loss of Eunice and others like her didn't make my job any easier.

I soon learned that working in CIC headquarters in Ottawa was a bit like doing "porridge" at ISHQ in Croydon. There were several experienced officers dotted across Canada with a huge amount to offer at national level, but they could not be persuaded to move to the capital from the Provinces, where they had built their homes and settled their families. This was entirely understandable. Ottawa was a lovely city, but an expensive one compared with many of the port and border locations. And the distances were enormous – far too great to be considered within "commuting" range, as was the case in the UK.

It also soon became clear that CIC HQ was not perceived by front-line officers to be a great place to work. Staff turnover was high, and morale was low. Having an Enforcement Branch in the midst of a Department that was otherwise committed to immigration and refugee protection was not a very neat fit, especially as it meant being nasty to people by arresting them and deporting them, or refusing them entry to the country, rather than welcoming them to their new home and turning them into new Canadian citizens. Unsurprisingly the majority of the Enforcement Branch later merged with Canada Customs and Revenue Agency (CCRA) into the Canada Border Services Agency (CBSA), where it was a much neater fit in the context of law enforcement.

It didn't take me long to figure out that in order to make an impact on the Canadian Border I would need to seek out alliances beyond the 8th floor of Jean Edmonds Tower North, where the CIC Enforcement Branch was based. Those alliances would be found in the ports of entry around the country, and a few blocks to the east at the Sir Richard Scott building, where the mighty CCRA was housed.

With regard to the ports, I am very grateful to a young officer who helped to plan my induction. Jamie Martin was an affable and popular young man who was attached to my section when I arrived, primarily to write a "Use of Force" policy for front line officers at the border. He was from Ontario region and served at the famous Peace Bridge at Niagara Falls, which linked Canada to the United States.

After a visit to the front line there, I could see where he was coming from. Niagara Falls was a night-time haven for many

Americans looking to let off steam after a hard week's work. Beer was cheaper north of the border. Casinos and strip clubs were plentiful. The last thing these guys wanted was some Canadian Border Officer stopping them and searching them and their vehicle en route. It was commonplace for Americans to carry firearms about their person or in their vehicle. CIC officers were unarmed and for the most part untrained in tactical defence techniques.

I worked long and hard with a Jamie on that file during my time there, including getting myself qualified in tactical defence and use of force. This involved some pretty brutal work in a gym in Ottawa getting beaten up by younger and fitter officers than myself but in terms of credibility, it did me no harm at all with the front-line staff, even though it raised an eyebrow or two amongst the senior pen pushers at HQ.

I travelled the length and breadth of the country in my first few weeks in Canada, and I was fortunate enough to spend some quality time observing operations at air, sea and land border crossing points. I also met several highly talented and motivated officers who were keen to do a good job and were desperately seeking some committed leadership support.

That was my strength. I secured a small budget which enabled me to set up the Port of Entry Working group, comprising the leading port managers from across the country. Every three months we would set up a road trip and visit each region in turn, to benchmark operations and discuss common issues and challenges. In my time in Canada, I was fortunate enough to visit every Province, and in the context of the border this would prove to be a very useful exercise, given the events that were to unfold the following year. Although I had little knowledge of that at the time of course.

Jamie stuck with me throughout this period and helped me a lot, particularly with the land border teams. I had no prior experience of managing land borders. The Channel Tunnel was the nearest thing we had, and that could only be traversed by train, which made border controls easier. The Irish land border was not a problem because we had a "Common Travel Area" between Great Britain, Ireland and the Channel Isles which allowed free movement of people, and there were no customs controls because both countries were in the EU Single Market and the Customs Union. Although this was something that would come back to haunt us after Brexit.

Jamie wasn't really cut out for the bureaucracy of headquarters. Like many front-line officers, he was cynical towards those who were appointed above and around him who immediately set about changing Border Programmes with very little knowledge or experience as to how things actually worked out there. He was a bit of a rebel, but he was a perfect foil for me. I knew how to manage upwards too. In the end we were all on the same side, and we wanted to do the best job we could for the government and the people of Canada.

Another young officer who I inherited in that team was Jeff Daly. Jeff was leading work on something called 'co-mingling" which involved the segregation (or not) of international and trans-border passengers at Canadian airports. One thing I learned whilst I was in Canada was the propensity of civil servants to argue with each other on policy questions over long periods of time, to reach entrenched positions and to leave policy files like this one hanging for years, much to the dismay of the airport operators who had to manage passenger flows on a daily basis. After a lot of hard work and stakeholder engagement across the Canadian government and with the Provinces we were finally able to come up with a solution – but it was far from easy.

Jeff, Jamie and I became good friends. We formed the bedrock of the POE working group, and I expanded their respective portfolios with Jamie leading on land and marine issues and Jeff focusing on air issues. Jeff has kept in touch with me ever since and is himself a senior manager in Immigration Canada nowadays – and he never spares my blushes by taking me out with his team when I go to Ottawa to tell them how I was the greatest leader he ever worked for in his entire career. Kind words indeed.

One of the many programmes I inherited in my role as Director of Ports and Borders in CIC was called "Our Missing Children". This was one of the few files that required cross-agency working on both sides of the border. There were often reports of children being abducted and taken across the land border. Mostly these were domestic cases, where one parent decided to avoid the jurisdiction of the courts and take their disputed custody case into their own hands. At the other end of the spectrum was the much nastier business of child trafficking, where kids were being moved around North America for slave labour and sexual exploitation by organised crime groups. Each Department had a nominated lead for the programme. On the Canadian side this was CIC, CCRA and RCMP. On the US side it was US INS, US Customs, and the FBI. I recruited a young officer named Jason Daigle to work on this project for me, whom I nicknamed "Jaise". Little did either of us know how much our engagement on this project would impact upon us just a few months later.

Turning to Customs, I went to see my boss one day to recommend a joint engagement strategy for the border with CCRA. She laughed out loud. "Oh, Tony you have got so much to learn about Canada. We don't talk to Customs. They do their job and we do ours."

Now I knew there was something seriously wrong with the Canadian Border set up. I had already heard of dust-ups between immigration and customs managers at the ports of entry around the country over roles and responsibilities, but I had put these down to a cultural divide at local level rather than a complete stand-off at national level. This was really weird. We always got along fine with HM Customs back home – they did goods, we did people. It seemed that in Canada they did pretty well everything, and we had no real idea what we were supposed to be doing. This needed fixing, and it certainly wasn't going to be fixed by ignoring them.

So, contrary to the advice of my line manager, I set a few hares running with CCRA. After all, the worst that could happen was that they would send me back to the UK prematurely. After a few enquiries I managed to track down a DG in Canada Customs called Mark Connolly. Mark was a senior customs guy from an operational background, who saw his top priority as protecting the Canadian Border from bad people and bad stuff. He spoke my language when it came to disrupting organised crime gangs, smuggling, illegal immigration, and the like.

Before too long I found myself drinking jugs of Canadian beer with Mark and his customs mates, who wondered how it was that this English guy was the first person from Canada Immigration to actually talk to them for ages – let alone to drink with them. This took me back to a lesson I learned from Vic Hogg – becoming accepted into the culture of another law enforcement agency is often better achieved by sharing stories over a drink than in a formal meeting. This was time well spent, given that the upper echelons of CIC, CCRA and RCMP would be thrown together shortly in response to one of the biggest catastrophic events to hit their border in North American history.

CHAPTER 13

THE 9/11 ATTACKS AND THE NEW AGE OF BORDER SECURITY – NORTH AMERICA

The phone in the hotel room rang. "Hey Tony – you awake yet?"

"Well, if I wasn't already, I am now Jaise. What's up?"

"Turn on your TV and take a look."

"Holy shit!"

I switched on the TV to see the second plane smashing into the Twin Towers, accompanied by smoke and screaming.

"What are we going to tell the conference?" I murmured, trying to take on board the fact that the USA was under some kind of attack. And most of the US and Canadian Border Management teams were in Calgary with me.

"Well, when you've figured that Tony, the guys are gonna want to know what they should do."

"About what?" I asked.

"About the border. Word is that the US are closing their airspace and 300 flights are being diverted to Canada."

"Blimey!" I said, reverting to my native tongue as my mind

raced around the scenario.

"Blimey for sure Tony – you had best get down to the lobby. In case you forgot, you are the Director for Ports and Borders round here."

Jason and I were in Calgary on that fateful day, at the annual "Our Missing Children" conference. This group met annually in different locations across North America, and in September 2001 it was the turn of CIC to chair the conference, and the chosen location was Calgary. So, on 10 September 2001, a crowd of law enforcement officers from both Canada and the United States were assembled together at a hotel in Calgary, many miles away from their usual workstations.

The attacks of 9/11 took us all by surprise. There was no advanced intelligence or heightened threat level to suggest that a terrorist attack was imminent. All we could do was watch the TV footage in horror. Of course, the by-product of this was that several of us had important roles to play in handling the crisis. We commandeered all the telephone lines we could find, and set up a small operations room in the government office opposite. Our first reaction was to get back to our base stations in Ottawa and Washington DC as soon as possible. However, it soon became clear that the US government had closed US airspace, so there was no chance of getting any flights out of Calgary that day. A few hardy souls decided to start the long drive back, but we knew that even with a fair wind it would take two days of non-stop driving to cover the 2000-plus miles back to our base cities. The more sensible thing to do would be to try and establish communication with HQ by telephone and take it from there.

After two hours, I finally got through to my boss in Ottawa.

"Hey Tony, there you are. How's it going?"

"Well sorry, but it looks like I'm stuck out here for now. Obviously, we have cancelled the conference – but I don't know when I'll be able to get back."

"Well, I'm not sure what you could do even if you were here" she said, with a sigh. "Everyone's on strike today anyway, so there's hardly anyone in the office."

It was ironic that the Canadian public service union had decided to call everybody out on the very day that North America had come under the worst terrorist attack in history.

"Is nobody there at all?" I asked. "Anyone from my shop?"

"I haven't seen them, but Jim Bissett and Neil Cochrane are here." Jim and Neil were Directors of inland Enforcement and Immigration and Refugee policy, respectively. Both really nice guys. In the end we agreed that Jim and Neil would set up a central communication centre in the office in order to liaise with officers out at the Ports. Several of my team – including Jeff and Jamie – joined the operation and set up single points of contact in the regions, something we had established already under the POE working group. Given the circumstances, it was the best we could do. This was a critical incident, but neither CIC nor the wider government was prepared for this. All we could do was react to each new crisis as it emerged.

The first was how to react to the decision by the US government to close the border. Not just the airspace, but the land border too. There were already some 300 flights bound for the US that did not have enough fuel to turn round and go back whence they came. Many of these were transatlantic flights from Europe. In very short order, we secured Ministerial approval to allow these flights to land at Canadian airports. A great many of them ended up at a small airport in St John, Newfoundland – where we had one officer on duty.

It sometimes takes a crisis like this to bring out the best in people. That was certainly the case in St John that day. The local people opened up their hearts and their homes to literally thousands of stranded passengers. Most of these had no intention of landing in Canada, and many didn't have the right papers or permission to do so. But this was not a time for enforcing regulations. This was a critical incident, where preservation of life was paramount. Our job was to ensure that everybody was safe and well and had food, water, and somewhere to stay. And – in time – to help them to either get to their intended destination or return whence they came.

I finally made it back to Ottawa about four days later, by which time it really was hitting the fan. Especially in my area. The US administration had gone into overdrive and was quickly looking for someone to blame (sadly often the case, in my experience, when it hits the fan). Who did this? How did they get into America? Who let them in? Must be the fault of those Canadians. Maybe the terrorists had been hiding in Canada? Most self-respecting Americans knew only too well that Canada was full of screaming liberals, immigrants, and asylum seekers. It's only a short hop from there to becoming a terrorist haven, right?

Sadly, even the fickle Canadian press believed that the Canadian government must have been at fault. I was astounded at their capacity to beat themselves up in this way. More and more senior officers would rush into my office waving a copy of a Canadian rag which had accused us of having an open-door policy for terrorists, and demanding an urgent briefing for the Deputy Minister on the story. I spent a lot of my time there trying to reassure them that just because some hack had taken it upon himself to have a pop at the administration, it didn't mean that CIC should be held accountable for the tragic events that had taken place in another country a week earlier. Our energies would be much better focused upon contact and liaison with our partners south of the border. If anyone was going to find out the facts first, it would be them.

Slowly the facts began to emerge. The four hijacks had been perpetrated by an Al Qaeda cell of 19 foreign nationals, all of whom had been granted visas to enter the USA by the US Immigration and Naturalisation Service. None of them had any connection with Canada. They had simply exploited a gap in intelligence sharing between the US Federal Agencies. There was no security assessment undertaken for young Saudi men visiting the USA in those days. This was a straightforward immigration test. Would they go back or not? Invariably, the answer was yes. These men had plenty of money and would be able to secure more gainful employment in their homeland than in the US.

Slowly and painfully, it became clear that there had been a major failing in the US Government, primarily in the lack of co-ordination and information sharing between agencies. The 9/11 report later identified no fewer than 15 separate occasions when the plot could have been disrupted with better collaboration between the US agencies, including the INS.

The response was immediate. The INS in its current form was abolished. Senator Tom Ridge was brought in by President George Bush to oversee a new department called the Department for Homeland Security. And US Customs took over jurisdiction at the border, under the leadership of judge Robert Bonner (who was to become a good friend of mine in later life). A new Department called US Customs and Border Protection was formed – effectively merging the immigration and customs functions at the US Border into a single command (a trend that would be followed by Canada, the UK and Australia in later years).

It didn't take Tom Ridge very long to recognise that in order to deliver a stronger border in the US going forward, a lot of work would have to be done with his "cousins" north of the border. On 12 December 2001 he signed a declaration with John Manley, Canada's Minister for Foreign Affairs, to develop a "smart border" between Canada and the USA. This would require a draft Memorandum to Cabinet known as "Hands Across the Border" and a good deal of work between the law Enforcement Agencies on both sides – especially the Director for Ports and Borders in the Enforcement Branch of CIC. My journey into international collaboration on Border Security was about to take on a whole new dimension.

In the immediate aftermath of the 9/11 attacks, the US border remained closed. Nobody could get in or out of the country. This was causing havoc – not just for those passengers stranded in St John, but also to the tens of thousands of people who relied upon cross-border trade for their livelihoods. Some people were even commuting to work every day across the land border. Then there were "just in time" supply chains where goods were moving to and fro daily, to keep production lines going. As time went by, the bigger crisis was how to get the border open again.

I was one of the first to get into the USA after the attacks, as part of a joint Canadian/US task force on border security. My encounter with US Customs on the way to Washington from Ottawa was quite extraordinary. Customs Officers had just taken over primary inspections at the US Border, and obviously there had been no time to train them in the art of passport control. All they had to go on was intuition. I marched up to the US Border Pre-Clearance zone at Ottawa airport on my first (of a great many) flights to Washington DC, clutching my British passport and US Customs Declaration.

After thumbing through my passport, the Customs Officer said, "So, tell me sir, what is the purpose of your trip to Washington?"

"Three days business trip" I replied.

"And what kind of business are you in?" said the officer, still thumbing through my UK passport as though he had never seen one like it before.

"Border management" I replied. "I am going to DC to meet with you guys to figure out how to get the Canada/US border open again."

"And what has this to do with a Brit?" came the swift reply.

"Well, I am the Director of Ports and Borders here in Ottawa and I think we have a lot of work to do, don't you?"

That was that. "Joker, eh?" He replied. "Secondary."

Not for the first time – and certainly not the last – I found myself being referred to "secondary" for a more detailed examination. This was how things worked over there. If the front-line officer had any concerns about a passenger, they could immediately direct them to secondary. This might be Customs secondary, or Immigration secondary. Given that the US INS had all but imploded, it was very likely that I would be spending some considerable time trying to explain to a cynical US Customs Officer how come the Director of Ports and Borders in Canada was a Brit, and why on earth some limey foreigner should be headed to their own HQ in Washington to talk about border security.

After a great deal of painful questioning and some embarrassing phone calls to verify I was indeed who I said I was, they finally let me through.

The fact that I found myself in secondary – both in Canada and the US – was a great source of amusement for Jeff, Jamie and the team. I recall one night out after a POE Working Group in Niagara Falls where we agreed to go over the bridge to the US for dinner. I use the term lightly – this was more for beer and chicken wings than anything else. On entry to the US all these Canadian guys were waved through upon production of their Canadian ID, whereas the Brit had to get out for an interview to go through the whole damned story again, just to spend a few hours in a bar on the US side. The humiliation was even worse on the way back when I found myself being examined by one of my own officers! But it was all done in good spirit and I was beginning to make a name for myself over there, which wasn't such a bad thing at all.

One thing that gave me an advantage over my colleagues at the Canadian border was my experience of border control, and the different methods of exercising it. As soon as the opportunity for legislation and new regulations came up, I wasted no time in putting forward suggestions for extending the powers of immigration officers at the Canadian border. At the time there was a huge fight over possession of "primary", with many officers pressing for immigration to take over passport checks from customs. Of course, this made sense to me – this was a system I grew up with. Immigration Officers were more effective at examining passports and passengers than Customs Officers, who were primarily focused on goods. However, this was never going to happen at the Canadian border. Customs was a bigger and more influential agency than Immigration, and we would always be outvoted on the idea.

But there were other ways of skinning a cat. Immigration Officers in Canada were by necessity empowered to examine inbound passengers, but despite common practice there was nothing in the regulations to say that they could only do so upon referral from a customs officer. I ensured that the new regulations were tweaked in such a way as to empower Immigration Officers to examine passengers seeking entry to Canada at any place within the port area, and I also introduced the "24- hour rule" which empowered immigration officers to overturn an earlier permission to enter within 24 hours of arrival if new evidence came to light. This rule was originally introduced in the UK to enable us to withdraw leave to enter from any person who was found in the Customs Hall to be importing illegal materials – mainly drug mules. This then gave us the opportunity to detain and remove them under immigration powers rather than taking them through the cumbersome criminal justice system, which might only lead to a short sentence and a recommendation for deportation anyway, depending upon the seriousness of the offence.

I also introduced CIC surveillance teams at Canadian airports who were empowered to roam the airport and interview arriving passengers before they arrived at the primary line – often by meeting a flight at the gate. This was (and still is) a very useful tactic, particularly where we had intelligence to suggest that there was somebody on board who might attempt to destroy their identity documents before seeing an officer in order to conceal their true nationality and identity. This tactic is still used to this day by human smugglers who often advise their clients to adopt a nationality of convenience (other than their own) to support an asylum claim.

These were not controversial changes, but at operational level they were highly effective. Suddenly immigration officers at Canadian ports of entry were released from their offices in "secondary" and free to intercept passengers before they arrived at the Primary Inspection Line (PIL) – or even afterwards, if they suspected some form of fraud had been perpetrated at the PIL.

This took many Customs Managers at the ports by surprise, and it wasn't long before they were trying to get Immigration Officers "back in their boxes". But the die was cast. The next step was to get both agencies working alongside one another rather than against one another – and 9/11 provided the foundations for that to happen.

I didn't realise just how bad the silos were between the enforcement agencies in North America until I started working on the "Hands Across the Border" initiative. At one of those early meetings in Washington I recall a very difficult exchange with US Customs officials over minimum standards for registration in NEXUS, a programme which would allow "trusted" travellers to cross the border without prior interview on every occasion, using automated border controls. Prior to 9/11 we already had the "Canpass" family of programmes which offered this service on entry into Canada, and US INS had a similar initiative their end, known as INSpass. NEXUS was designed to bring these two programmes under one umbrella, both at airports (NEXUS AIR) and at land border crossing points (NEXUS LAND).

After some debate, we agreed that US and Canadian citizens would become eligible for enrolment on production of evidence of citizenship and after a criminality and security check on both sides. This was compulsory – those who chose not to go through the process would have to queue up and see an officer alongside everybody else. I then raised the question of permanent residents, in other words people lawfully resident in either Canada or the US who had not become citizens (e.g., "green card" holders).

"Why would we want to do that, man?" said a particularly heavy-set US Customs Officer.

"Why not?" I replied. "If they are lawfully resident in North America and we undertake the same checks as we do with citizens, what is the risk?"

"Have you not seen what's been going on here?" he snorted. "In case you missed it, my homeland has just been blown up by a bunch of Arabs. And now you want me to give them a fast pass entry to a whole load of them who are living up north?"

"Well, I think you'll find that a great many Canadian citizens were born in other parts of the world – and American citizens for that matter. But we just agreed to let them into the programme" I replied, trying hard to ignore the racist overtones that were creeping into the conversation.

"We will want to check everything" he said. "School, employment history, family background, the works. We can't do that if they are not citizens".

Trying not to get too exasperated by this conversation, I pointed out that a great many permanent residents of Canada had in fact lived there longer than many Canadian citizens. The fact that they had chosen not to seek citizenship didn't mean that we couldn't conduct background checks, or that they presented any greater risk than their counterparts who had.

There were many similar conversations and negotiations in those early days which were extremely difficult. It was hard to agree policy on risk-assessing travellers across the border with

Customs Officers who had little or no knowledge of immigration policy and practice, or of risk-assessing people. The fact was that we were trying to build a new system for risk-assessing travellers against a backdrop of the worst terrorist attack in history. At the same time, we had to accept the fact that the vast majority of people crossing that border presented no security threat whatsoever, and by impeding their capacity to do so we were causing serious damage to their livelihoods.

Of course, no policy ever works smoothly. The best-laid plans can always go awry. One strand of this project was aimed at "trusted truckers". A huge volume of trucks crossed the main arterial routes between Canada and the US every day. It was vital to keep these lanes open – there would be serious economic damage on both sides if we failed to do so.

Imagine the look on my face when the first 100 checks came back on US truckers, and over 30% of them came back with a criminal record that rendered them inadmissible to Canada. Of course, some of these guys had been crossing the border for years, and we were none the wiser. After digging a bit deeper we discovered that the US parole service saw long-distance trucking as an ideal occupation to rehabilitate offenders. It never occurred to them that crossing the border could be a problem! I often quote this example when discussing the need for joint agency collaboration and joined up government. All too often in my time in government on both sides of the pond, I found departments working against each other instead of in collaboration.

I worked with my good friend Caroline Melis on the Memorandum to Cabinet. Caroline was a great writer. We worked many a long day and even some weekends on this, but it was worth it. We came up with a series of proposals that would change the face of border management in North America – and ultimately beyond – for ever.

This is where my work with the regions and the other agencies came to the fore. We knew well before the 9/11 report came out

CHANGING BORDERS: A KINGDOM UNLOCKED

that we had a serious problem with keeping data in silos, and not sharing it between agencies for the greater good. I later learned that in fact it was US Customs who were able to link all the 9/11 hijackers together within 24 hours of the attacks, given their access to passenger name data held by airlines. Between the US agencies and ourselves, we set about drawing up new requirements for capturing data held by airlines – firstly "Advanced Passenger Information (API)" and secondly 'Passenger Name Records (PNR)". Airlines were engaged in working groups with us to negotiate what data elements would be required and in what format they should be sent to government. The US Agencies demanded that any airline operating either on international routes in and out of the US, or on domestic routes within it, or on trans-border routes, or even on overfly routes in US Airspace, must provide this data in advance.

We set up joint passenger analysis units (JPAUs) at all our major airports including Vancouver, Toronto, and Montreal. These comprised secondees from Canada Customs, Canada Immigration and the RCMP. In addition to standard watch list checks on inbound manifests, we set up data links, so each officer had direct access to their own back-office systems. This process – known as the "swivel chair" system – enabled us to conduct cross-agency risk assessments for immigration, documents, customs, identity, criminality, and security on all travellers quickly and efficiently without having to wait years for a new integrated data system. What's more, the system worked. By placing officers from different agencies into joint teams, we were able to break down some of the silos that had previously existed between government agencies. A spirit of trust emerged between them – so much so that they were coming up with ideas of their own about how to progress this. To this day I continue to promote international collaboration between border agencies – and the transportation companies and supply chains – as our best weapon to deter international organised crime and terrorism.

Having established the concept of joint units in Canada and the US, we then set about the next challenge – how to combine them into one single unit at the major international airports in North America. This was relatively easy in Canada – the US agencies were already pre-clearing flights heading south at all the major Canadian airports, so they had staff and systems in place already. Less so in the US. The Americans were already wary of letting other agencies inside the room, let alone agents from another country.

In the end they relented, and I was able to secure permission to post officers to selected US airports to work alongside US Customs to analyse data on flights heading to Canada via the USA. One such posting was to Miami, Florida. Suddenly this Brit Director of Ports of Entry had become more popular than ever – especially as I got to decide which officers would be selected for this role. Working at Miami Airport in temperatures above 25C was a far cry from working at Winnipeg Airport at temperatures of minus 25C.

And so the concept of targeting centres was born. As time went by both Canada and the US – and indeed Australia and the UK – would develop their own National Targeting Centres comprising officers from multiple agencies. Using data acquired in advance of the physical movement of people and goods across borders, we were able to develop the concept of the "multiple borders strategy". Thus, border control became a series of transactions which began some time before the physical arrival – and the concept of "intelligence-led" border controls was born, something I still lecture about to this day.

Although from a professional perspective I am sure that the time I spent in Ottawa was career defining, it was also hugely rewarding from a personal perspective. The Canadian people were extremely friendly and welcoming. We made a great many friends there, some of whom remain friends to this day. This was in part due to the efforts of my dear wife Jill who – unbeknown to me – followed up on an advertisement in the *Ottawa Citizen* for footballers to join the Ottawa Falcons over 35s for the upcoming season. What's more, she even forged my signature on the registration papers and booked me in for the first game of the season, not long after we arrived in the country.

"You did what?" I said.

"I've signed you up for the Ottawa Falcons to play football on Friday evenings this summer" she replied.

"But you know I haven't played for years, and I don't have any boots? Plus, there's a big difference between over 35s and over 45s, which is more my age group these days."

"Well, you're playing and that's that. I'm not spending the next three years mixing with people from your workplace, and I know you can't live without your football. I told them you'd played before in England, and that was that. You're in the Ottawa Falcons OT 4th squad for the game on Friday!"

I couldn't help thinking how I'd landed on my feet with Jill. She knew me so well – better than I knew myself. I have always loved the beautiful game, and she wanted me to be happy.

My eldest son Mark came to Canada with us. He was 18 at the time and had run into a few problems at home, so I thought a new start in Ottawa would help him along in life. I registered him in Algonquin College in Ottawa, and he also joined up with the Falcons. We went along to the first session together and he ended up playing for them as well.

The soccer season there runs from April to September and although there isn't a professional league – or at least there wasn't then – there was a very healthy amateur league with expats from all over the world playing in the evenings or at weekends. I started out in the Old Timer 4ths and surprised myself by winning the most valuable player (MVP) award in my first season there. This led to a promotion for the rest of my time in Canada to the 2nds and even the odd game for the first eleven.

This was great fun, but also fiercely competitive. Players had to show proof of age before every league game, and because of the cosmopolitan make-up of Ottawa many games were like mini-internationals. The Falcons were predominantly English expats, but we played other teams made up mainly of French, Korean or West Indian expats. I vividly remember one game in particular which ended up in the match being abandoned and a 22-man punch up on the field. Not quite the behaviour expected of a British government representative abroad, but something that wasn't completely alien to me from those early days in the West London Sunday League. In particular there was a fierce local rivalry between the Ottawa Falcons and the Ottawa Royals, who were composed mainly of Scots. This also took me back to playing football in UKIS alongside several very loud and very talented Scotsmen.

Joining the Falcons brought with it huge social benefits off the pitch, where we forged new friendships which have stood the test of time. The Falcons regularly gathered together with their families in local bars to watch any England games on big screen TV, most dressed in England shirts. This often extended on Saturdays to English Premier League games – and with the five-hour time difference it was not unusual for these sessions to start quite early and go on for most of the day.

My enduring memory of Ottawa was of the friendly welcome we received from the community there. Jill gave birth to both our sons in Ottawa General – Daniel in 2000 and Ben in 2003 – and we received huge support from our friends there in terms of baby showers, pre-school groups and so on. I have kept their passports up to date so both the boys can make best use of dual nationality in their lives in future – Canadian by birth, British by descent.

One of our friends was in a similar position to me, having been posted to the Canadian government on a secondment from the British government. She decided that she liked the Canadian lifestyle so much that she would take out Canadian citizenship and stay there. I admit the thought did cross my mind, and I often wonder how my life would have turned out if I had chosen the same course. I suppose the two main factors that mitigated against doing so were (a) the extremely cold winters, where the temperature often dropped to – 30 degrees centigrade, and (b) a culture of discrimination in the Canadian government in favour of officials from French descent over those from British descent. I'm all for diversity and supporting ethnic minorities to achieve their maximum potential, but not at the expense of denying posts to others on those grounds alone, especially where there is a specific differential in capability and competence. I'm afraid I saw too much of that in the Canadian Federal Government in my time there to place me in a comfort zone that I could accept. Besides which, London was calling and reminding me that my specific skills sets were needed back home. Although even then, I had no idea what was in store for me back in the Home Office in London. Another new chapter in my life was about to dawn.

CHAPTER 14

BACK TO THE HOME OFFICE – DEPUTY DIRECTOR, IMMIGRATION ENFORCEMENT LONDON

One of the benefits of overseas postings in those days was that Government policy was to offer staff and their families the opportunity to return from post directly to London in business class, or to purchase an alternative route home in economy class for the same amount. I first picked up on this policy during my posting to Dhaka in 1984. Although that was an unaccompanied posting, I was able to afford a trip to Singapore, Malaysia and Thailand on the way home.

Similar rules applied to my posting to Canada. Jill and I took mid-tour leave to return to the UK to have Daniel christened in Lichfield, Staffordshire, but instead of returning across the Atlantic we chose the long way round and had a great holiday around the Far East and Hawaii before landing back in a frozen Ottawa in February. We were fortunate to have a great many holidays and trips from our Ottawa base. We still joke that Jill would probably win a competition for the most exotic places she has breast fed – the space centre in Houston and the Star Ferry in Hong Kong amongst them.

We closed up our house in Ottawa in September 2003 to head home. It turned out that this was a "one off" posting, meaning that I would not be replaced. Meanwhile there had been a lot of changes back in the Home Office – driven mainly by the asylum influx crisis – and a lot of people had been promoted. Indeed, having come from a small team of Assistant Directors running the Immigration Service (Ports) Directorate, I would be returning to an army of about 40 of them, many of whom had worked for me before I went to Canada. So, what job would I return to?

My post at Heathrow had been filled by my good friend Ian Neill. A huge new Directorate had sprung up in Manchester, and one thought I had was to go for a post there. The boys were still pre-school age, and we could live in the Peak District. However, it soon became clear to me that the Department had other plans for me. This had after all been a development posting, and London beckoned. I was invited to apply for a Grade 6 (Deputy Director) post in Immigration Enforcement, reporting to the Enforcement Director (Colin Allars). This involved attending a video interview board from Ottawa – chaired by my old friend Dave Wilson – and before I knew it, I was a substantive Grade 6 and a Deputy Director in the Immigration Service Enforcement Directorate.

Returning to London after three and a half years in Ottawa was a bit of a challenge in itself. My renewed lease of life on the football field – coupled with achieving my ambition of learning how to ski at the age of 49 – had taken its toll on my knees, and I had to face up to a cartilage operation. I was on the waiting list for this for most of that summer and I finally got a slot the week before we were due to fly out. Fortunately, technology had come a long way and they were able to operate using keyhole surgery, but this would still leave me on sticks for the journey home. What's more, we had booked a flight back via New York, Miami, and Antigua.

Travel wasn't easy on crutches with a double buggy and two small kids on board. One of the favourite children's entertainers of that era was an Australian band called "The Wiggles", and one of their songs favoured by my two-year-old son was called "Can you stand on one leg and wave your hands?" which he liked to target upon me whilst I was on crutches! We still laugh about that to this day.

I also had the job of disposing of the furniture. Now this was officially government property – but without anywhere to use it, the Home Office suggested I put it up for sale at the market value and return the proceeds to Accounts Branch. In the end we bought some of it ourselves and brought it back with us, as a reminder of a fabulous time in our lives in a Canada.

We returned to our house in Sutton and started on a long programme of renovations. The flat roof had leaked several times whilst we were away, and the whole place needed a complete overhaul. This took an age, and it was a difficult time for us all working around the builders, particularly given that we had become accustomed to living in nice big houses in Ottawa. At the same time the Home Office had changed beyond all recognition. The asylum influx had become the most pressing political issue of the day, and the Blair government had introduced a new target of "tipping the balance". This meant – in effect – that the UK Immigration Service was required to remove more "failed asylum seekers" (FAS) than "new asylum seekers" (intake) every month. This was a very big ask. The Ports Directorate was responsible for intake reduction, and the Enforcement Directorate for delivering FAS removals.

My role as Deputy Director Enforcement in London put me in charge of two former offices where I had previously served – the Intelligence and Investigations Unit (IU) and the London Enforcement Office at Becket House – although the landscape had changed completely. The IU had moved from Harmondsworth to Eaton House in Feltham and was now known as the West London Enforcement Office. New buildings had been acquired by the Home Office in Croydon and City Road in Central London – known as Electric House and Communications House, respectively. Only Becket House remained from the Estate I had left behind three years earlier.

There had been a consequential increase in staffing across the board at all levels and a huge expansion of "Reporting Centres" where asylum seekers were required to report from time to time as their cases worked their way through the system. It is important to note here that although my domain was to enforce removals, it was not to conduct casework. There had also been a huge growth in asylum casework teams across the country, who remained part of the Asylum Directorate. So the challenge for us was to identify those people who were "Appeal Rights Exhausted" (ARE) and who also had a valid travel document from those who were still caught up in the system and not removable at all. A problem that has continued to haunt the Department ever since.

The four London Enforcement Offices (LEOs) had been deliberately set up in competition with one another. The objective was to become the top asylum removals office in the weekly stats, which were pored over with ever increasing scrutiny by senior civil servants and Ministers. I inherited a team of four Assistant Directors – Maria Cavilla, Steph Hudson, Jackie Eastham, and Geoff Lockwood – who presented me with some of the most difficult challenges in chairing meetings that I can recall in my entire career. I am not one for shouting or banging tables when chairing meetings, but I still recall many long meetings there where everyone was talking, and nobody was listening. Except for Geoff, perhaps. Despite this, there was no denying the passion this team had for the task in hand, and the ingenuity they put into their work to deliver their targets. Something that made me smile in later life when I heard a Home Secretary tell a Home

Affairs Committee that they didn't have targets in Immigration Enforcement.

I have said many times that the Immigration Enforcement portfolio is a banana skin for Ministers, and for Home Secretaries. David Blunkett was the Home Secretary at this time, but he was forced to resign in 2004 following allegations about his personal life and the fast-tracking of a visa application. He was succeeded by Charles Clarke, who himself was forced to resign after a row over the charge that we had stopped removing foreign criminals.

Political interference in immigration decision-making was commonplace. These cases were ultimately a matter of judgement against a set of immigration rules set down by Parliament, and a good deal of constituency casework comes from people who have fallen foul of the immigration laws but don't want to go home. It was always far easier to grant leave to remain in an individual case than to refuse it. Even then many did not see refusal as a reason to go home, but rather as a reason to perpetuate their argument in the hope that somebody somewhere in the system would eventually change the decision.

Immigration enforcement is a thankless task. It means arresting and detaining people who are seen as innocent in the eyes of many. Although illegal entry, overstaying and working in breach of conditions were all criminal offences, breaching immigration conditions was not seen as serious by many observers. If the offender is a hard-working and popular member of the community, then illegality of status can become coincidental. Many a time I attended immigration raids to be spat at and abused by people in the community simply for doing my job. I was not alone in that.

Meanwhile back at the ranch, not delivering enforcement and removal targets was seen as failure. The thirst to deliver "Tipping the Balance" amongst Ministers (because it was a PM requirement) – and therefore Senior Civil Servants (anxious to please) – was massive. We were called in every Monday morning to explain why it was that we hadn't removed more failed asylum seekers (FAS) than the week before. The fact that most of them had lodged last-minute appeals, judicial reviews or fresh applications (thereby removing themselves from the removable pool) was lost in translation. It was all our fault. Yet if we ever put anybody on a plane when such an application was pending, we were potentially placing the Home Secretary in contempt of court. It really was a "no win" situation.

I recall one occasion when I was in charge of immigration enforcement in London where we had arrested a very large number of "illegals" in various intelligence-led enforcement operations over the course of a week. Back in the JOE days, this would have had our bosses leaping with delight. Not now. Unfortunately for us, most of them – whilst certainly in the country unlawfully – chose to play the "asylum card", thereby disbarring any chance of removal for the immediate future. Worse still, this fuelled the asylum intake figures to the extent that the "tipping the balance" target was damaged.

I recall a very heated exchange with one of my superiors around that time that led me to storm out of the office and seriously contemplate resignation for the first time in my career. I was in effect being encouraged to stop arresting immigration offenders altogether in my area, because it was "messing up the asylum intake target".

Now if Ministers wanted to level with the public and admit that they were stopping immigration enforcement operations in London in order to reduce the number of new asylum claims in and hit the "tipping the balance" target, then that was fine by me. But this was not the agreed policy position. In fact, this hadn't even been put to Ministers at all. It was in effect an attempt to bully me – and therefore to bully a lot of dedicated enforcement officers in my command – to allow illegal immigration to go unchecked in my region. Immigration Officers operate under powers mandated by Parliament to arrest and remove immigration offenders. It is a policy that no government of any colour had ever tried to overturn. In fact, immigration enforcement laws have been steadily strengthened over many years to facilitate this. Any statement to the contrary would cause huge political damage to the party advocating it. Yet here was I being told to ignore the rule of law and pull back from operations, in order to manipulate a government-targeted reduced asylum intake. If we don't arrest them then they can't claim asylum, right?

So why did I bite my lip and turn around? Because – as with many other occasions in my career – I was counselled by immigration officers junior to me in grade, but certainly wiser than me in knowledge. "Tony, you have to roll with the punches. We've finally got one of our own up there now. Don't let the buggers get you down!" This was the message that came back to me from the front line. I relied upon it many times for inner strength as I continued my climb up the slippery pole. For many senior civil servants, respect from the front line wasn't very important at all. For me, it was everything.

Asylum removals were very hard to achieve. They still are. The dice are loaded against the executive, regardless of the fact that it may be a government priority. Nonetheless we persevered, and by introducing closer working arrangements between the asylum caseworkers and the enforcement teams, we started to turn a corner. Not least because our colleagues on the ports side of the business were making great strides in reducing asylum intake at the border.

The main tool they used for this was to agree the implementation of juxtaposed controls on the cross-Channel routes, where the vast majority of illegal entry was occurring. If we could stop people before they arrived in the UK, then they couldn't claim asylum here. They were in France or Belgium – both safe countries in their own right. They could claim asylum there if they were genuinely in fear of persecution in their homeland. Figures started to come down as we ramped up our detection teams in Calais and Dunkirk.

The ports side of the business was working well under the leadership of my friend and colleague Dave Roberts, who was by now the Director of Immigration Service (Ports). I was one grade below him, as a Deputy Director of Immigration (Enforcement). Given my experience of leading Border operations in Canada, I felt a move back to the UK border would be beneficial both to myself and to the Department. Fortunately for me, my next big break was just around the corner.

CHAPTER 15

INTO THE SENIOR CIVIL SERVICE – DIRECTOR, PORTS AND BORDERS, UK IMMIGRATION SERVICE.

Towards the end of 2004, Colin Allars decided it was time for him to make a career move. Colin was a really nice guy, but he wasn't a UKIS veteran like many of us in the upper echelons of the Immigration Service at that time. He was a generalist with excellent policy skills that were in demand elsewhere.

This meant that a vacancy was to arise as Director of Enforcement. This was in effect a Grade 5 post – the first rung of the Senior Civil Service. To my surprise, Dave Roberts – then Director of Ports – decided he wanted a new challenge and threw his hat into the ring for the post. This in turn left a vacancy in his role. This was effectively the Head of UK Ports and Borders, but unlike the Canada role, it also included line management for over 4,000 officers stationed at UK ports and borders as well as overall responsibility for the operation itself.

By now Brodie Clark had taken over as Senior Director (Grade 3) of the UK Immigration Service. In effect, this was the Chief Inspector of Immigration role. Brodie was a former prison officer who had moved across from the prison service to the Immigration and Nationality Department whilst I was in Canada. I don't think Brodie ever actually saw himself as the Chief Inspector of UKIS, although in effect this was his role, alongside one or two other things.

Brodie chaired the promotion board for the Director of Ports post. A jump from grade 6 to grade 5 was a big one. It didn't just involve an interview. As it was the entry point into the Senior Civil Service, I had to go through a whole raft of psychological and psychometric tests along the way. Some of these involved puzzles and multiple-choice questionnaires. In fact, I found the whole experience to be quite good fun. I will never forget going through one of the questionnaires with Jill on the sofa at home one night. One question came up – "Have you ever literally jumped for joy?"

"No" I replied out loud. I always saw myself as a pretty laid-back kind of guy, who never got overly excited about anything much.

"Yes, you bloody have," remarked Jill.

"No, I haven't" I replied. "When then?"

"When you took me to see QPR and Kevin Gallen scored the winner, you literally jumped for joy," she replied.

Ah yes, of course I did. As did every other true Rangers fan in the ground. Indeed, football had always been the thing to get my passions up. Especially at Loftus Road. This would be hard for most people to understand – but if any Rangers fans are reading this book, they will get it.

I learned a lot about myself during those exercises. They certainly helped me through my leadership journey thereafter. As for the promotion – all I could do was take the tests, go through the interview board, and then wait and hope.

Brodie gave me the news when I was least expecting it. We were at one of those interminable Home Office 'awaydays' when he sauntered up to me after lunch and asked if he could have a private word. We spent a couple of minutes wandering around the hotel trying to find a quiet spot before he sprung it on me.

"Congratulations Mr Smith – you've got the job. You are the Director of UK Ports and Borders. Now don't you dare let me down, will you?"

So that was that. I had made it into the Senior Civil Service, as Director of Ports and Borders in the UK Immigration Service, exactly 30 years after reporting for duty as a young "sprog" immigration officer at Heathrow Airport. What's more, it occurred to me that I was probably the only person on the planet who had been the Director of Ports and Borders in two different countries. Certainly – as I was soon to discover – during times of crisis.

I made it my business to get out to the ports and talk to the front line as quickly as I could. The role put me in charge of around 4,000 staff dotted around the country at ports and airports and a small number working around the world as airline liaison officers (ALOs). I wasted no time in building up my personal development folder. I joined a new leader's course sponsored by the Home Office and attended a Command & Control Course at the police college at Bramshill. I also registered on a programme management course to gain an external qualification as a Senior Responsible Owner. All good moves, as things turned out.

As Director of UK Ports of Entry, I had lost none of my enthusiasm for international work. The new European Border Agency (FRONTEX) was forming, and it was part of my job to represent the UK at their Management Board meetings in Warsaw. This was my first real taste of EU politics. Because the UK and Ireland had opted out of the borderless Schengen zone, my Irish colleague and I found ourselves being excluded from some of the key decisions – and even had to leave the room in a couple of occasions at the request of the EU Commission, who were keeping a very close watch on the formation of an operational cohort who might challenge their area of competence.

Once again, my operational experience came to the fore. As most former Heads of Borders will tell you, we tend to flock together based on our common desire to collaborate to protect our respective borders from threats. After the formal meetings, the informal meetings took place in the bars and hotel lobbies around Warsaw, where lasting friendships were formed. Secretly most Heads of Borders from EU countries were fiercely opposed to Schengen, and the dismantling of their internal border controls. Many – notably the Scandinavians – were already building "alternative" check points at hot spots within their own territories, in some cases just a few hundred yards up the road from where the original border post was located. The Dutch were acquiring internal passenger data on intra-Schengen flights into Schiphol to identify illegal migrants coming to Holland from Southern European countries. We drew up plans to exchange intelligence and officers with each other, and to collaborate to take out criminal gangs and smugglers operating within the EU wherever we could.

The EU Commission was not too keen on all this operational collaboration between us. I can remember proposing a 5-year plan to Frontex to enhance cross EU Border Agency collaboration – which I know had widespread support from the Management Board – only to be shouted down by the Commission representative on the grounds that "they didn't really like long-term plans". My dear friend Ilkka Laitinen – who served as the first Executive Director for Frontex – was increasingly perplexed by the Commission's failure to deliver promises on all kinds of things including budgets, jurisdiction, accommodation, and infrastructure. Frontex is in much better shape these days than it was then, but it is clear that the political agenda around integration and the desire to protect our borders was always going to be a challenge – as we were to find out later in our quest to "take back control of our borders". But more of that later.

CHAPTER 16

The London attacks,
July 2005

The next big turning point in my career took place on 7 July 2005 – the London bombings. I was actually with Brodie at a pre-arranged liaison meeting at Heathrow with our colleagues from the Department of a Justice of Ireland when the news broke. There had been multiple terrorist attacks on the London transport system by a team of suicide bombers. For the second time in four years, I found myself playing a leading role in the national border security response to a major terrorist attack.

At least this time I was within easy range of headquarters, and not stranded thousands of miles away. We apologised to our Irish colleagues and headed back to our stations. Brodie went to the Home Office in Central London. I went to ISHQ in Croydon to take charge of the Gold Room.

Fortunately, following my recent training in command, control and co-ordination, I had already commissioned a review our capabilities in this area. I had been able to procure a small control room in ISHQ for this very purpose. It was kept under lock and key for most of the time, but it contained all the necessary equipment to participate in a major crisis, including hotlines to key people in government and major news feeds. In fact, media play a very significant role at times like this. They are on the scene very quickly indeed – sometimes even before first responders – and can convey images of disaster scenes around the world in an instant. I recall driving back from Heathrow to Croydon that day listening to radio interviews with eyewitnesses talking about explosions on the underground, and on a London bus.

Of course, memories of my experiences of 9/11 in Canada flashed through my mind. Who had done this? Were they foreign fighters? If so, how did they get into the country? And when? I had been Director of UK Ports and Borders for six months, so, there was a good chance that this was on my watch. Did we know they were coming? What intelligence did we have in advance? What did we do about it? Could we have stopped them? Would this be the end of the Immigration Service, as it was for the INS after 9/11? Would I get the blame?

One thing my 9/11 experience had taught me was not to jump to conclusions based on speculation, but to chase down the facts. The Government announced that a state of emergency had been called. This meant that a critical incident command structure would be set up. A gold group would be installed, reporting direct to Ministers through the "COBRA" system.

Despite its sexy title, COBRA is no more than an abbreviation for the Cabinet Office Briefing Rooms (COBR) with many briefings taking place in room A. There is a web of tunnels and passageways running through the cabinet office to Downing Street, where the key strategic decisions are made. When the country is under attack, COBRA would almost certainly be chaired by the Prime Minister. However, it did not follow that the UK Immigration Service would be called in. This would depend to a great extent upon the need (or not) to implement additional measures at the UK border, which would in turn depend upon the facts. At this stage there had been no "knee jerk" reaction to close the border. Resources were focused upon identifying the attackers and mitigating the threat of any repeat attacks. And caring for the injured, of course. The first responders – police, fire, and ambulance – were on the case, but there was a very good chance that we would be called upon to act. We needed to be ready.

When I got back to base, I opened up the Gold Room and set about establishing a command structure. Again, my training and experience kicked in here. I had already arranged for specific officers at ISHQ and at the ports to step up at a time like this. A designated command team were relieved of their "business as usual" duties and directed towards the incident. Whatever had happened in London that day, we still had flights to clear and cases to manage. The whole point of a critical incident structure is to shift resources towards the problem, whilst mitigating the impact on "business as usual". The long-term goal was to close off the critical incident as soon as it became possible to do so, thus restoring normal operations.

The Anti-Terrorist Squad at New Scotland Yard took the lead on the investigation and fed out information to us through the gold group as the facts came out. Four suicide bombers with rucksacks full of explosives had attacked Central London during the rush hour, killing 52 people and injuring hundreds more. This was the worst single terrorist attack on British soil in history. The four bombers – Mohammad Siddique Khan, Shehzad Tanweer, Hasib Hussain and Germaine Lindsay – were all British citizens. Khan, Tanweer and Hussain were all born and bred in Yorkshire; Lindsay was born in Jamaica but had lived in Yorkshire from the age of five.

It soon dawned on me that the facts of this case were vastly different from those I had encountered in North America four years earlier. Although in both cases all the terrorists were prepared to die in pursuit of their cause, the US attackers had all breached the US border and visa system to perpetrate their deadly acts. By contrast the UK attackers had in effect turned on their own country, something that gave rise to the new concept of "home grown terrorism", and a new challenge for border and enforcement agencies worldwide. Indeed, it was something that would change the entire complexion of border control forever. Border control wasn't just about foreigners and immigration anymore. It was about national security, including checks on our own people.

As these were British citizens, attention turned to the intelligence services and the police. What did we know about these people? Were they under surveillance already? Why didn't we see this coming? Who had they been in touch with? Who had masterminded the operation? Were there more in the pipeline?

Now it so happens that the Home Office was already leading a significant programme of work to transform the UK border. Driven by the events of 9/11 and the huge growth in passenger data, they had set out a vision for a new "electronic" border system in the UK known as "e borders".

I was not directly involved in the e borders project at that time. There was a separate governance structure in place for that. I was in charge of running the border, whilst others developed the new e borders system. I was nonetheless described as one of their major 'stakeholders' – unsurprisingly, given that I was in charge of UK border operations. This was where I experienced my first real taste of "consultants". Ironic really, given that I was destined to become one myself in later life.

I learned a couple of lessons about consultancy during that time. The first was that it was a very expensive business. I vividly remember going out to an e borders meeting at Heathrow one day and driving around Status Park looking for a spot to park my Vauxhall Zafira, amongst all the Mercedes and BMWs already there. During one budget review I asked for a list of the highest earners in my Directorate and found out that I was number 43 on the list, despite being the most senior officer there. We had several companies involved in the project at the time and although they certainly had good skills in things like project management, they didn't have the first idea about border management. I remember being interviewed by a couple of them in Croydon one day, asking me what I thought the future strategy for the UK border ought to be. I gave them both barrels and agreed to meet them again a week later. The following week they turned up again with some very pretty slides and graphics, basically telling me everything that I had told them the previous week. Ingenious.

Now maybe I was a bit of an old soldier by now, but one thing I had learned over the past 30 years was not to believe everything you hear. Particularly in an area where you have been bitten before. I was given all sorts of advice on how I should run the border, much of it from people who had very little experience of working there themselves. My main loyalty was to my workforce (I was after all one of them) and to the British public. That meant keeping the border moving as freely as possible but not compromising on security.

Although it was clear that the 7/7 attacks were not directly attributable to a failure in our immigration vetting systems as was the case with 9/11, it was equally clear that we had not been looking in the right direction in preventing terrorist travel. We had been focusing all our attention on potential threats posed by foreign nationals subject to immigration controls at the UK border. Further checks after the event revealed that all four of the attackers had in fact travelled abroad – albeit with their own identities and on genuine British passports, but for nefarious reasons - in fact, to train to become terrorists. This meant that we needed a new approach to border security which demanded a much closer working relationship between the UK Immigration Service, the police, and the security services.

Before we could get too far down that road, we still had operational issues to resolve directly after 7/7. We were getting daily intelligence reports that there were more attacks in the pipeline. COBRA was sitting throughout this period, and I was in daily contact with colleagues in Special Branch. Ports and borders were on heightened alert to watch out for any potential terrorists entering or leaving the country. The latter was particularly difficult for us. We had abolished our physical embarkation controls by now, and we relied entirely upon passenger data and watchlists to identify any suspects seeking to depart the country. (This was something I opposed vigorously at the time, and still do).

Sure enough, on 21/7 another group of terrorists tried to repeat the exploits of 7/7 group. Four explosions took place at Shepherd's Bush, Warren Street and Oval underground stations, and another on a London bus in Hackney Road. Fortunately, on this occasion the main devices failed to fully explode – apparently due to faulty detonators. However, we now had "live" terrorists on the run in a London, and a manhunt was under way. Obviously as custodians of the UK Border we were part of the response, and our focus shifted quickly from the arrival controls to the departure control. The police response was led by officers from the Anti-Terrorism Branch (SO13) and Special Branch (SO12), who were to merge the following year into the new Anti-Terrorism Command (SO15). We had always enjoyed a good working relationship with SB, going back to my early days at Heathrow in the seventies. My contact at SB was Jon Donlon, who went on to become a great friend and colleague of mine.

Special Branch deployments to UK ports at that time were variable. Officers were appointed to SB on a constabulary basis, depending upon the ports served within the Force Area and the resources available there. This meant that there were generally enough SB officers available in the regions around the country to watch outbound departures there, but not so in London and the South East, particularly in the aftermath of 7/7 where the police were already stretched to the limit following up on the investigation itself.

To supplement SB checks, we scrambled what resources we could to outbound controls at Heathrow, Stansted, Gatwick, Luton and Waterloo International whilst the intelligence teams worked overtime to develop profiles of the 21/7 bombers for dissemination to the front line. Things moved at an electric pace at CCTV images emerged on live television of suspects running through the London Underground network.

During the manhunt, the police mistook a Brazilian student, Jean Charles de Menezes, for one of the suspects and shot him dead following a chase through Stockwell underground station. Records suggest that Menezes had entered the UK via Ireland on 23 April 2005, although he was previously an overstayer in the UK and therefore unlikely to benefit from the terms of the Immigration (control of entry through Ireland) Order 1972. Either way he was probably running away from the police because he believed he was unlawfully in the UK at that time. Certainly, he had nothing to do with the terrorist attacks – he was in the wrong place at the wrong time. But I often use this as an example to others that they should not try to run away when challenged to stop by a police officer. You never quite know what might be going on around you, and what the risk level might be.

This was a torrid time for all of us involved in law enforcement. We were all driven by a desire to capture the suspects and to keep the public safe from further attacks. By 29 July, the police had arrested all four suspects: Muktar Said Ibrahim, 29, Yasin Hassan Omar, 26, Ramzi Mohammed, 25, and Hussain Osman, 28. Muktar, Omar and Ramzi were born in either Eritrea or Somalia and had all been granted asylum in the UK. Osman was originally from Ethiopia but had been naturalised as a British citizen.

Although all four of the terrorists were lawfully in the UK, we did not emerge from the incident completely unscathed.

Osman had managed to escape on the Eurostar to Paris using his brother's passport before being arrested in Rome. He had slipped through our net, amidst all the chaos.

These events led to the development of a new UK counter-terrorism strategy, known as CONTEST. The strategy comprised four strands: Prevent, Pursue, Protect, and Prepare. We signed a new operational agreement with the Counter Terrorism Branch so as to clarify roles and responsibilities of the various agencies at the border, in the event of another critical incident. Our security checks were expanded so as to cover not just foreign nationals crossing the border but EU and UK nationals as well. Immigration Officers were given additional powers at the border to detain and examine British citizens who were suspected of being involved in acts of terrorism. Ports were asked to develop their own operational plans and to test them regularly. This included a plan to introduce blanket embarkation controls within a specified timeframe, in every case. These plans were developed, operationalised, and tested. The UK border would never be the same again. A whole new approach to border security was developed during this period, and I was a key participant in it, something that would serve me well in the years still to come.

CHAPTER 17

HOME OFFICE NOT FIT FOR PURPOSE

During my tenure of the post of Director of Ports and Borders in the UK Immigration Service, I was fortunate enough to avoid too many confrontations with Ministers, and even less with Home Secretaries. That is not to say that I didn't like them. In fact, I always had a huge amount of respect for any politician who was prepared to step into the Home Office. Survival rates weren't traditionally good for politicians in that Department.

The problem was that the usual reason for operational staff to be called into Ministerial meetings on matters of immigration and border control was that something had gone badly, rather than well. It was a rare event indeed for senior civil servants to be called in to see Ministers to be congratulated because something had gone well. No news was good news. But when things did go wrong – as they often did – contact between officials, Special Advisers and Ministers became much more frequent.

Apart from managing my way through the 7/7 incident and the aftermath, things went fairly well for me in this post.

As Director of Ports and Borders I was answerable directly to Brodie Clark, alongside three other Directors – my old mate David Wilson (Intelligence); Dave Roberts (Enforcement); and Brian Pollett (Detention). We got along quite well as a team, and most of our board meetings revolved around the asylum figures and achieving the "tipping the balance" target. This was a top priority for the Blair Government at that time.

Things were working well on my side. Dave Roberts had already broken the back of the asylum intake target through the establishment of the juxtaposed controls in Calais. I kept this chugging along by working closely with my colleagues on the French side and establishing some joint initiatives with them to stop smugglers. This was where my Canadian experience came to the fore – good fences make good neighbours. An effective border is much more likely to accrue where there is collaboration behind a common purpose on both sides. We introduced additional security checks on the freight side, including our magnificent dog teams who were always more effective at finding illegal immigrants concealed in vehicles than any technology. Meanwhile our entire enforcement effort was focused on arresting, detaining, and removing failed asylum seekers. The strategy was working – we were indeed tipping the balance.

However, there is never any space for complacency in the Home Office. No sooner did we shut one door than another one opened. Whilst the asylum casework teams were racing through cases and the enforcement teams were chasing down and removing Failed Asylum Seekers (FAS), the criminal case working teams were struggling. These teams were charged with the duty of liaising with the Prison Service to ensure that any foreign criminals coming towards the end of their sentence would be deported before their earliest release date (EDR). This didn't always work smoothly – many of them had no desire to be deported at all, and would adopt many of the traditional measures to avoid it. This included failure to engage in the documentation process, or lodging late applications for asylum, or under the Human Rights legislation. Or simply "kicking off" to such an extent that it was virtually impossible to get them on board an aircraft, even with an escort. The Prison Service were of course keen to see the back of these inmates as soon as the release date came round, and were therefore very happy to pass them into "immigration" custody at the end of their sentences. Which was fine – assuming that the Immigration Department had enough spaces in their detention estate to accommodate them, and, of course, enough case workers to progress them to removal stage.

In 2005 Lin Homer took over as Director General of the Immigration and Nationality Directorate, succeeding Bill Jeffrey. I knew Bill well, and always had a lot of time for him. He was always a big supporter of the UK Immigration Service and although never an immigration officer himself, he understood the culture and the business model very well. In contrast, Lin was an unknown entity to most of us. She came from a local government background, having previously served as Chief Executive Officer at Birmingham County Council. Lin made it her business to get to know her entire SCS team very quickly. We were invited into her office on the 12th floor at Lunar House, one by one, for an introductory meeting. I remember being struck by her openness and honesty, from the very start. It was pretty clear to me that she saw significant changes ahead, and that she was not going to be one to shy away from delivering them. Little did I know at the time just how radical those changes would be – and what a personal impact she would have upon my own career from that moment onwards.

It wasn't long after Lin's arrival that the Criminal Casework scandal engulfed us like a tsunami. Once the press gets hold of a story – invariably a bad one, when it comes to the Home Office – they smell blood and run with it. So do the opposition. This was clearly a major scandal. The one thing that the Home Office and its Agencies pride themselves on is keeping their citizens safe. That's less likely to happen if they are seeing foreign national prisoners who would otherwise have been deported being released back into the community. It soon became clear that Foreign National Offenders (FNOs) were being released not just from prison but also from immigration detention pending deportation. They were out in the community, with a consequential increased risk to public safety.

As with everything else in the Home Office, the buck stops with the Home Secretary, who had the thankless task of reporting all this to Parliament. An urgent policy review demanded that all those who had been released should be immediately tracked down and re-detained, something that was far from easy, given that a great number of them had no wish to be deported at all. Again, it fell to the Home Secretary to report the progress of this operation – or lack of it – back to a hungry opposition and an anti-Government press who were keen to see heads roll. To say that along the way we had actually achieved the PM's top priority of "tipping the balance" – which is why our enforcement and casework efforts were focused in that direction – was lost in translation. Something had to give.

It fell to the Home Secretary of the day – Charles Clark – to take the blame. I met Charles a few times and he seemed to be a very nice man, and very committed to the role too. But sadly, he was returned to the back benches in May 2006 to be replaced by John Reid, a Whitehall veteran who had served in many different Departments as a Minister under the Blair administration.

John Reid arrived at the Home Office with a tough reputation, and he wasted no time in setting out his pretty candid view about the state of the Department. Something that led to the famous phrase "not fit for purpose" – which was to haunt us for many years to come.

Now unless you have actually worked in the Senior Civil Service, you might be forgiven for assuming that crises like these pass us by. Ultimately it is Ministers who take the blame. They come and go, whilst civil servants remain unscathed to pick up the baton where the last Minister had dropped it.

The reality is that nothing could be further than the truth. In my experience, Senior Civil Servants always take their jobs extremely seriously. We were mortally wounded at the loss of Charles Clarke, an honourable man who had served his country well and didn't deserve to be treated in this way. The loss of any Minister of State was always a tragedy to us. If anything, it drove us even harder to right the wrongs of the past and get things right next time round. We suffered many sleepless nights along the way during that period – and there would be many more to come.

John Reid was a reformist, as was Lin Homer. They led a thorough review of the Department. One area we had been described as "not fit for purpose" was in leadership. This was particularly painful for those of us in leadership positions, particularly on the operational side of the house. Consultants and coaches were called in from all over the place to help us develop our leadership skills. I took full advantage of this opportunity. Leadership had always attracted a high marking on my report – unlike political acumen, where I was usually bottom of the class. But I had learned from my own coaching that sometimes it is better to focus on your stronger skills for development, not just your weaker ones. I convinced myself that the mark of a true leader was best measured by the esteem in which one is held by one's peers, workforce, and stakeholders, and not necessarily by one's superiors. There is no doubt that my career was enhanced considerably by the introduction of 360-degree reporting, where these measures had to be considered. Without that, I doubt I would have reached the dizzy heights that I did.

Reid's agenda for fixing things at the Home Office wasn't entirely unwelcome to all of us. He was right to demand a reduction in staffing in the centre – there were far too many sections and units watching and checking what the rest of us were doing, in my view. In particular, I was fully behind his ambition to move us towards Agency status and for us to become a uniformed disciplined force, like the police. I had by now travelled far and wide to meet with Heads of Border Control in other countries, and there was no doubt that we were very much in the minority in operating within a Civil Service Department. I could never quite understand why I had been given significant enforcement powers by Parliament which I was then discouraged from using as a law enforcement officer because of political interference; or why so many people were taking leadership roles in the Department without ever having exercised them themselves.

Although the most significant casualty of the foreign national prisoner scandal was Charles Clarke, the Senior Civil Service did not emerge entirely unscathed. Ultimately it was immigration enforcement that had dropped the ball on criminal deportations, and they formed part of the wider Immigration and Nationality Department, which had already come under a great deal of public scrutiny and criticism in the past. One way to resolve such crises was to identify the senior officials who were most closely involved in the area that had failed, and to arrange a "career move" for them. The two officials subsequently named by the press as having been moved as a result of this issue were Digby Griffith – a Director in Immigration Enforcement at that time – and my boss Brodie Clark. It was reported that they were not held to be directly responsible for the crisis in the first place, but rather for reporting inaccurate figures in the follow up. Of course, they weren't personally involved in the collation and dissemination of the figures – they relied upon lower grade staff for that. But as with Ministers, the buck stops somewhere. Both were moved into new roles.

This had a direct impact upon my own position. Brodie was relieved of his responsibilities for immigration enforcement, intelligence and detention and put in charge of the UK Border, which at that time was in fact my job – albeit at Grade 5 level rather than at Grade 3.

Of course, I didn't begrudge this position for Brodie – he had after all chaired the Board that promoted me into that position some eighteen months earlier. I had no problem working for him either – I found him to be a tough and uncompromising leader but at the same time fair and just, particularly if you were fully honest with him and contrite when errors took place in your area.

Notwithstanding, it would be inevitable that this reorganisation would amount to an undermining of my own position as a Director of Ports and Borders in the UK Immigration Service. It wasn't long before this manifested itself in the operational structure. Brodie was able to secure two more Grade 5 posts at the UK Border, alongside my own. Firstly, at Director for Change Management was appointed. Then a Director for Heathrow.

Obviously, this didn't sit too well with me. My own position and authority became increasingly unclear. Did this mean I no longer had a role to play in UK Border Transformation? Had a big chunk of my operational command been taken out of my control? I was never one to be backward in coming forward when I felt my position in the workplace was being undermined – another area that frequently appeared in my annual report as one for "development". I soon began to make some noise about this, including to both Brodie and Lin. Which was to lead to the next milestone in my extraordinary career.

CHAPTER 18

PROMOTION TO SENIOR DIRECTOR: THE END OF UKIS, AND THE BIRTH OF THE BORDER AND IMMIGRATION AGENCY (BIA)

As is often the case in times of crisis, the government responded with a structural change aimed at consigning the problems of the past to history with a brave new dawn. It was clear that the Immigration and Nationality Department – and the UK Immigration Service – were no longer "fit for purpose". They were ripe for reform, and with a new Home Secretary and Director General at the helm, now was as good a time as any.

The new Border and Immigration Agency (BIA) was formed as a replacement for IND in April 2007. Lin Homer had been busy augmenting her senior team, bringing in Senior Directors to sit alongside Brodie on the IND Board. This included new Senior Director (Grade 3) posts for Asylum, Immigration Enforcement, and Managed Migration. Her vision also included moving operations to a regional command structure at arm's length from government control, through agency status.

I remember one of many conversations I had with Lin around that time, one that was to frame the rest of my career. I was called up to see her one day, in expectation of receiving another rollicking for making a fuss about the diminution of my role as Director of Ports and Borders due to circumstances entirely beyond my control. Which was indeed part of the call – but there was a much more significant agenda too.

"Tony, we all know you are angry about what's happened round here, but you still have so much to learn about politics. You really need to understand when to hold your tongue and bear in mind that at this level you need to have a lot more political nous than you have now."

This was a familiar conversation with Lin, and she could point to several subsequent events in my career which bore that out. Good catch.

"Well, I don't know what I've done to deserve this" I replied. "My job was to secure the border and bring down asylum intake. I had no idea what was going on with FNOs and deportations. That wasn't my area. It's just not fair."

I guess with hindsight this might have come across like a petulant schoolboy complaining to the headmistress. I suppose I was. Although I was in fact deeply hurt that I was (apparently) being punished for events that were outside my sphere of control.

"Listen to me" she said. "There are some big changes coming up over the next few months, and I have every respect for your skills and experience. There are two big jobs in the pipeline, and I expect you to apply for both of them. One is the Senior Director post in Immigration Enforcement – I know you have a lot of experience of that. The other is a Regional Director post for London and the South East, running all immigration and enforcement operations across the region. These are Grade 3 posts. I know that would be a big step up for you – but I think with the right development you could do it. Starting with a bit more political nous and a bit less noise. Nothing stays the same for very long in this business."

I thanked her for her time and consideration and went away to consider the next stage of my journey. Sure enough, notices emerged shortly afterwards inviting applications for the posts of Senior Director (Enforcement) and Regional Director (London and South East) in the new Border and Immigration Agency. Both were grade 3 posts. I applied for both.

After another range of assessments, interviews, and tests I waited for what seemed like an interminable period for the results. These were both huge jobs which would take me to the next rung up in the SCS – a level that I could never have dreamt of reaching when I started out as a young immigration officer at Heathrow all those years ago. In fact, both these posts were pitched at Grade 3 level – one level above that held by the mighty Peter Tomkins, the last "real" Chief Inspector of the UK Immigration Service. Indeed, an appointment to either post would put me on the same grade as my boss, Brodie Clark – and would attract a significant increase in salary and consequential pension benefits. It seemed too good to be true.

I didn't get the Enforcement job, but I did get the Regional Director job. To be fair to the selection board, they brought in a broad mix of people to fill the six RD posts available. These were in Scotland and Northern Ireland; North East; North West; Midlands; Wales and the South West; and London and the South East. Three women were appointed from outside the Home Office with little or no knowledge of the business. Three men were appointed from within the Department, with a lifetime of experience in the business. Including yours truly.

My old friend and colleague Jeremy Oppenheim was charged with the responsibility of making this all work. Jeremy was a likeable personality, and a great mediator and communicator. He felt it would be a good idea to "buddy up" the Regional Directors into pairs. My post in London and the South East was by far the largest. Indeed, my workforce and budget were on a par with that of all the other five regions together. Which is why my post was set at Grade 3, and the others were at Grade 5. But in reality, that made little difference. We quickly formed into a new leadership team for UK immigration operations, and I was delighted to be paired up with Gail Adams, who joined us as Regional Director for Midlands and East. Gail had a strong "Brummie" accent and brought great knowledge of local and regional government with her to the organisation. Yet another chapter in my journey had begun.

Whilst my career had moved on at lightning speed between 2003 and 2007, climbing from Grade 7 to Grade 3, I inevitably took my eye off the ball at home. I had been warned many times by mentors and coaches that I needed to focus on my work/life balance, but I'm afraid that all rather washed over me during this time. The return to our suburban semi in Sutton was a far cry from our life in Ottawa by the Rideau canal, and before I knew it I was spending all the hours God gave me on this extraordinary career journey. It never really occurred to me that this might be affecting my family life. Jill had always been so proud of me and seemed keen to support me every step of the way, but she was of course herself a very able officer with significant potential in her own right, stuck at home for the most part with two pre-school children.

We agreed that she should also resume her career in the Home Office. In the end Jill got a job in immigration enforcement in Croydon and we hired a string of Canadian au pairs to look after Daniel and Ben whilst we were both working. They both started school at Barrow Hedges Primary in Sutton South, and Jill got back into the swing of things in the Home Office in Croydon – not far from my own office.

Anyway, whilst I was running around doing all this international Border stuff Jill had become embroiled in new circles at work herself, and it became clear that we weren't spending much time together at all. There were times when I wondered whether marriage number two was about to go down the drain. In the end we managed to come through it all, but not without some very dark moments along the way. I don't tend to share this much with friends and colleagues – but I always empathise when I see marriages break down due to distractions at work. I don't have the answer to this dilemma, but at least I can say hand on heart that I've been there and got the T-shirt. Fortunately, we managed to come through it, but I can recount many cases where others in a similar position to myself did not.

Meanwhile, back at work, the Home Office reform agenda was moving forward at breakneck speed. I remember taking up my post as Regional Director for London and the South East in the BIA in 2007. Each of the Regional Directors was required to report to one of the Strategic Directors, who had a seat on Lin's Executive Board. As I was the only Grade 3 in the Regional Director team, this created an interesting challenge for the Civil Service hierarchy – "same grade reporting".

Matthew Coats, who was then the Senior Director for Asylum, took over from Brodie as my new line manager. I remember Matthew speaking to me on my first day. He said I would never be more powerful in that post than I was on that day, so now was the time to make the most of it. To be fair to him, Matthew recognised that I had a depth and breadth of experience in the borders and immigration business that far exceeded his own, and he was prepared to give me my head. His big challenge was even greater – to deliver the "New Asylum Model" (NAM) across the Home Office.

The governance structure between the Regional Directors and the Strategic Directors was an interesting one. Although we didn't sit on the Executive Board, we did have our own Regional Directors Board. This met monthly in different parts of the country, and a Strategic Director was always invited to attend. Meanwhile we were rarely invited to the Strategic Board meetings unless something was happening "in our patch" that warranted their attention. Of course, in my region we had the small matter of the London 2012 Olympics on the horizon – but more of that later.

The idea behind regionalisation was that all of the operational functions of the Department – mainly asylum, immigration, and enforcement – would form part of the new Regional Command Structure (except Her Majesty's Passport Office (HMPO) which already had its own regional structure). The notable exception to this rule was the Border, which remained exclusively under the watchful eye of Brodie Clark. So here I was being moved away from UK Border Control operations – which I had been running pretty well exclusively for the past two years – to inland functions of processing immigration and asylum applications and delivering immigration enforcement. All areas which I had worked in to a greater or lesser extent over the years.

In dividing up the spoils between us, we needed to identify specific buildings and offices on our patch which would become part of our new command structure. I was already based in Croydon, where we had a massive estate which encompassed most of the buildings on Wellesley Road including my old haunt of Lunar House, where I had started my career as a young EO all those years ago.

The rest of the command was divided up largely along the lines of police force boundaries, so I inherited the entire Metropolitan Police District and the counties of Kent, Surrey, Sussex, and Hampshire. This amounted to over 4,000 staff and a budget in the region of £350 million. Laid across that were my "public service agreement" targets, which were set by the centre and agreed with Ministers. Each of the strategic Directors also had PSA targets for their respective areas. For Matthew it was the "case conclusion rate" for asylum; for the Immigration Strategic Director it was the introduction of the new immigration system; and for the Enforcement Strategic Director it was about removals, deportations, and penalty notices for hiring illegal workers.

As you might expect having read so far, I was very much at home with the enforcement targets (yes, we certainly had those in my day), but less so with the other two. Naturally, Matthew was very much focused upon the asylum targets. Indeed, he was happy to provide me with most of his best assets in order to deliver them. The immigration side of the house was split between the big battalions in Croydon and Sheffield who were trying to cope with ever-increasing numbers of applications to enter and remain in the UK (a policy which the Labour Party admitted years later to have been flawed), so resources were fragmented between my region and the North West. Meanwhile the Enforcement Teams already had a regional structure, based around the legacy UKIS system and the land of hybridity.

In order to set up my operational command structures, I was provided with a ring binder full of flow charts of names and grades of staff, nicely finished in different colours. Asylum was pink; migration was green; enforcement was blue. There were also reds, which represented those in the "enabling" departments of finance, HR, and corporate management. I don't know who devised the colours or why, but I could see the logic behind the enablers being red. They were first in line for the chop when the budgetary axe fell, on the grounds that shared services could be thinned out not just between the regions, but right across the Home Office and potentially beyond. Some of my team reckoned that asylum was pink because of the pink and fluffy nature of the business – although I couldn't possibly comment on that.

One of my first tasks as Regional Director was to sort out my leadership team. Although there was a little bit of wriggle room, the Strategic Directors had a major say in who would be farmed out to the regions and who would be kept in the centre, so I inherited a mixture of staff of all grades coming from completely different backgrounds, roles and competencies – all expressed visually in colour charts. I knew from my own background that integrating the immigration case-working battalions in Croydon with the new asylum teams across the region and the front-line enforcement officers was going to be a challenge. They came from different cultures and had a different philosophy to the work. My immediate reaction was that this would be like mixing oil and water.

And then it came to me in a flash – "mixing the paint". This soon became my catchphrase, and it was soon picked up right across the Department and beyond as the new world that we were about to enter into. Matthew told me that this was inspirational on my part, which was very kind of him. Although I was grateful for the compliments, I knew at the same time that it was something that just came naturally to me. The key to delivering a successful transition hinged upon winning the hearts and minds of the staff. And for the most part, they loved it. They wanted to be a part of this brave new world where we all worked together rather than against each other. The journey to regionalisation had begun.

The first thing was to sort out my senior team. Given the grading structures that exist in the Civil Service, I first had to discover how many posts I would be given in the upper grades, from each of the three strategic directors.

I inherited two Grade 5 posts – one from Asylum and one from Migration. There were also several Grade 6 posts allocated to me, from all three Directorates, as well as from Corporate Services.

It soon became clear to me that I would need all of my leadership skills and more than a bit of luck to mould all this into a cohesive team. The divisions between the respective parent departments were far worse than I had thought. I recall attending an early meeting of the asylum leadership team, who told me that the biggest risk to delivering the asylum case conclusion rate was as a lack of support from enforcement to deliver removals. There was a deep-seated suspicion that the enforcement teams would simply "do their own thing" and ignore any instructions from asylum caseworkers to arrest and detain failed asylum seekers. I could see why – anyone who ever worked in enforcement knew full well that the chances of getting someone from the asylum process onto a plane was riddled with loopholes and difficulties. It was far easier to focus on criminal cases and other forms of fraud, such as immigration crime. At the same time, the enforcement teams were for the most part legacy UKIS immigration officers. They couldn't quite understand why we had recruited all these new people from outside to do removals casework, which they had been doing for years.

Meanwhile, the immigration groups were simply in a race to clear as many cases as they could. If someone was refused an extension that was the end of the matter, as far as they were concerned. There was no liaison between immigration caseworkers and Immigration enforcement on that side of the house either.

Given that the Department (or Agency, as it was now known) had opted for a regional model, I felt the best thing to do would be to extend that down the line as far as I could and identify Deputies who could take charge of specific areas across the region.

After a great deal of deliberation and poring over maps of council, district and police boundaries we came up with a model which allowed for three "areas" broadly slicing the region into three – West (covering all of West London and the Thames Valley) South (covering Croydon, South London, Surrey, Sussex and Hampshire) and Central/East (covering Central, North and East London and Kent).

There were three main offices that could act as area headquarters – Status House in Feltham, Lunar House in Croydon, and Becket House in Southwark. The next challenge would be to find an Area Director for each, and to persuade the powers that be of the need to allocate me a third Grade 5 post to facilitate the new structure. Hugh Ind – who had competed with me for the Regional Director post and was already a Director (Grade 5) - got first pick and decided he wanted South. He knew Croydon well, having worked there for many years. I had already decided to have my regional HQ in Croydon – something that was sneered at by some colleagues, who felt I should be in the new Home Office building in Marsham Street in Westminster. Some of them were very condescending towards Croydon, even to the extent of telling me what a dump it was. This was something I found disappointing, given that the vast majority of our staff lived and worked there. Sure, Croydon was not blessed with the great glass-fronted buildings that occupy the City or Canary Wharf - but as a transport hub it was second to none, and it had a huge catchment area to draw staff from at all levels.

With Matthew's help I was able to persuade the Board that a third Grade 5 post at that level was warranted in my command. Following an extensive selection process, we appointed Gareth Redmond to cover West and Sharon Flannery to cover Central and East. Gareth had previously served in David Blunkett's Private Office and had considerable experience in policy areas, whereas Sharon joined us from Probation Services in the Midlands, where she had a good track record in operational delivery. The process of "mixing the paint" was under way.

CHAPTER 19

THE BIRTH OF UKBA, AND MORE TURMOIL IN THE HOME OFFICE

One area that survived the move to regionalisation was the border itself. I'm not quite sure how or why this happened. Under the Canadian model, staff at the ports of entry were managed by the Regional Directors, and not by the Centre. Not so in the UK. Whilst we were busy mixing the paint and creating regions on the immigration side of the house, Brodie was busy installing a parallel regional team at the border, but still under the central control of ISHQ.

With immigration enforcement now firmly embedded in the BIA, the last vestiges of the UK Immigration Service remained out at the ports, where the Immigration Branch had been formed almost a century earlier. But by now the writing was on the wall. UKIS had run its course. Another major reform was about to evolve, one which would see its final demise. The BIA became one of the shortest serving Departments in the history of Whitehall and on 1 April 2008, BIA merged with UK Visas and the Customs Component of Ports of Entry to create the new UK

Border Agency (UKBA). The old Immigration Service (Ports) Directorate was merged with the HMRC front line staff at the UK Border to create the UK Border Force (UKBF). Brodie Clark became the first Head of UKBF, reporting to Lin Homer, who became the first Chief Executive of the UK Border Agency. This meant that Brodie inherited a significant number of "legacy Customs Officers" to add to his team of "legacy Immigration Officers".

The UKBF model was based loosely upon the changes introduced in the US and Canada after 9/11. Both countries had merged immigration and customs functions at their ports and borders into a new single Border Agency. In the US, this became US Customs and Border Protection (CBP). In Canada, it became the Canadian Border Services Agency (CBSA). In the UK, UKIS was subsumed into the UK Border Force (UKBF).

This merger presented us with some significant challenges, which would take many years to unfold.

Firstly, pay and conditions for Customs Officers working at UK ports of entry were significantly different to those that applied to Immigration Officers. Shift disturbance and other "allowances" had been bought out by HMRC prior to the merger, in return for "annualised hours working" (AHW) which enabled managers to deploy staff on more flexible shifts in line with business need. Immigration Officers were invited to move across to the AHW system – but many resisted this in favour of retaining their existing terms, which caused management issues at the ports for some years thereafter.

Secondly, although the two organisations had worked well together for many years, there had been little cross training. If we had an issue with goods, we would refer it to them. If they had a people issue, they would send it to us. They operated under separate legislation to us, with different powers and authorities. It would take a long time to cross train and cross empower the workforce. Particularly in the older officers, who were more set in their ways. Many still call themselves Customs Officers or Immigration Officers to this day. The idea of being a Border Force Officer (BFO) was an anathema to some of them.

Thirdly, the policy lines became blurred. There was hardly any corporate knowledge of Customs and Regulatory checks in the Home Office, which is where the UK Border Force was housed. Yet HMRC kept a firm grip on policies relating to the movement of goods across the UK Border, something that was to become a big challenge for government in later years, as Customs made a huge comeback after Brexit.

That said, there were advantages to the merger too. By sharing intelligence, information and systems with each other we became much better at identifying and intercepting threats at the Border. If bad stuff is crossing the border, then bad people are behind it, somewhere down the line.

Career options were also broadened, as officers moved between different functions at ports of entry. Plus, UKBF inherited a fleet of five cutters and a surveillance aircraft from HMRC, which proved increasingly valuable in identifying illegal entry via the coastline, something that would also haunt government in the years to come.

As UKBF continued to evolve at the border, so did we away from it. My "mixing the paint" agenda in London and the South East was working. With the Area Directors, I continued to drive regional delegation through towards my vision for "local immigration teams" (LITs). These would be led at Grade 7 level by Assistant Directors running their own "mini regions" with the dual task of delivering results and expanding our footprint in the communities. This led to a much better framework of engagement with local authorities than had previously been the case. I empowered my Area Directors to take decisions and to delegate authority within their command, so that we could focus more on stakeholder engagement and partnership working.

The thing I remember mostly about my senior team in the UKBA London and South East Region is its diversity. Despite what many people think, the Immigration Enforcement and Border Force Directorates of the Home Office are extremely diverse – and have been for some time.

Of course, in keeping with wider society, that hadn't always been the case. The Immigration Service I joined in the 1970s was largely a cadre of ex-military types, almost exclusively white and male. But that changed over time as the older brigade retired and new officers came in from all walks of life, and from all corners of the country. My ambition was to support the Home Office aim to bring more officers from different backgrounds into the upper ranks of the organisation.

Many people complained then (and still do) that this has taken too long. I would like to think that the first Board I set up in UKBA in 2008 bucked this trend. My senior team comprised people from diverse backgrounds including black, white, straight, gay, and registered disabled people. All there on merit. Indeed, I was blessed with a superbly diverse workforce right across the region, and I made sure that I spent time working with Home Office representative groups to promote diversity. I was fortunate enough to win a great many awards in my career, but one that stands out and sits proudly on my mantelshelf alongside my CBE medal is one from the Home Office Network for my services to leadership in diversity. It's something that still sends a shiver down by spine when I am trolled by people on social media for being a racist and a bigot, simply for arguing for strong borders and effective immigration controls. Indeed, I remember doing some work with a leading journalist in later life who expressed some surprise (and admiration) for the diversity of our ICE teams when he was introduced to them.

Of course, a role such as this was always going to take me deeper into the realms of political controversy. The Immigration Minister at the time, Liam Byrne, decided that we should be much more transparent with the public - so much so that all the Regional Directors were sent off on a media course and encouraged to involve the media in operations. This was a huge turnabout from the previous administration, who would hang an officer out to dry if they dared to say anything to a journalist who managed to get through to us on the phone. The message "Home Office Press Office" had been drummed into us. Yet here we were being quoted widely in the media, and even appearing regularly on television.

Something I was facing in London at the time was the perennial issue of community engagement. I was pulled into Scotland Yard a few times to talk to the Commissioner and his Deputies about this. Some even suggested to me that we ought to have "no go" areas in London for immigration raids, where sensitivities were high. The Minister hit the roof when I told him about this. He made it very clear to me that he wasn't interested in immigration "no go" areas anywhere. We needed to be out there tackling illegal working, and the public needed to know it. My Comms team developed a standard catchphrase to go out to local media: *Tony Smith, UKBA Regional Director for London and the South East, said 'it's not OK to hire illegal workers in (XXXX). Any employers doing so will face significant penalties, and illegal workers will be arrested."*

The Comms team had authority to issue this release every time we conducted a raid in the region. It wasn't long before I became a household name in some places – indeed Isle of Wight radio insisted on at least a radio interview, if not a TV interview, every time we sent a team over on the ferry to conduct an enforcement operation there.

One of the big challenges we had in London was in Chinatown. Our cupboards were bulging with intelligence to suggest that the Chinese catering sector in Soho was riddled with illegal workers, which was probably true, but we could not do anything about it without the agreement of the local police community team.

This became a very big deal indeed. I sent up a submission to Ministers and the message came back loud and clear: "We will not tolerate illegal working anywhere in the country. We must send a very clear message to all communities about this. We should mount a major operation in Chinatown." I was also told that we should ask the Press Office to engage local media when conducting the operation itself.

After extensive negotiations with Scotland Yard, Charing Cross police, and a few selected Chinese community leaders, I led a team of police and immigration officers into the heart of Chinatown to conduct simultaneous raids on a dozen restaurants believed to be in breach of the illegal working rules. We were accompanied by a BBC camera crew who decided that as the operational leader, I would be the centre of their attention. The operation was both chaotic and successful at the same time. We saw people jumping out of windows and escaping from rear doors in droves at the sight of us. In fact, apart from the managers, it was hard to find anyone in the target venues who had a work permit. We rounded up about 30 individuals and served notices of potential liability for hiring illegal workers (NOPLs) on several of the managers before a crowd started to gather. That was it for me – we had made our point. Time to beat a hasty retreat, all under the watchful gaze of a BBC camera crew.

Our instincts were right. All those who were arrested were in the country illegally. Most of them had entered in the backs of lorries via Dover. Hardly any of them had passports. The employers had made no effort to check their immigration status before hiring them, as the law required. Back in the day this would have been classed as a highly successful upper tier operation.

But that wasn't the end of it. The media coverage led to a huge row about the rights and wrongs of conducting immigration raids in specific areas. We were accused of picking on the Chinese community in particular (even though some of those arrested weren't from China at all). The Chinese Ambassador even got involved. I found myself out in the media again some days later, defending our approach. For every commentator who supported us, there was another that opposed us.

Now I knew what Lin meant when she talked about "political nous". Even when you are right in law, you might be wrong in the court of public opinion. Fortunately, I had Ministerial cover for this one – but not for others, which almost brought an early end to my career a few months later.

By now Jackie Smith was in the hot seat as Home Secretary. The Home Office had been working for some time on an accreditation system for security guards. The Security Industry Authority (SIA) was established as a non-Departmental Agency to issue licences to workers in the security industry. Policy makers thought it would be a great idea to make bouncers and their like get a licence to ply their trade. That way we could conduct criminal record checks on them all and clean up the industry.

Now one thing that the Home Office and its Agencies has always struggled with is being "joined up". You would have thought that somewhere in the policy machine, somebody might have checked with immigration to make sure these people had permission to work here in the first place before issuing a licence to them. Sadly not. As time went by, we found ourselves arresting more and more illegal workers in the security industry who were producing their SIA licence as a statutory defence for permission to work. So one bit of the Department was giving them a licence to work, whilst another bit was arresting them for not having permission to do so. Of course, the SIA licence didn't count as permission to work. It simply indicated that the worker concerned did not have any outstanding convictions, which most illegal workers don't, to be fair to them. They are simply working under false identities or with false papers to conceal their immigration status.

This problem came to me. We were provided with a full list of SIA licence holders, and after some research we had to tell Ministers that quite a few of them were definitely working illegally. Even more were likely to be so. The only way to know for sure would be to investigate each case individually. This led to a series of immigration raids – to home addresses where we had them, but to workplaces if not – and a large number of arrests and removals.

As time went by, this became ever more embarrassing. Some of these SIA licence holders were popping up in sensitive jobs. We found them working in government buildings, often without having established their true identity and status at all. For the most part, this was just illegal working, but the very fact that there were security guards working in sensitive positions in the heart of government in false identities sent a shiver down my spine. The terrorist threat was under control, but my no means eliminated. The fact that an imposter could be controlling the entry of people and goods into secure buildings was worrying, not just in terms of their own conduct, but (potentially) in terms of facilitating the passage of others, including dangerous materials.

I reported my concerns in a private submission to Ministers, advising them that it was highly likely that there were people working in the Palace of Westminster under false identities. These were not exclusively security guards – some were cooks, cleaners, and caterers – but with stringent checks supposedly in place to prevent unauthorised people entering the building, it was pretty clear that deception had been employed to get past security checks.

Written submissions are standard forms of communication between senior civil servants and Ministers. These can go up under different levels of security. They are then sorted into boxes by the Private Office, for the Minister to read. Mine was highly classified and submitted by hand to the Private Office.

I got a call from the office late one Saturday evening, telling me to report to the office first thing Sunday morning. A major broadsheet had printed a copy of my submission about illegal workers in the Palace of Westminster on the front page. My name was clearly visible. I spent most of that day and the following week trying to explain why I had embarrassed the Minister in this way. Why did I write this down? Who did I copy it to? How did it leak? Where was my political nous?

Of course, the fact of the matter was that I had ruffled feathers high up in other parts of Whitehall. Somebody somewhere had approved access to sensitive areas of government buildings, and they had been duped. This led to a mad scramble to review Home Office vetting procedures. But it was all my fault for exposing this in public, thereby embarrassing the Department. The fact that I had acted entirely within Departmental guidelines was lost in translation.

I had been taught from an early age that leaking documents to the Press was an absolute red line for any civil servant. Anyone caught doing so would face disciplinary action which could easily lead to dismissal. In more extreme cases, criminal prosecution could ensue.

A senior civil servant was appointed to lead an investigation into the leak. The police were called in. Several people (including myself) were interviewed in the course of the investigation. Some time later the culprit was found. He was actually working in the Minister's Private Office, and obviously had access to sensitive submissions like mine which he was systematically leaking to the press in order to embarrass the government he worked for. I presume he felt his action was justified in the public interest (forgetting entirely that this was a complete breach of Home Office security procedures). I doubt he even had a second thought for hapless officials like me, who were put through the wringer as a result of his actions. I must confess I would have quite liked five minutes alone in a room somewhere with him – but that would certainly have curtailed my career.

The ensuing enquiry caused another huge row in the Home Office. It even led to the arrest of Damian Green, the MP for

Ashford, who was the opposition spokesman for immigration at the time. Damian was cleared of any wrongdoing, and I came to know him quite well when he became Immigration Minister in the next government. Indeed, he attended my retirement party some years later, when I was able to assure him that I had had absolutely nothing to do with the decision to arrest him – although I was indeed the author of one of the submissions that led to the leak investigation in the first place.

The *pièce de résistance* was still to come though. This time I really thought I was for the high jump. I was having Christmas lunch with my team in Croydon when I got a call from Hugh.

"Hi Tony, Hugh here. Sorry to disturb your lunch, but we have a problem".

"Hi Hugh – OK, what's up?" I replied.

"Well one of the teams has got hold of the papers used by a Home Office Security guard. Clearly illegal, it's a dodgy landing stamp. We've been to his address, but he's not known there. And he's on late duty today".

My mind was racing now. What should we do? Normally we would defer this and pick him up at home later on, out of sight. But that wasn't an option.

"What do you think?" I said.

"Well, it's come up to me and they want authority to arrest him at work".

Again, normally not a problem. This was standard practice where we didn't have an address. But in this case, he was in our own back yard. Unlawfully, as it turned out.

The rest is a bit of a blur. I think we discussed how we might be able to arrest him quietly, maybe upon exit from the building or out of site, without creating a fuss. Either way, in the end, I authorised it. Not one of my better decisions, but one I felt entitled to make. There were no Ministers around on a Friday, and it was Christmas. Things would be pretty quiet at the Home Office. Nobody would notice.

The offender was duly arrested at the Home Office, but sadly not out of public sight or mind. On the contrary, the arrest was seen by people who were not sympathetic to our cause, and keen to create a stink about it. By the time I got home it was airing in broadcast media that the Home Office had "raided itself" and arrested a person posing as a security guard. The news editors were rubbing their hands with glee.

Lin rang me at home and told me in no uncertain terms what she thought of me. Best not to go into too much detail here – suffice to say that she left me in no doubt about her feelings. Hugh and I were both told to report to the Home Office first thing the next day (Saturday). Not something that filled me with joy, not least because Rangers were at home that day. I wanted to go to Loftus Road, not Marsham Street.

I can remember picking up a copy of the *Standard* on the way in and glancing through the "jobs vacant" pages. I wondered if anyone was looking for an ageing civil servant with a few war stories to tell. I did have 35 years under my belt, after all. Would they still pay me my pension? Maybe now would be a good time to write my book?

Lin was still very angry with me when we got there. She had a team of people in the office, scurrying around getting documents. After reminding me a great many times about my shortcomings on political nous, she brought me a copy of the person's passport. I breathed a sigh of relief. One look at it and I could tell it was fake.

"That's Mickey Mouse" I said, reverting to my native Immigration Officer tongue. This was common language when presented with a fake document. Someone had made a poor attempt to place a fake landing stamp in the passport, indicating the holder had indefinite permission to remain. Of course, I was the only one there that morning who could see this for a fact. Nobody else there knew what a fake stamp looked like.

It didn't get me out of jail – but it gave me a lifeline. Are you seriously telling me I should leave a security guard on duty in a major office of state – guarding access to the Home Secretary herself – in the certain knowledge that he had secured a pass by fraud and was himself an illegal immigrant? Well yes actually, that's what they were suggesting, because had I done so then we wouldn't all be in the office on a Saturday morning trying to comfort a distressed Home Secretary and placate a noisy media. And of course, I could be at Rangers instead. They had a point. But I was pretty sure I could bin my copy of the *Standard*, at least for now. The decision might have been wrong, naïve, embarrassing – but it was reasonable, and defensible in law. And of course, a decision not to act on the intelligence immediately I received it could also have raised serious questions as to why I had allowed a security risk to continue because of potential political embarrassment.

Lin gave me a really hard time for a few weeks after that. She had her inner office man marking me. Every little thing that I did which might cause the slightest controversy led to a call from her office, sometimes from herself. It got to a point where I was seriously upset by all this. I couldn't seem to do a thing right. My confidence went, something that I wasn't used to at all.

Eventually I went to see Lin in her office. I think she was a bit surprised at how upset I was. I told her that I was very proud to be a part of her senior team. That I knew I wouldn't be there without her support. That I had tried my best to build a regional command for her to be proud of. But I couldn't carry on if she had lost trust in me.

To be fair, she was very sympathetic. We agreed that things like this would happen from time to time, that we all make mistakes, we are all human. She then went on to say some really nice things about me, which actually brought me to tears. Not something I was renowned for either.

I guess it was an outpouring of relief – that I could finally sleep again and get back to doing what I do best. I could finally put this whole episode behind me. Although even now, over a decade later, people still remind me about the day I sent an enforcement team into the Home Office to arrest a security guard. I promised to put my side of the story in my book, if I ever wrote one. So here you are.

Another *cause célèbre* at the time was the case of Baroness Scotland. As Attorney General, the Baroness had helped to steer legislation through Parliament which placed a legal obligation upon staff to check and copy documents of their employees to ensure they had a right to work in the UK. Failure to do so would result in a civil penalty. But after a very public investigation by the popular media, it came to our attention that she had employed a home help who, as it turned out, was an illegal worker from Tonga. By appointment through her office, I sent one of my Deputy Directors to interview her one evening. He referred the case to me by mobile phone, just as I was stepping out of my car after a very long day at work.

After a long conversation on my front lawn, during which all the twists and turns of my previous experiences of political cases flashed through my mind, I authorised the service of notice of potential liability on the Attorney General. Despite being given ample opportunity to do so, she had been unable to produce any evidence that she had kept copies of right to work documents, as required by law. I was sure that this was no more than an administrative oversight on her part, as was often the case, but that was irrelevant. It would be wrong to avoid the decision because of her political status, in my view.

As usual, there were a number of questions asked of me in hindsight. Why didn't I ask Ministers? Why didn't I defer to think about it? Didn't I think this would be embarrassing for the government?

Sometimes an omission can be as compelling as an act. We had all the necessary evidence, an admission, and we were empowered to act. Putting a decision to another Minister was bringing politics into the rule of law. Would any other course of action get through the court of public opinion? What would the man on the Clapham omnibus have said if we had turned a blind eye in this case, but not in others? I was pleased to see that the Baroness herself subsequently conceded that she had erred in law, and that we were right to act as we did. But it didn't make the decision any easier.

There were a great many other instances that I could refer to during this time which tested my political nous. The words of my old friend Bob Perks from Isis House kept coming back to me: "You can't win old son, you know that. Best you can do is spread the blame."

Some of my most difficult decisions involved casework. I had to make some difficult decisions on admissibility. Three cases spring to mind which I still refer to in case studies about visa applications.

1.   Mike Tyson, US citizen. A professional boxer but a convicted rapist, he sought entry to come to the UK to participate in a boxing match which would raise a lot of money for charity. The back pages of the tabloids were all for it. The front pages of some of the broadsheets were against. We had demonstrations from women's rights organisations outside the Home Office, and rallies in boxing communities around the country arguing the case.

2.   Martha Stewart, US citizen. Businesswoman, writer, and television personality but convicted of fraud. Sought entry to come to the UK to meet HM Queen Elizabeth as part of a promotion campaign to promote Wedgewood pottery in the United States. Widespread support from the Department of Trade; widespread opposition from the law enforcement community and campaign against fraud.

3.   Nick D'Arcy, Australian citizen. International swimmer, sought entry to compete in the London 2012 Olympics but convicted of GBH. Former Australian champion, gold medal

prospect. Widespread support from the Australian Government and the IOC. Widespread opposition from the law enforcement community and campaign against violence.

I certainly spread the blame on all three, but someone had to make the final call. What would you do?

Answers on page 350.

CHAPTER 20

THE NATIONAL
IDENTITY DILEMMA

Although my role was primarily operations, I was sometimes drawn into some significant policy discussions in my time at the Home Office. One such area was identity management.

We had known for many years that the best way to circumvent UK immigration laws was to adopt a false identity. We knew from debriefing illegal entrants that they were coached to do this from the outset. Get through the border, destroy your passport, identity card or anything else that might show who you are. Change your name, and even your nationality if you can. If they don't know who you are or where you are from, they can't deport you.

I had lots of experience of this and saw a potential solution – biometrics. For those that don't know, biometrics relates to the measurement of biological and physical characteristics that can be used to identify individuals. They include things like fingerprints, iris scans and facial recognition. Unlike names on passports, these are very hard to change or conceal. The police had been using fingerprints for many years to identify criminals on the Criminal Records Database (CRB). However, they were less common in immigration cases.

By now, we had become increasingly aware of the value of biometrics to immigration and border control. The US had been using them for several years – all citizens from outside the US and Canada were required to provide ten fingerprints and a digital image on entry to the country, through the US VISIT programme. They had already amassed a huge store of biometrics for use by a range of enforcement agencies, including Customs and Border Protection, Border Patrol, and Immigration Compliance Teams.

In the UK, we began our journey into biometrics by introducing fingerprint checks. All new asylum seekers were fingerprinted (save for children), and their details were recorded in the UK immigration and asylum biometric system. Over time, this was supplemented by fingerprints from visa applicants around the world. Then we added deportees and other immigration offenders. We started to share our biometric database with EU countries, through the EURODAC system. We found people who had claimed asylum in multiple identities in different countries, and others who claimed to have come in the back of a lorry but had actually come through the visa system and overstayed. As time went by, we were able to cross-match immigration fingerprints with police fingerprints, to identify the immigration status of criminals.

Meanwhile, we were making much greater use of e-gates to clear passengers who were not subject to control. British, EU, EEA and Swiss people who had e-passports could enter without seeing an officer, simply by looking into a camera and matching their live image to the one in their passport chip.

In my view, one thing the Blair government got right – and subsequent governments got wrong – was its proposal to build a UK National Identity Register. Tony Blair subsequently confirmed this in his own autobiography – the only real way to tackle the problem of illegal immigration was to set up a National Identity Register. His plan was to introduce national identity cards, starting with biometric residence permits (BRPs) for foreign nationals.

Because Croydon was in my jurisdiction, I was leading the first teams to issue BRPs. People seeking extensions of stay or permanent residence in the UK would henceforth provide fingerprints and photographs, and would be issued with a card bearing details of their immigration status. These cards had biometrics embedded in them to prevent fraud, and could be produced by the holder as evidence of immigration status, right to work, etc.

I thought this was an excellent idea, and argued long and hard that we needed to offer the BRP service to people who were not British citizens but had "settled" status in the UK. I knew from experience that there were many people living in the UK at that time who were in this position, and I had seen for myself the application of the "green card" system in the US and the "permanent residence" card in Canada. I also thought this would help us a lot with illegal working and "right to work" checks, so we could distinguish those who were entitled to live and work in the UK from those who were not. For example, some of the "Windrush" generation who had lawful status as long-term Commonwealth migrants or their descendants – but had never been registered as such. More of that later.

As Regional Director for London and the South East, I was asked to provide immigration officers to help with the National Identity Register project. We were very well placed to do this. We had officers in our command who were forensic experts on document fraud and forgery, and others who were well versed in immigration history and law so that they could clarify immigration status when documentary or official records were lacking. We even planned to send officers over to the passport office to interview new and first-time renewal applicants for British passports. We knew that some people had been able to secure British passports in the past based on fraudulent source documents such as fake UK birth certificates and dodgy references.

I still argue that some of our better achievements in the Home Office involved the introduction of biometrics into our border, visa, and immigration systems. By opening up interfaces between the Immigration and police databases – and particularly the CT cache of latent prints at Scotland Yard – we were able to identify some very serious threats to our security, as well as countless cases of identity abuse. However, the coalition government of 2010 abolished the National Identity Register, and that was that. Despite my warnings to the contrary, they pressed ahead with the "hostile environment" in the blind assumption that everybody with a right to live in the UK would be able to prove it. Despite all the noise about Home Office culture and behaviours, the fundamental reason for the Windrush scandal was the failure to introduce the National Identity Register which would enable everybody with a right to live and work in the UK to prove it. The rest is history.

CHAPTER 21

SRO and Gold Commander – the UKBA London 2012 Olympic Programme

One of my more remarkable memories of the 7/7 terrorist attack in London was the timeline. On 6 July 2005 – the day before the worst terrorist attack in our peacetime history – the International Olympic Committee (IOC) announced that the 2012 Olympic and Paralympic Games would be held in London. This was against the odds. Paris was the favourite. There was an outpouring of national pride, with union flags waving in Trafalgar Square and across the land at the prospect of hosting the most prestigious international sporting event in the world.

Actually, I had done some work on the Olympic bid – notably the immigration and borders chapter. In return for awarding the Games, the IOC expected to be given considerable control over immigration, border and customs facilitations for the period of the Games. For us, the most challenging demand was a requirement to suspend visa requirements for "Games Family Members". This meant that national teams would select their "squads" (which included the entourage, not just the competitors) and submit a list of names to the host country for "accreditation". There was an expectation that accreditation would be granted, unless there were strong reasons to refuse it. Immigration credibility was not seen to be such a reason. So, if you were particularly good at sport – or even sufficiently well connected with your own National Olympic Committee to get on their delegate list as a bag carrier – there was a very good chance that you could get into Britain under the "Games Family" rules. Then you could either disappear or claim asylum after the event. We knew very well that it was highly likely that some people from some countries would do exactly that - but Ministers considered it was a risk worth taking, when weighed against the overall prestige to UK plc of hosting the Games.

The 7/7 attacks put a new perspective on all of this. What better target for any terrorist than the Olympics? The event had a history of terrorist attacks. Nobody who was around at the time would ever forget the images of kidnappers from the Palestinian group Black September appearing on the balcony in the Olympic village in Munich in 1972, or the killing of nine members of the Israeli Olympic team and a German police officer after a failed rescue attempt. Did we really want to get involved, given that we now had our own terrorists right here in London?

Construction of Olympic venues began in earnest, including the new Olympic stadium. This played neatly into the structure I was building in my region, and the local immigration team in Stratford took on a life of its own as more and more new construction workers were brought into the site.

Unlike previous hosts, the UK did not need to bring in low-skilled workers from abroad to help build the venues. Under EU free movement rules, we already had access to a very large pool of EU workers who could come in and help. All you really needed to get a job on the Olympic Park was an EU identity card, or some other form of documentation to show you had lawful status to work in the UK. We knew that this surge in unskilled work at the Olympic site would trigger a rise in the black market for forged and counterfeit documents, and that it wouldn't be long before we started to see illegal workers turning up at the site in large numbers in order to work there.

Readers will have their own views on how much of a threat this was to the security of the Games.

My own thought process followed the same lines that got me into trouble with the Home Office for lacking the political nous to leave a security guard on the premises even though I knew he was an imposter. For the most part, illegal workers don't pose a security threat. They use false papers to assume the identity of a person allowed to work in the UK, in order to earn money. Some would go so far as to say that this was a noble gesture on their part, and they should not be penalised for it. If they were honest people simply trying to earn a crust – and they were doing work most people didn't want to do anyway – then what's the problem?

Well, firstly because it's illegal. But secondly because there was always a chance that more sinister motives were at play. My mind raced back many years to Canada, and the case of Ahmed Ressam. In 1994, Ressam tried to enter Canada illegally on a forged French passport. When caught at the airport, he said he was an Algerian and was fleeing persecution by the Algerian government. Although his asylum claim was denied sometime later, he disappeared into the community, then managed to procure a Canadian passport in a false name, after producing a fake Canadian baptism certificate and claiming to have lived in Canada all his life.

Ressam was in fact a member of Al Qaeda. Having secured a genuine Canadian passport in a false identity, he was able to travel via circuitous routes to Afghanistan for terrorist training and back without raising suspicions at the Canadian border. It was also much easier for him to access the USA. On 13 December 1999, he hired a car packed with explosives in the trunk and crossed to Canada/US border with the intention of carrying out a terrorist attack at Los Angeles airport. Although he was able to elude US INS pre-clearance checks when boarding the ferry at Victoria (he was after all travelling on a genuine Canadian passport, albeit obtained by deception) he was stopped by a US Customs Officer who had some concerns about him (maybe using the sixth sense I came to develop during my own time on the line). They found enough explosives in his car to detonate a devastating explosion that could have killed countless civilians, had the plot succeeded. Subsequent enquiries showed that Ressam also had links to the 9/11 attackers. He was jailed for 22 years in 2005, but on later review this sentence was extended to 37 years.

I often used Ressam as a case to demonstrate how fake identities had been used in the past by terrorists to defeat border controls and gain access to public targets. This was not the first time this had happened, and it wouldn't be the last. The work under way at Olympic Park involved sophisticated construction projects. It would not be beyond the gift of a terrorist to get into the Park under a false identity and plant an explosive device or perform some other act of sabotage to wreck the Games. This would lead to the inevitable steward's enquiry in Whitehall as to how this could have been allowed to happen, and who was to blame. It wasn't going to be me.

The case for strict identity checks on the site was supported by several journalists at the time. They were hungry for stories to show that the Olympic venues were riddled with illegal migrants, many of whom had fake documents. I deployed a team of forgery experts to the admissions office at the Olympic Park, and sure enough, we found fake documents and imposters turning up every day. For the most part they were simply illegal workers, but there was always a chance that another Ressam was somewhere in their midst. The terrorist threat level was severe. We had to do everything in our power to mitigate it. Political nous went out of the window (again).

It is worth noting that during this time I was not in charge of the UK border. The UK Border Force was a separate Directorate within UKBA, led by Brodie Clark. Although I was in charge of all the Immigration Enforcement work going on at the Olympic Park – and as such I was being pulled into meetings across the Home Office and with other government departments as the senior Olympic spokesman for UKBA.

Early in 2009, Lin summoned me to a UKBA Board meeting to deliver a presentation on planning for London 2012. I explained that work would need to be done across all the Directorates of the Agency. Time was of the essence. We couldn't delay the Olympics because we weren't ready on time, as had been customary with other Home Office Programmes. UKVI would need to liaise with the National Olympic Committees in source countries to identify Games participants and participate in the screening and vetting service, outside the standard visa system they were accustomed to. UKBF would have to manage the arrivals process, including the designation of the Olympic port and the likely arrival of record numbers of visitors, including over a hundred heads of state. Immigration enforcement would need to engage on illegal working, as I was doing already in Stratford. Then there was the matter of accreditation, and how and where it would be managed.

The Board decided unanimously that I should be appointed as Senior Responsible Owner (SRO) for the UKBA London 2012 Olympic Programme. This meant setting up a Cross-Departmental Programme Team and a series of projects across the Agency, including UK Visas, Border Force, and Immigration Enforcement.

As work on the Olympic Programme escalated, it soon became clear that my SRO role would become a full-time job. Increasingly I was delegating regional issues to Hugh, to give me the bandwidth I needed to cover the Olympic work. Eventually this led to another conversation with Lin, and a discussion about what my role would be. We agreed that I could no longer do both, so she gave me a choice. I had already decided that I would retire after 40 years' service, in October 2012. What better way to go out than having delivered one of the biggest challenges ever faced in the history of the Home Office? Sure, there would be risks. Many people would want us to fail. But I wasn't going to let that deter me. I was always one to walk towards a problem. I wasn't the only one, by a long chalk, but there were plenty of others who would rather walk away from one. I knew which gang I wanted to be in.

I went for the Olympics job, which would be my final swan song in government service. (At least, that's what I thought at the time). Hugh took over my previous post as Regional Director, and off I went to set up my new Olympics Programme team in the heart of UKBA headquarters, in the Home Office building at Marsham Street. I was also given a seat at the UKBA Board.

Moves were already afoot elsewhere in the Home Office to prepare for the Games. It was decided to create a new "Olympic Security Directorate" (OSD) on the fifth floor. They would take the lead on overall Home Office briefings for Ministers, covering the full range of security issues ranging from site and venue security through to security vetting and policing. Robert Raine was brought in as Director of OSD, reporting to Charles Farr who was the Director General of the Office of Security and Counter Terrorism (OSCT).

Outside the Home Office, the rest of the Whitehall machine was also preparing for the Olympic challenge. As this was first and foremost a sporting event, it was right that the Department of Culture, Media, and Sport (DCMS) should take the lead. The Department for Transport (DfT) would have a big role to play in getting people to and from the venues. A London Organising

Committee (LOCOG) would need to be set up.

I soon got to meet with the SROs in other government departments. Jonathan Sharrock was appointed as Olympic lead for the Department for Transport and became a great friend and ally of mine. Nicky Roche was leading the cross-government work over at DCMS, under the watchful eye of Tessa Jowell, Minister for Sport. Tessa had played a massive part in securing the Games for the UK in the first place, and I never met a nicer Minister in my entire career (apart from Alan Johnson perhaps – although he was the only Home Secretary in my time to be a QPR fan, so I suppose I was biased there). Paul Deighton and Jean Tomlin were leading the London Organising Committee (LOCOG), for Seb Coe. I got to meet them all, on a regular basis. We shared a common purpose – to deliver a safe secure and inspirational Olympic Games in 2012. And we were all people who were prepared to walk towards the problem.

One of the big challenges for us was how to manage the accreditation scheme. The traditional split of responsibility between border security and homeland security didn't really work. The first proposal was that UKBA would lead on accreditation for all the non-UK delegates; and OSCT would lead on the UK delegates, with police support for criminal record checks.

Fortunately for me – and for the wider Department, as it turned out – I had retained my strong connections to Canada. They were hosting the 2010 Winter Olympics in Whistler, British Columbia. There was a rule in the IOC that host countries would help one another to prepare for the next Games, learning lessons from last time.

I secured an accreditation to go to Canada, together with a small selection of other UK government representatives. One of the major achievements of the Canadian government was to agree new specifications for the Olympic Accreditation card. This was the document that would provide qualifying access not just to the country, but also to the venues themselves. As such, it would be hugely valuable to any terrorist who wanted to get into the UK and the Olympic park.

The Canadians had learned that the card used for the Beijing Games in 2008 was not a secure document, probably because the Chinese government had their own plans for managing security and access, which might not be along the same lines as ours. The Beijing card could easily be reproduced on a high-quality photocopier and handed to an imposter. The Canadians had therefore spent a lot of time negotiating new standards with the International Olympic Committee, which included the introduction of forgery safeguards into the document. These were shared with us, and I was able to engage with our National Document Forgery Unit (NDFU) – widely believed to be one of the best anti-forgery units in the world – to build an even better and more secure document for London 2012. I learned a lot from our Canadian friends on the risks and issues involved in hosting the Olympics and will always be grateful for their support. They even seconded a couple of officers to my team to help us through it all.

I also knew that there would be some serious negotiations to be done with the IOC and LOCOG. Obviously, their prime concern was facilitation – both into the country and into the venues. They did not want the host country introducing any onerous measures either at the border or in country which would create long queues. At the same time, they understood our concerns about security and were keen to work with us on that. The question for me, and for my colleagues working on the security aspects at the time, was how we could put in place enough mitigations to minimise the security risk, without placing undue obligations upon the Games Family Members. Our mitigation would be two-fold. Firstly, we would undertake as many checks as we could in advance, so that we could weed out any people whose background suggested that they may pose a risk. Secondly, we would ensure that site security was robust enough to ensure that harmful materials could not be imported into venues, without appearing to be overly oppressive to spectators.

Some ground rules had already been laid down in Games gone by. The first of these was the amount of data that the NOCs would need to provide to us when making their application for accreditation. This was limited largely to the data held on the applicant's passport or travel document. The second was the timeframe under which accreditation would be granted. This would get shorter and shorter as Games time approached. And the third was the decision-making process. There was a difference between denying a medal hope and denying a bag carrier. Politics was creeping into the decision-making process – again.

In the end the Home Office decided that it would need its own "Olympic Accreditation Clearing House (OACH)" – and the best people to run that would be the UKBA team. Trying to split responsibility for checking British and non-British applicants just wouldn't work. After all, the UKBA was already responsible for checking "British" people and others crossing the UK Border for security and criminality, on behalf of all the agencies.

What was needed was a central repository to which all incoming data would be submitted by LOCOG, and a system which would enable accreditation to be generated automatically to those who did not pose any risk to any of the agencies. This would be achieved by a "hub and spoke" system to ensure the data reached all the agencies with an interest in the security of the Games, whilst preserving the firewalls that existed between their respective intelligence systems.

Where a risk was flagged by anyone, the cases would be held on the system pending escalation to determine what risk had been identified; by which Department or Agency; and what we were going to do about it. The upshot of the decision meant that the person concerned would not be "accredited" and would not therefore be given an "accreditation card". This meant that people coming from overseas to participate in the Games would not be allowed to travel. And people who were already in the UK and wanted to gain access to any of the venues – for example to provide services – would be denied access. As such, it was a pretty big deal.

The next big question to arise related to biometric capture for Games family members. I knew full well the benefits of introducing fingerprint checks into the UK visa system. It had helped us to identify a great many imposters who posed a security threat and had been deported from the country in another identity. What's more, the store of latent prints lifted from terrorist events both at home and abroad provided us with another useful security tool to identify potential threats. However, under Games Family Rules, visas were disallowed. We would be able to conduct name-based checks only. This became an issue of significant political debate within the UKBA Board and also with the wider Home Office Board – and with other Departments as well. In my quest to win the argument to capture fingerprints from Games family members I found myself presenting my case to a significant group of people including the Home Secretary (Theresa May), the Mayor of London (Boris Johnson), the chairman of the London Organising Committee (Sebastian Coe), and the British Representative to the International Olympic Committee (the Princess Royal, Princess Anne).

In the end we agreed that we would be allowed to capture and check fingerprints from those Games family members who would ordinarily have provided them under the visa system (i.e., visa nationals). This would be optional prior to travel, but compulsory on arrival. In order to minimise the potential for backlogs on arrival, we put in place an extensive programme to send fingerprinting officers out to training camps around the world. Thus, the London 2012 Olympics became labelled the first "Biometric Games".

I should pay tribute here to former colleagues in UKVI and the Foreign and Commonwealth Office. Some of our Ambassadors and High Commissioners around the world came up with some ingenious ideas to help us meet the requirement. In one case, they managed to secure an agreement to send a team of officials into Mogadishu to meet their Olympic contingent airside at the airport to perform the necessary checks and to issue them with the necessary papers to enable them to come to London 2012. It was just as important to us to have all countries of the world represented as it was to minimise any chance of a security threat. In the end the Somali team was able to make it to the Games and play their full part in the event. The fact that most of them subsequently claimed asylum after the event and never went back was lost in translation – especially as one of the true heroes of London 2012 was our own Mo Farah, who had himself entered the UK at the age of eight as a child refugee from Somalia.

We dealt with a great many difficult cases in the run up to the Games, too many to list here. These were hard to adjudicate. Some were escalated to Ministers to make the final decision. Suffice to say we got it right most of the time because there were no significant representations from any one country about a significant refusal of accreditation, yet we know with hindsight that nobody got into the country or into the Games venues to perpetrate a terrorist attack on our watch. Sure, some innocent people may have been denied access, but we were operating at a threat level of "Severe". A terrorist attack on London 2012 was "highly likely". Not on our watch – we had learned the lessons of the past.

I became the UKBA Gold Commander during Games time, and part of the wider "Gold group" structure. The decision to have a private security firm managing venue security was reversed after it became clear that they had neither the manpower nor the bandwidth to complete the task. The British military were called in, a decision which received widespread public support.

I found myself on daily calls with senior police, military, and security officers and attending regular meetings at COBRA with the Home Secretary. In this time, I was blessed with several silver and bronze commanders from across the Home Office, who responded magnificently to the call of duty when needed. We had planned meticulously for all eventualities. There were too many of them to list in person, but I was delighted to ensure that each and every one of them was presented with a commemorative medal from the Prime Minister as evidence of their achievements. The Games went off without any major security incident. I had learned the lessons of the past in mitigating potential threats – and could finally breathe a huge sigh of relief.

After the Games were over, realisation dawned on us. Despite all the prophets of doom telling us that London 2012 was doomed to failure, we had delivered the greatest show on earth, and the flags were out everywhere.

Of course, we weren't the heroes of the hour. They were our magnificent team GB who had netted a record haul of medals at both the Olympic and the Paralympic Games. We didn't want the limelight. Media spotlight on us would be bad. It would mean there had been a terrorist attack, or huge delays at the border, or civil unrest. But there wasn't. The whole country was gripped in a wave of enthusiasm and optimism. Britain was great again!

Some of us had been rewarded with VIP passes to the closing ceremony on Sunday. We found ourselves mixing with Boris Johnson, Tessa Jowell, Jeremy Hunt, and other political leaders enjoying the celebrations. My 40 years of service were nearly up. Retirement loomed large. I had managed to dodge the bullets. I would be leaving the Home Office with a slap on the back rather than around the face, which had happened to other senior civil servants less fortunate than myself who came before. Today was our closing party – the Olympic team that had worked so long and hard together for the past four years was about to disband.

In fact, I believed I had already reached the pinnacle of my career. I had served over 40 years in the Department, rising up through the ranks from Immigration Officer to Senior Director (Grade 3) in the UK Immigration Service, the Border and Immigration Agency, and the UK Border Agency. I had served as Director of Ports and Borders in two countries, Canada and the UK, both during severe terrorist attacks. I had taken on the role of SRO for the UKBA and UKBF London 2012 Olympic Programme, and Gold Commander for the Games period itself. I had nothing else to prove.

Some of us were invited to the Olympic parade on the Mall, where we had prime seats in the structure that lined the route from Trafalgar Square down to Buckingham Palace as Team GB walked past, proudly waving their medals in the sunlight. My spot was directly opposite the seats occupied by the Cabinet of the day, including David Cameron and Theresa May. I had attended several COBRA meetings during the Games and had met the PM and several close members of his cabinet during that time. And I had briefed the Home Secretary every day on issues relating to accreditation and border security. We knew each other well. One of my fond memories of that day was seeing Theresa May wave to me from across the Mall, only for a rough-looking bunch of rather drunk people in the row in front of me to jump up and wave back to her. I later learned that they had won a competition run by the Sun newspaper to secure those seats at the parade – and they assumed this was the Home Secretary welcoming them!

We later adjourned to a pub near Marsham Street for our closing party, which was hugely emotional. I worked with some very tough people on the Games – military, police, law enforcement officers not known for showing emotion. Yet here we had grown men crying and hugging each other in celebration. It really was a monumental achievement, and something that will be dear to my heart for the rest of my days.

Meanwhile, life went on around us in the broader UKBA

– and not without problems, as usual. The whole point about running the Games period as a critical incident was to enable the command team to take control of it, leaving the rest of the Department to continue with business as usual. This meant that I had to go through a tortuous set of submissions and reports to Senior Civil Servants and Ministers setting out the scope of my authority as Gold Commander. Even then I was frequently challenged about some of my decisions by others in the Department after the event – a favourite pastime in the Home Office. But in every case, I had learned my lessons well and was able to produce my decision logs, setting out my thought processes at the time and my reasoning behind each decision taken. I knew the decision didn't have to be right – that was always a matter of conjecture. But it did have to be reasonable, and nobody could say it wasn't. I have kept all my decision logs for subsequent scrutiny by those with an axe to grind, right up to the present day. In effect I had taken most of the Olympic problems away from other Senior Directors, enabling them to focus upon some of the wider challenges facing the Department. And there were a fair few of those.

Firstly, the contract to deliver the much-vaunted e-borders programme was terminated in July 2010, after a series of delays and adverse reports. This left us with the legacy IBM Semaphore Programme, which was already delivering significant levels of Advanced Passenger Information to us, and the Fujitsu Warnings Index system, which had been there from inception. Also, the new flagship immigration casework programme (ICW) was struggling to meet its requirements, requiring ongoing renewal of the existing legacy CID system, run by ATOS.

I was summoned to several Programme Boards to discuss ICW and e-borders, and argued long and hard for the continuation of existing programmes and novation of existing contracts to give us business continuity until after the Olympics. I even managed to secure permission from the Home Secretary to pause any new

IT initiatives during 2012, to ensure that the Olympics work went ahead as planned. So rather than taking advice from many who promised me brand spanking new IT systems for the border and for casework for London 2012, I stuck to my guns and kept the old systems renewed, renovated, and running, because I knew they could do the job. One of my better decisions, as it turned out.

Secondly, the Border Force was thrown into turmoil after a report by John Vine, the independent Chief Inspector of Borders and Immigration (ICIBI), found that there were inconsistencies in the checks being conducted on inbound passengers at Heathrow. This created a press storm and led to the resignation of Brodie Clark in November 2011, leaving the Border Force without a substantive Director General in the year leading up to the Olympics.

Thirdly, Rob Whiteman succeeded Lin Homer in September 2011 as the new Chief Executive of UKBA. In April 2012, the Home Secretary decided to reform the Agency by separating the Border Force from UK Visas and Immigration and Immigration Enforcement (effectively removing the "B" from "UKBA"). Brian Moore, formerly Chief Constable of Wiltshire, was appointed as the first Director General of the UK Border Force in March 2012. This meant I was now reporting to Rob on the accreditation and immigration components of the Olympics, and to Brian on the border components.

With great respect to both, they brought a huge amount of leadership skill and knowledge to UKBA from local government and policing respectively, but neither had my depth and breadth of experience of immigration and border controls. And to be fair to them, they respected my authority to deliver for their respective Departments on all matters relating to the Olympics. Indeed I was particularly grateful to Rob, whom (I know) was instrumental in nominating me for an honour later that year, even though we only worked together for a limited period.

Brian remained in post until September 2012 but decided to leave after that, leaving the Border Force without a leader.

Most textbooks will tell you that the biggest risk to delivering a successful programme is turbulence and change in the operating environment, especially in the leadership and governance structure. I can vouch for that. It was hard to steer a steady ship through these stormy waters.

There continued to be more talk of reform, breaking up the remainder of UKBA into UKVI and Immigration Enforcement – something which was to finally come to pass in March 2013. I had been following all these developments throughout the Games period but remained fixed upon my own desired outcome – a safe, secure, and inspirational London 2012 Olympics. And that job was now done. It was time to go – or so I thought.

CHAPTER 22

BECOMING DIRECTOR GENERAL
OF THE UK BORDER FORCE

As I was sorting through my papers in my office in Marsham Street, the phone rang.

"Tony, it's the Home Sec's Office. She wants to see you."

Uh-oh. This was not good news. I knew Theresa May well. I was at the Home Office when she arrived there, and I had briefed her regularly over the past couple of years on our readiness for the London 2012 Olympics. In fact, every day during the Games period, I had accompanied her to COBRA meetings with David Cameron, Boris Johnson, and the rest of them to give assurances that we would not have five-hour queues at the border; nor would we be granting entry to anyone who posed a risk to the safety and security of the Games. Despite a hungry media seeking to suggest otherwise. And I had been proved right. The Games were over, and my 40 years' service in the Home Office was nearly done. I didn't need any grief at this stage of my career. Retirement, a pension and even a possible medal was within sight.

"What's happened?" I asked. We received a daily brief of all the latest media stories. Any hint of complaints from Heathrow about long queues at arrivals would be picked up by the Special Advisers. Any suggestion that we had let someone in who was a serious criminal, or a security threat, would attract their attention. And the thing I had come to learn in almost 40 years in the borders business is that shit happens – no matter how hard you tried to avoid it.

"Nothing we can see guv. All seems pretty quiet out there at the moment. Apparently, it's personal – and she's waiting for you now."

I walked along to the third floor and knocked on the door of her office, wondering how many SPADs and officials would be surrounding her. To my astonishment, there were none.

"Hi Tony, thanks for popping in. Cup of tea?"

I had to pinch myself to ensure I wasn't dreaming. It was virtually unheard of for a senior civil servant to meet a Home Secretary alone without some third party in the room – let alone over a cup of tea.

"How is your mum?"

Mum wasn't at all well, as it happened. She had just had open heart surgery in St George's Hospital, and it was touch and go.

"Not great, Home Secretary, but thank you for asking. She's a tough old cookie, so we are hoping she'll pull through."

"OK well, give her my best wishes, won't you."

I was still trying to figure out why I had been called into one of the highest offices in the land to have a chat with the Secretary of State about my mum over a cup of tea. There must be a catch, surely?

"Tell me Tony, how serious are you about retirement?"

This knocked me back a bit. I already had a deal with HR that I could take early retirement in return for taking on the role as Senior Director and SRO for the UKBA London 2012 Olympic Programme. Officially I wasn't due to go until I was 60 years old in December 2013, but my 40 years was up in October 2012, which seemed the perfect time to bow out. But surely, she knew all this already?

Before I could reply, she said, "Look Tony, I know you have done your time here and we really are very grateful for everything you have done. But the problem is I haven't been able to find anyone suitable to take over as Director General of the Border Force. And my boss over the road at Number Ten wants a name now."

Even then the penny didn't drop. I started to blurt out a few names of people that I thought might be suitable. She interrupted me and said:

"Actually, Tony I thought of all of them already – but I would really quite like you to do it. What do you say?"

I gulped, then heard words coming out of my mouth that someone inside me seemed to be controlling: "It would be an honour and a privilege to serve you and the Home Office in any way you see fit, Home Secretary."

So that was that. I had just been appointed to the post of Director General of the UK Border Force, upon the personal invitation of the Home Secretary herself.

CHAPTER 23

UK BORDER FORCE:
THE FINAL LAP

My first impression on taking over the Border Force was the sense of panic that prevailed amongst the senior team. I decided to pull them together for a strategic conversation in the first week. The Chief Operating Officer at the time was Mandie Campbell. I knew Mandie well from UKIS days and we had worked together on the Olympics, but she was now facing bigger problems in resourcing the border. The Olympics had gone, but the student arrivals season was upon us. Heathrow Airport was watching us like a hawk for delivery of service standards – woe betide any Terminal manager who allowed a queuing time to slip above the 45-minute limit. And woe betide any officer who didn't check every single passport or ID card thoroughly against the warnings index.

In order to hit the throughput targets, Mandie was going cap in hand to Rob Whiteman to find officers from within the residual UKBA who were capable of working at the border.

Many of them had day jobs in immigration enforcement and other targets to meet.

Once again, fortune was on my side. I knew that around this time, arrival numbers at our ports would start to decline. It was ever thus. There would be a surge at Christmas, but apart from that I would have about six months' breathing space to enable us to gear up to summer 2013. Added to which, I wasn't sure if I would still be around by then. In fact, I had suggested to the Home Secretary that Mandie might be an appropriate candidate for the top job herself. But my first mission was to try to restore some kind of order to an organisation which was clearly struggling to inspire confidence in Ministers.

I wrote a submission to the Home Secretary shortly after my appointment, recommending a range of measures we could introduce to smarten up the UK border. These included principles I had picked up through many years of experience relating to pre-clearance, biometrics, advanced risk assessment and automated border controls which would inspire confidence both in our ability to check all arrivals thoroughly prior to entry whilst at the same time facilitating flows. I knew it could be done. I also mentioned the need to "get a grip" on the border operation. In my following meeting with her, she left me in in no doubt that her top priority was to "get a grip". I gained the distinct impression that she felt we had lost it – notwithstanding the successes of London 2012.

Another advantage of securing the DG post – only the second one in history for the UK Border Force – was that I was now operating at Grade 2 level. I was therefore a member of the Home Office Board. My new reporting officer was the Permanent Secretary, a post that was occupied by Dame Helen Ghosh. Helen herself left the Department soon afterwards, to be replaced by Helen Kilpatrick. I expect this huge turnover of staff at the upper levels of the Home Office senior civil service was also disconcerting for Ministers at that time. If there was ever an organisation crying out for some stability, this was it.

Of course, I should make it clear at this point that although I was formally appointed as Director General of the UK Border Force, my appointment was only "interim". Indeed, that was the same status afforded to my predecessor, and to my new boss. In order to achieve a substantive appointment to the post, I would need to go through a selection panel. That said, it was rare to get round to running selection panels at that time. Many of us were in "interim" positions, some for considerable lengths of time. In reality it made little difference. If I were to oversee huge delays at the border or the admissibility of people without the proper checks during my tenure of the post, my head would be on the block. Arguing that I was only an interim DG wouldn't avail me.

One of the happier memories I have of that time is the reception I received from so many officers at the front line. There were messages in my inbox from Falmouth to Aberdeen, and all ports in between, congratulating me on my appointment. Many were heartfelt indeed – here we had an immigration officer who had come up through the ranks, sitting in the top seat at last. I was one of *them*. I asked my office to set aside an hour in my diary every week to enable me to respond to their emails directly, and to ensure I was out on the ground with them every Friday. Not just preaching to them in the office – getting my hands dirty too. I was going back to the border – and I loved it.

It wasn't all plain sailing though. I met with the Home Secretary and her special advisors, Fiona Hill and Nick Timothy, on several occasions. It was clear that despite the success of London 2012 they still had little confidence in the Border Force. There was a constant worry that we might not be checking all passengers thoroughly at all the ports of entry – Theresa May had staked her reputation on that. Plus, Heathrow Airport continued to complain very loudly – frequently in the press – if any sort of a queue built up at passport control. This was the same old story – facilitation v control, and how best to balance it.

One tool that had proved very useful to us in this regard was the development of the e-gate. I had been heavily involved in the introduction of automated border controls in the past. I had worked with Accenture and others to introduce the first automated clearance system (ACS) at Heathrow when I was Director of Ports in 2005. We installed automated kiosks in Terminal 3 so that pre-registered passengers could pass through simply by inserting their passport and matching a biometric. Whilst I was away working in London region and on the Olympics, the e-gates had taken on a life of their own. They were now installed in most major airports so that British and EU passengers with e-passports could use them to enter the country without seeing an immigration officer. The airport authorities saw this as the answer to their prayers – so much so that they were prepared to invest their own money in more and more e-gates, in the hope that the Border Force would disappear altogether and stop creating queues.

They missed the small point that it was actually the Home Office and the Border Force who were responsible for border security, and we needed to be sure that any new technology they installed to clear passengers met our requirements. Heathrow had decided to go on a frolic of its own and build a new-style e-gate – known as ACS+ – without getting prior agreement from the Department. The upshot was that the ACS+ e-gates were decommissioned and mothballed, pending resolution of an ongoing dispute between the airport authority and the Department over costs. This did nothing to thaw relations between Heathrow Airport plc and the Home Office – an essential ingredient if we were to balance facilitation and control.

I met with the CEO at Heathrow to discuss all this, and we agreed to lock our respective teams in a room at Heathrow to thrash out a solution between them that would meet the concerns on both sides. If we could crack this at Heathrow, we could build a long-term policy and funding model for the use of e-gates at all our airports. This would meet all our security requirements, whilst at the same time provide them with more opportunities to clear passengers who did not require leave to enter (ie, British, EU, EEA and Swiss) through e-gates.

After three days we had white smoke, and I was able to take a solution to the Home Secretary and the SPADs which would resolve the problem. However, this wasn't quite enough on its own. The SPADs demanded that the Heathrow hierarchy attended meeting in the Home Secretary's office to apologise for briefing the press against us. So, I spent a good deal of time trying to persuade a reluctant senior Heathrow team to come into Marsham Street and apologise to the Home Secretary. It wasn't so bad – I had done it myself on many occasions where we had screwed up. Honesty was the best policy, and bygones could become bygones. In the end the meeting took place, the apology was delivered, and e-gates were back in play at Heathrow. After that the UK Border Force went on to become the world leader in automated border controls, moving more passengers through e-gates than any other country in the world. With Heathrow at the helm. Although to this day I often smile when I see airports complaining to the press about queues at the UK Border.

CHAPTER 24

HM REVENUE & CUSTOMS: COLLECTOR OF THE REVENUE

Although I had amassed a huge depth and breadth of knowledge about immigration and border security throughout my 40 years of service, I was less well informed about the Customs side of the business. My appointment as Head of the UK Border Force was another rude awakening in my extraordinary journey.

I received several letters from Cabinet Ministers after the Olympics thanking me for my work on the Programme, including Jeremy Hunt (DCMS), Boris Johnson (Mayor of London), Theresa May (Home Secretary) and David Cameron (Prime Minister). So, when one arrived on my desk from George Osborne (Chancellor of the Exchequer) I presumed it would be something in a similar vein. Not so. In fact, it was written authority to confer upon me the official title of Her Majesty's Collector of Revenue at the Border.

Although the UK Border Force had acquired responsibility for checking goods at the border in 2008 alongside people, my personal engagement with Her Majesty's Revenue and Customs

(HMRC) had been limited. I had been to Custom House a few times during my time as Regional Director in the UKBA to discuss how our respective enforcement teams would work together (alongside the police, the National Crime Agency, and others) to investigate organised crime regarding smuggling of dangerous and prohibited goods (firearms, drugs, and the like). I had also worked with them on the London 2012 Olympic Customs Manual, which set out specific terms under which licensed and restricted goods and livestock may be admitted temporarily for the purpose of sport (horses, rifles etc). But in terms of customs declarations, regulatory requirements on animals and products of animal or plant origin, or collection of revenue at the border, I had very little experience.

In fact, the UK Customs Service was steeped in history going way back beyond the creation of the Immigration Branch in 1905. I had many an argument with colleagues about which came first – immigration or customs controls – in the context of borders.

The Roman Empire provides us with the first signs of "Border Control", in the form of a physical barrier erected to mark the boundary of a territory, and "controlling" those who crossed it. Emperor Hadrian ruled from 117 to 138 AD and is famously remembered for constructing a great wall in Britannia, later to become known as "Hadrian's Wall". The wall ran from the Banks of the River Tyne near the North Sea to the Solway Firth in the Irish Sea and comprised milecastles and turrets along it. This is where we find the first evidence of the existence of a "Border Officer", charged with controlling the movement of people between the Empire and those beyond it.

Other Empires came and went with wars over the years, with borders being redrawn as territory was won and lost. The concept of "sovereignty" can be traced back to two peace treaties signed in October 1648 in the Westphalian cities of Osnabrück and Münster. Known at the Peace of Westphalia, this essentially gave countries rights over their own territories and boundaries, without interference from external powers. Although of course it did nothing to prevent further wars and conquests, or the colonization of New Territories.

At its height, the British Empire was the largest Empire in history, and the foremost global power for over a century. By 1913 it held sway over 412 million people – about 23% of the world's population at that time. In return for colonisation, it became customary to offer the indigenous community some form of citizenship of the Empire. Prior to 1949, any person born within either the UK or the British Empire became a "British Subject". This included the dominions of Australia and Canada. Although many Commonwealth countries declared "independence" and created their own "citizenship", they retained the title of "British Subjects". But prior to the 1960s, all the British Subjects in the world could come and live in the UK, if they wanted to. These laws would have a massive impact upon those who could or could not cross international borders and under what conditions, in future.

As empires were built and countries were formed, the military took primary responsibility for managing the borders. But the primary government agency to take on the smugglers were known as "Customs".

In England smuggling first became recognised as a problem in 1275, following the creation of a national Customs collection system by King Edward 1.

UK Customs Officers can be tracked back to Geoffrey Chaucer, famous author of *The Canterbury Tales*, in the 14th century. Chaucer was himself "Comptroller of Customs" for the Port of London between 1374 and 1386.

By the start of the 19th century HM Customs had 75 "Custom Houses" at ports of entry in England and Wales, each staffed by two "collectors" who supervised other officers collecting revenue for the Treasury. In addition to the fixed locations at ports, HM

Customs also deployed "riding officers" to patrol the coastline on horseback looking for "suspicious activity". This supplemented the 33-strong fleet of "revenue cutters" patrolling the coastline.

The history of UK Customs is steeped in folklore and has been the subject of many famous books, including *Kidnapped* by Robert Louis Stevenson, who wrote:

> *Few places on the British coast did not claim to be the haunts of wreckers or mooncussers. The thievery was boasted about and romanticized until it seemed a kind of heroism. It did not have any taint of criminality and the whole of the south coast had pockets vying with one another over whose smugglers were the darkest or most daring. The Smugglers Inn was one of the commonest names for a bar on the coast.*

Indeed, smugglers back then did portray a sense of justice in acting against draconian state powers to facilitate the illegal entry of grain and other necessities to evade revenue and tax requirements for the poor. Some even saw human smuggling as humanitarian to support people fleeing wars in France. Some still do – although that's another story.

It wasn't until after the introduction of the Aliens Act 1905 that a new "Immigration Branch" was formed, to manage the increasing movement of people. Customs Officers have found themselves in several different Whitehall Departments over the years; but in terms of border management, their history transcends other enforcement agencies by many centuries.

Upon receipt of my letter from Mr Osborne I took advice from my good friend and colleague Kevin Franklin – himself a former HMRC officer with a much greater depth and breadth of knowledge of Customs than I – and together we opened a dialogue with senior civil servants at HMRC about how this requirement actually worked in practice.

The reality at the time was that Customs was not a priority

at the UK Border. Membership of the EU Single Market and the EU Customs Union meant that goods moving between the UK and the EU could flow freely with very few checks, other than for VAT and Excise purposes. Goods arriving at our deep sea ports from outside the EU were subject to more stringent checks and could only be released once we were satisfied that all the necessary regulatory checks had been completed, but this accounted for only about a fifth of UK imports and exports at the time. When weighed against the broader challenges of preventing terrorist travel, controlling immigration, and border security, this did not feature very high up on the priority list. This was about to change as the political clamour for the UK to leave the European Union (including the Single Market and the Customs Union) gathered pace.

Although my experience of customs control was limited, I did try to get out to those parts of my command where our officers were active in clearing goods entering the UK. This included visits to our customs warehouses where goods were being routinely screened and cleared for importation, or detained pending further investigation and potential seizure for failing to meet standards or pay duties.

One of my favourite stories about my time as Head of the Border Force is one that I have told at many after dinner speeches, where I became the Grinch who stole Christmas. We had a huge warehouse in the Midlands where air freight was examined for potential Customs infractions. This included several consignments from the Far East including importation of counterfeit products destined for the Christmas markets. Headphones, trainers, designer gear, perfumes – you name it. We had a veritable Aladdin's cave of seizures there.

I was listening to the radio on my way into work one day when I heard that the UK Border Force had seized a huge number of Manchester United football shirts. These were in all shapes and sizes, mainly ordered online by UK families for their children.

But when the shirts failed to turn up on doorsteps, it became increasingly apparent that they had been seized by the nasty Border Force – thus ruining Christmas Day for a large number of Manchester United fans.

I was summoned to the Press Office to go on air to explain why we would do such a thing. The message that importation of counterfeit products was illegal wasn't going to land well with young Johnny from Wythenshawe, or his angry parents. We contacted the club for advice – after all it was their copyright that we were protecting – only to be told that they weren't particularly concerned by the breach. Sure, the club would make a lot more money by selling official club merchandise through their own outlets at five times the price. But after all, this was free publicity for the club – and if it helped them to build their fan base, so what?

I always found it hard to enforce the law without identifying the real mischief we were trying to eradicate. Of course, we do a great job preventing the importation of harmful drugs, fake medicines, and dangerous materials – but fake football shirts? Yes, I was the Grinch who stole Christmas in 2012.

Another big challenge facing UKBF at that time was the incremental growth in responsibilities for implementing border controls on behalf of other Departments and Agencies. As a Home Office Department, the Border Force would always be led by Home Office priorities which at the time involved strict checks on people entering and leaving the country, primarily for security purposes but also for immigration. Although we had now inherited a significant number of legacy Customs Officers, an inevitable consequence was that they would be directed more to passport controls than to traditional customs controls. Indeed, in some meetings with staff representatives I was told in no uncertain terms that the legacy Customs staff were feeling unloved – and worse still we were abandoning traditional checks on goods in the red and green channels at the border in favour of clearing passengers through the ports to meet service standards on queuing times at passport control. This was something I was keen to address – although time was running out.

CHAPTER 25

A NEW UK BORDER STRATEGY

One area I was keen to develop whilst I was still in post was the UK Border Strategy. I was concerned about the siloed, separated nature of the business, and the fact that we were being stretched in several different directions without any clear sense of long-term vision or purpose. I had worked on border strategies in North America, and had a good idea of what the main components of such a strategy ought to be. A senior civil servant, Stephen Kershaw, was invited to hold the pen on this task, and I attended weekly meetings with other Directors General from UKBA, OSCT and elsewhere to compile a document to agree with Ministers.

I had already presented my own blueprint to Theresa May after she appointed me to the role, so I had a good idea about what the strategy should look like. Firstly, we needed a clear vision and mission statement to facilitate the movement of people and goods across the UK border to promote growth, whilst deterring and preventing movements that may be non-compliant or harmful. We didn't need to open every box to do Customs, or even to open every passport to do immigration anymore. What was needed was data. Accurate, timely, comprehensive data that could be run against government systems – preferably prior to arrival – to distinguish those people and goods that passed the test from those that did not.

Secondly, we needed to embrace the multiple borders strategy. Modern-day border controls are best described as a series of transactions that begin way before travel and continue throughout the end-to-end journey. By verifying identity and entitlement (for people) and commodity and compliance (for goods) in advance of arrival, passage through the physical frontier at the port of entry can be facilitated using automated border controls. Likewise non-compliant and harmful people and goods can be offloaded earlier in the process and prevented from travelling at all. As we know to our cost, it may be too late if they are already airborne before we spot the danger.

Thirdly, we needed to embrace and implement integrated border management. This required a fundamental review of all the many Departments and Agencies with an interest in the border, and an examination of how well they worked together behind the common mission. There was always going to be a tension between different Departments with different mandates. Some wanted more facilitation; some wanted more control. Getting the balance of priorities right required a flexible governance structure and a control strategy. Merging immigration and customs at the border is a form of integration, but it will not necessarily deliver the desired outcome.

And finally, we needed an end-to-end identity management system. This meant capturing and "locking in" the identity of all travellers at first encounter and using biometrics to verify their identity at each stage in the process. In some countries – such as Singapore – this means from cradle to grave.

I set about drafting the strategy with Stephen and we did make some progress, although getting agreement even within the

Home Office was a challenge. Taking it out to other government departments would be an even bigger one. In fact, it would take another seven years, until December 2020, before it would finally be published. But at least we had set the ball rolling.

Another area that required attention at that time – and still does to this day – was the introduction of new technology at the UK border to meet the requirements of the strategy. The failure of the e borders programme had left the Home Office with a number of legacy systems based on different platforms, with limited connectivity to each other. A similar picture had emerged with HMRC. Several companies and consultants had been hired to fix the problem, but for the most part most of the effort was geared towards business continuity and keeping things running in the face of ever- increasing volumes. I recall being asked to attend a meeting with Justin Holliday – the Senior Finance and Commercial Lead in the Home Office at that time -to talk to industry leaders about the challenges we were facing, and how they might help us to fix them. Which was an interesting turn of events, as I moved from gamekeeper to poacher role in later life.

As we moved into 2013, it seemed to me that my card was being marked for a longer spell at the top of the Border Force than had first been envisaged. I had developed a relationship of trust with Ministers and SPADs, which hadn't always been there in the past. Things were moving forward well, and I had managed to dodge most of the bullets that were flying around at the time. I was by now well into my 41st year of service, but there had been no sign of any serious competitor for the role. On the contrary, I was being encouraged by most of the workforce and many senior civil servants to apply for the job substantively. The troops were for the most part happy that I was there. I developed a good working relationship with the unions, and most of the Border Force senior team accepted me as their leader.

I was eventually called to a Selection Board chaired by Helen Kilpatrick with other Home Office Board Members, including

Rob Whiteman and Charles Farr, and I was beginning to wonder whether I might end up staying even longer in the post. Indeed, had the post been subject to an election by the workforce rather than scrutiny of the cabinet office, I expect I would have won by a landslide. I was therefore a bit surprised – although not disappointed – to discover that I was to be released after all. After a further round of selections, Sir Charles Montgomery had been identified as the new Director General of the UK Border Force. Helen called me in to say thanks for all my service and say that they could probably find something for me to do for the rest of 2013 (I would be 60 in December) but the offer of early retirement was still there. In the meantime, I had appeared in the New Year's Honours List of 2013 as a Commander of the British Empire (CBE) for my services to Border Security during the London 2012 Olympics. So that was that.

I arranged an induction programme for Charles and started preparations for my exit strategy. Perversely, Sir Mark Sedwill was appointed as the new Permanent Secretary just around this time. Mark was a good friend of mine. We had worked together in the past when he was in charge of UK visas, and we always had a healthy respect for each other. We have kept in touch, and he subsequently confided in me that had the timings been different he would have fought tooth and nail to keep me in his senior team for longer at the Home Office, which was very kind of him.

Theresa May was also very kind to me. She invited me to the Houses of Parliament to have a drink with her personally, and to thank me for my service. She also delivered a speech at my retirement party in Marsham Street, presenting me with a range of gifts including a letter from the Prime Minister (David Cameron) thanking me for my service. She also gave me a handwritten letter of her own, framed with my Border Force epaulettes. Both these letters, together with one from Sir Mark, now hang proudly on my office wall.

In fact, it was unusual for both a Home Secretary and a

Permanent Secretary to speak at a retirement party for a senior official, and I was honoured that both Theresa and Mark did so at mine. My lasting memory of that event was having my family there to witness it – especially Mum and Dad. Theresa asked me to introduce her to my Mum, who was overwhelmed. Mum was a great fan of hers and started gushing out stories about how on earth I ever did all those things when I could hardly find my way to school in the mornings. I think Mum took that story to her grave with her, together with memories of our day out at Windsor Castle where I picked up my medal from HM Queen Elizabeth.

Both Theresa and Mark went on to greater things, of course. Theresa became Prime Minister herself in 2016, and Mark became the Cabinet Secretary (and top civil servant) in 2018. I am frequently asked about the time I spent working with each of them in government service, and I can honestly say it was an honour to serve with both of them. I have met Theresa a few times since. To me she will always be the Home Secretary, because that is where I knew her best. Politics is a messy business, and there will be plenty who will brief against her. But I can only speak from personal experience, and her sense of public duty and service to the country was unsurpassed, something that shone through clearly on the steps of 10 Downing Street when she tearfully announced her own departure from office in 2019.

At my final meeting with Theresa May, I took the opportunity to seek her advice on how I could continue to help the Home Office "from the outside" – particularly the border and immigration space, which had after all been a major part of my life for over 40 years. We agreed that I would stay in touch on matters of policy – my depth and breadth of experience in these policy areas would be useful to the next generation of civil servants. Also, the government had a range of experts who had served in the military or the police and could respond to media requests if there was a major incident such as a war or a riot – but there wasn't an independent expert who could talk about crises at the border. So we also agreed I would keep in touch with the Home Office Press Office, should the media come calling. Which they certainly did – and still do, all these years later.

My day at the Palace was also another great moment for me. Mum hadn't been well, and Dad had limited mobility due to back problems, but both wanted to come along. They were both great royalists and supporters of the Royal British Legion in their time. Having their eldest son step up to receive an award from Her Majesty herself was a day to behold. The staff at Windsor Castle were wonderful. We were given priority parking and assistance into the hall. Mum, Dad and Jill all sat in the audience with all the other proud family members who had come along to watch the ceremony.

I was diverted into another room for my briefing as to how to approach her Majesty, with a few other successful appointees including the singer Kate Bush. I wore my Border Force uniform. When my turn came round, I had a brief chat with the Queen and talked about the challenges of managing border security during the Olympics. I also reminded her of our first meeting back at London City Airport all those years ago. It was another great day in my extraordinary life, and one that I shall remember forever.

Chairing the World Borderpol Congress, Budapest, Hungary, 2014.

Being interviewed live on BBC Breakfast TV following the disappearance
of flight MH 370, 2014

With daughter and business partner Sharon Ayley, Fortinus Global Ltd, Trade Show Johannesburg, South Africa, 2017

Training Border Agencies in New Delhi, 2018

Reunion with Senator Tom Ridge, International Summit on Borders,
Washington DC, 2018

Discussing the UK migrant boat crisis on the Victoria Derbyshire Show,
BBC, 2018

One of many media interviews on migration at borders with
BBC News, London, 2018-2020

Media interviews on a new Border Strategy for Malaysia, 2017

Discussing Alternative Arrangements for the Irish Border after Brexit with
Nigel Farage, LBC radio, 2019.

(Above and below) meetings at the EU Commission with the expert panel for Alternative Arrangements for the Irish Border after Brexit, 2019

On Sky News discussing the migrant crisis in the English Channel, 2020.

Being interviewed on TV - hopefully the viewers
could not see my slippers!

Completing the ASICS London 10k run for Alzheimer's charity in 2021
(aged 67), in memory of my dad.

My legacy to mankind – with daughter
Sharon and sons Mark, Daniel and Ben

PART THREE

LIFE ON THE OUTSIDE – 2013 - 2021

CHAPTER 26

Into the Private Sector – Fortinus Global Ltd

Ordinarily my story would end there, but although my work with the government was done, my work in Border Control was not. I have often said that you can take the man out of the Border Force, but you can't take the Border Force out of the man. Although for me, of course, that also included the Immigration Service, even though it had long since been abolished.

I had become a founder member of the ex-Immigration Service Team (EXIST) whilst I was still serving in UKBA. Although the Home Office did have a network of retired officers, it was not widely known or used or recognised by former immigration officers. As I have said before, many Immigration Officers stayed in the UK Immigration Service (or the UK Border Force, as it was to become) for their entire careers.

One day whilst I was serving as Regional Director in the UKBA I was contacted by Bill Vincent, a former colleague from my days at Isis House, to say that our mutual friend Dave Green had suddenly passed away. Dave was a great friend of mine. We had joined the Home Office around the same time, and he was one of those officers who was always ready to keep my feet on the ground and take me out for a pint as I climbed the promotion ladder. His untimely death came as a great shock to me and to a great many of our colleagues.

Dave had suffered an unexpected brain haemorrhage at his home in Streatham. He was taken before his time and whilst still a serving officer, so I suggested to our HR Department that they should issue a Departmental Notice advising all his friends and colleagues of his unfortunate and untimely passing, and funeral arrangements. To my dismay they declined to do so, saying it was not "Home Office policy" to do such things. I was livid and decided to do it myself anyway, and spread the word across my command and in the Border Force. The outcome was a massive turnout at his funeral in Streatham, and a thereafter a group of retired colleagues decided to form the EXIST network so that retired officers could keep in touch with one another. We still have a regular UKIS annual reunion in a pub near Waterloo station every year, known affectionately as the "Cape to Cairo" after legendary drinking sessions at Heathrow in years gone by. Sadly, our numbers have declined as the years have passed, but the both the EXIST network and the Cape continue to preserve contact between those UKIS veterans of us that remain. Long may it continue.

One of my first acts after leaving government service, having been given the Home Secretary's blessing to do media interviews, was to accept a bid from *The Sun* newspaper to talk about the state of the UK Border. I had thought that my experience in dealing with the media whilst in the job would see me through this. My ambition was to point out to the public that in reality we had a very strong border control in the UK - much better than most other countries – but there was still work to be done in specific areas. This included identity management, an entry exit system, and a replacement for the failed e-borders and ICW programmes.

The outcome was a front-page photo of me in uniform adjacent to a headline "Our Border is Out of Order, says former Border Force chief". Worse still, this didn't just go out in the newspaper one day and become fish and chip paper the next. Media outlets were now online and immediate, and stored indefinitely on the internet. Anyone who googled me after that would see that headline associated with me before anything else, making me look like just another disgruntled former civil servant taking the first opportunity to take a dig at his former employer. The fact that I never once said our border was "out of order" (obviously made up by the journalist or his editor to sell newspapers), or that I said many positive things about our border controls, was lost in translation. I soon learned that the media were a lottery, and a great many reporters were more interested in having a pop at the government rather than reporting the facts.

I was also surprised at the level of interest in my profile. I was always confident that I had achieved a great deal in my time at the Home Office, but I didn't realise that so many people had been tracking my progress until after I retired.

I wasn't ready to sit in my garden and write my memoirs just yet. The fact that I am only publishing this book now, eight years after retirement, is testament to that.

I remember vividly my encounter with my GP around that time.

"So, Tony have you thought about what you might do now you are hanging up your boots at the Home Office?" he said.

"Not really", I replied. "I might do a bit of consultancy work and a bit of writing".

"Well make sure you do something. I don't want you dying on me."

I gulped. I hadn't really thought about dying. My mum and dad were still alive. They were now living in Carshalton, close to me so I could keep an eye on them. Mum had survived her heart valve operation in 2012 against all the odds. Dad still complained of a bad back, but both were in their eighties. For a sixty-year-old, I was pretty fit. My kids were still young (or at least two of them were). I wasn't ready to pop off just yet, although I was increasingly concerned about the number of funerals of ex-UKIS colleagues I had been attending recently, many from my peer group.

"Why, what's wrong with me?" I gulped.

I knew I had high blood pressure – that ran in the family and went with the job. But apart from that I thought I was OK. I braced myself for the worst.

"Don't worry, your tests are fine" he said. "But I have known you for long enough now. Your body has been running on adrenalin for some years now because of that job. You need to do something. If you don't do anything, you may just shut down completely and that will be that."

So, if I needed a jolt to stay in the game, that was it.

Little did I know that I was to continue to play such a significant role in events yet to come in the increasingly thorny field of border security and Immigration.

Offers of work started to roll in from the private sector. Having already secured my Civil Service pension, I was not interested in a full-time position with any one company, but I was keen to work with like-minded people whom I respected. There was some talk of keeping several of the UK Home Office Olympic Security Team together. The Games were such a success (off the field as well as on it) that the Foreign and Commonwealth Office and the Home Office asked us to keep in touch with a view to exporting British excellence to other countries in areas such as policing and security (which in my case included border security) as part of the "Great" campaign.

In order to take up work as a private consultant, I was advised by my accountant to set up my own limited company. The next question became, who I could persuade to partner with me in the company – and what would I call it? In terms of the former, I turned to my elder two children, Sharon and Mark. Both were between jobs at the time. Sharon already had some experience in business herself, and Mark was taking a keen interest in accounts and book-keeping. In terms of the latter, I spent many hours trying to think of a company name that would reflect the nature of my speciality – border security.

The answer came from an unlikely source – my mum. It was customary for us to visit Mum and Dad every Saturday evening for a takeaway, and I mentioned that I was struggling with this. Mum had always been interested in Latin and asked me if I had thought of using that. I looked up the Latin words for strong borders and came up with "Fort" (strong) and "Terminus" (borders). After some playing around with words, Fortinus Ltd was born.

Before very long I found myself at the heart of several high-profile incidents involving border security, immigration and so on, either as a border security consultant or as a media commentator. My experiences in these key areas – many of which remain in the public domain – are set out in the chapters that follow.

CHAPTER 27

Smart security and the checkpoint of the future – 2013

I had discussed going into border consultancy work with my old mate Tony Mercer. He had jumped ship a couple of years before me and was now working in the private sector, and we had kept in touch. I had known Tony on and off since we were teenagers working in Croydon together. He had put me up in Dhaka for a while, and also in his home in Hampton when I was in between marriages. In fact, we had become so close that he was my best man at my wedding with Jill in 1999.

Tony's main achievement in the Home Office was the rollout of the biometric visa programme – something he deserved more credit for than he was given at the time. However, his inability to secure a senior post in the Home Office after that had pushed him into early retirement, and he now had a couple of pretty big contracts in the private sector.

I had also developed a friendship with Matthew Finn, whom I had met on the conference circuit over the years. Matthew had never actually worked in the Home Office, but he was an expert in passenger information and border systems and was now running his own border and aviation security company.

My first real work proposition in the outside world came from Matthew. He was putting together a bid for a contract for the International Air Transportation Authority (IATA) and the UK Department for Transport (DFT) on the viability of the "Checkpoint of the Future" programme. The work would entail interviews with airlines, airports and border agencies around the world, and the production of a comprehensive report for the client. He was putting together a team to work on this which would include Stephen Challis (a former Head of Innovation at Heathrow), Tony Mercer, and myself.

The question we were asked to consider was whether a "data-driven" approach to aviation security checks (as opposed to border control checks) was possible, practical, and worthwhile.

Many people confuse aviation security checks (or security screening, as it is sometimes called) with border security checks. The main difference is that aviation security checks (AVSEC) are there to ensure the safety of the aircraft and the passengers and crew on board it, whereas border security checks are more related to the eligibility to travel and enter the destination country, including any security threats the person may pose once admitted. So traditionally AVSEC checks are performed when people are about to board aircraft, through a comprehensive search of their luggage and their person. It is a function of government overseen by the Department for Transport (DFT) and the Civil Aviation Authority CAA) rather than by the Home Office and its agencies. Similarly in other countries different agencies perform AVSEC, such as the Transportation Security Agency (TSA) as opposed to Customs and Border Protection (CBP) in the United States.

Meanwhile Border Security checks are conducted by the relevant Border Agencies, and involve a more sophisticated risk assessment based upon passenger data and associated intelligence relating to the individual. The question was whether a more sophisticated risk assessment of the passenger (such as those being conducted by Border Agencies) might inform a more selective search and screening process rather than the "one size" fits all approach conducted at most airports.

The response to 9/11 was a failure on both fronts. Firstly, as we have noted previously, the US Agencies managing the US border at that time had failed to link intelligence held in different departments of the administration to disrupt terrorist travel to the United States through the US visa system. Secondly, those responsible for the physical search and screening of passengers boarding those fateful domestic US flights that day had failed to detect the presence of "box cutters" concealed by the hijackers, which ultimately enabled them to overpower the crew and take control of the aircraft.

Aviation has long been a target for terrorists, with the first bomb aboard an aircraft reported in 1932. Hijackings in the 1960s and 1970s, where terrorists were able to smuggle weapons on board to overpower crew and take control of the aircraft, led to the global implementation of pre-boarding "screening" systems. The downing of Pan Am flight 103 over Lockerbie in December 1988 showed the devastation that could be caused by detonating explosives concealed in hold baggage. This demanded increasingly onerous pre-boarding inspections of both passengers and baggage at airports across the world, and – as I knew from personal experience – the 9/11 hijacks on domestic US aircraft had led to a fundamental change to border security requirements. There was now a much greater emphasis not just on physical screening at point of boarding, but also advanced risk assessment and intelligence gathered prior to travel.

In general terms, governments have tended to react to terrorist events in the aviation sector with increasingly onerous physical pre-departure checks. Richard Reid's attempt to blow a hole in the aircraft fuselage by concealing explosives in his trainers in 2001 meant that all passengers were required to submit their shoes for inspection prior to boarding. In August 2006, the Metropolitan Police and the UK Security Agencies identified a terrorist cell in the UK that was in an advanced stage of planning to bring down several flights from Heathrow to the United States and Canada using peroxide-based liquid explosives which could be passed off as soft drinks to be detonated on board. This plot – known as the "Liquid Bomb plot" – led to a new requirement that all liquids, aerosols, and gels (LAGS) above a certain volume could no longer be taken on board aircraft.

However, it was the case of Umar Farouk Abdulmutallab – otherwise known as the "underwear bomber" – that raised the possibility of a more data driven risk assessment to security screening. Abdulmutallab was a Nigerian-born terrorist who flew from Ghana to Amsterdam on Christmas Day 2009, where he successfully boarded a connecting flight to Detroit with explosives concealed in his underwear. Fortunately, the device failed to detonate. He was subsequently convicted of attempted use of a weapon of mass destruction and the attempted murder of 289 passengers and sentenced to life imprisonment.

It later emerged that Abdulmutallab was known to the intelligence services, although under a slightly different name. He had been in contact with Anwar Al-Awlaki, a suspected leader of Al Qaeda in the Arabian Peninsula (AQAP). He had also recently travelled to the Yemen. Despite this, he had been issued with a US tourist visa and had not been subjected to any additional screening at airport security when he boarded North West Airlines flight 253 in Amsterdam, bound for Detroit.

This raised two questions. Firstly, despite the lessons learned from 9/11 and 7/7, how was it that terrorists were still able to evade capture and board aircraft – even when there were indicators such as travel history and intelligence to suggest they may pose a risk to the safety and security of the aircraft? And secondly, why could we not distinguish people like Abdulmutallab from other innocent passengers boarding the flight – especially given the amount of data that was now available in airline registration systems and government databases?

This project was precisely what I was looking for to keep myself active after government service. Before long I found myself chairing workshops involving former colleagues from the Home Office and the Department for Transport, port and airport operators, airline security officers, and border and security agencies worldwide. Fortunately, I had taken the opportunity to renew my developed vetting (DV) security clearance shortly before retirement, which gave me access to several colleagues both at home and abroad to inform the study.

We travelled far and wide to interview senior officials from government agencies around the world and gather information on international policy and practice, which informed a comprehensive report for the UK government and IATA on the options available for the Checkpoint of the Future. Whilst the final report was classified, it was abundantly clear to me – and still is – that it is imperative that government agencies and transportation companies continue to share information and intelligence with each other, not just at national level but also at international level.

The flip side to this coin is the privacy debate, where a person's right to privacy sets out specific parameters as to the sort of data that could and should be shared, with whom, and for what purpose. Whilst those arguments all have merit, I continue to promote the need for collaboration in international data sharing to this day – and to applaud our magnificent police and security services in the UK, who have thwarted so many terrorist attacks, such as the liquid bomb plot, which would otherwise have been just as devastating as the 9/11 and 7/7 events that I knew so well.

This did not mean that we could ignore the requirement for physical screening of passengers and their baggage when boarding aircraft, either on domestic flights or on international flights. Although artificial intelligence and data analytics have advanced to the point where they have become critical tools in identifying risk, they can't tell us what is in a person's mind at the time of boarding. At the same time, it is clear to me that those passengers who are prepared to submit additional data about themselves to control agencies in advance pose less risk than those who do not, especially terrorists, whose ambition is always to try to keep a low profile until the point of impact. This could lead to a more segmented approach to AVSEC checks based on data, and already does in some countries such as the United States, through programmes such as TSA Pre-check.

I thoroughly enjoyed working on this project and went on to engage on a great many adventures in the field of border and aviation security thereafter. It also enabled me to keep in touch with an alumni of international border specialists – many of whom held high office in their respective countries prior to retirement and were "still in the game". It also enabled me to develop new relationships with other key leaders in this field, as my path through the world of international border management continued to unwind.

CHAPTER 28

THE BIRTH OF THE AUSTRALIAN BORDER FORCE, 2014

One aspect of my work in the Home Office that I had always enjoyed was international liaison. Ever since I had attended the Four Country Middle Managers Conference in the 1990s, I had been fascinated by the way that different countries had approached border management and transformed their controls in response to major events, and how they worked together to resolve matters of mutual concern.

Having been Head of Ports and Borders in both Canada and the UK, both during times of significant border transformation following terrorist attacks, I felt I still had a good deal to offer in this area - particularly in the EU and in the "Border 5" (which had now taken over from the "Four Country Conference" with the addition of New Zealand). I had enjoyed significant operational experience in the UK and North America during my career, but less so in Australia and New Zealand, although I had visited Australia on a couple of occasions in the past and developed good working relationships with my peer groups in the Immigration and Customs Departments there. They were always very keen on international liaison, and I had met some of them at international meetings in various parts of the world where we had discussed matters of mutual concern around things like passenger facilitation and intelligence led controls. One such person was Mike Pezzullo, who was by now Head of Department for Immigration and Border Protection (DIBP) in Australia.

The Australian border was already viewed by many experts (including myself) as a model of excellence. In the run-up to the Sydney Olympics 2000 they were the first country to develop the concept of "Advanced Passenger Processing" (APP) and the "Electronic Travel Authority" (ETA), which provided the foundation for the global platform for exchange of passenger data between airlines and government. This process (now known as "interactive Advanced Passenger Information" [iAPI]) enabled them to risk-assess passengers before they arrived at their ports of entry. The interactive element, coupled with the universal introduction of "machine readable travel documents" (MRTDs), also enabled them to deny boarding to passengers at the point of disembarkation where necessary. Because of the geographical context for international flights, Australia has been able to implement this system on all international routes into the country – thus meeting the strategic objective of "exporting the border". This strategy is now endorsed globally as best practice in modern day border controls, based on the founding principle that it makes sense to risk assess people (and goods) at the earliest possible point in the journey.

Despite being a "country of immigration" (planning levels for 2014-15 catered for 190,000 new immigrants and 13,750 humanitarian refugees), Australia also had one of the toughest immigration enforcement regimes in the world. Undocumented arrivals were few and far between, and detention was widely used for illegal immigrants awaiting deportation. They had also responded vigorously to the challenge of undocumented maritime asylum seekers by establishing "offshore" processing centres and interdiction on the high seas – something that would become a challenge for the UK government a few years later.

Whenever I deliver lectures about border controls, I always say that if I were to pick any border in the world to take charge of, it would be Australia. They are an island nation, miles from anywhere, with no land borders or near neighbours to contend with. Far easier to deliver the multiple borders strategy there than in other countries such as the USA (with extensive land borders to both North and South) or even the UK (with very short maritime and air crossings to mainland Europe) . So all this talk about the "best border in the world" is fine – but the fact is, we are not all on a level playing field.

In March 2014 I received a call from Jim Canham, an International Borders Manager for Accenture. Jim was based in Australia at that time, leading a major piece of work with Australia Customs in Canberra. Accenture was part of a private sector consortium bidding on a tender to provide strategic support to the Department of Immigration and Border Protection (DIBP) on the merger of specific components of DIBP and the Australia Customs and Border Protection Service (ACBPS) into a new consolidated Australian Border Force (ABF). Jim felt that I would be a major asset to their bid team- not least because I had lived through similar reforms in both North America and the United Kingdom during my time in government service. There would be lessons to be learned from those exercises that might help the Australian government through this transition. Their border model until that time had been very similar to the one that I inherited when I arrived in Canada in 2000, with Customs operating primary inspections of ports of entry and immigration officers in secondary.

The call from Jim came very late in the day, on a Friday evening in London. Tenders had to be in by close of play in

Canberra the following Tuesday, and they were 12 hours ahead of us. There followed a frantic exchange of documents between Jim and myself, and I ended up burning the midnight oil reviewing materials and submitting new ones to him over that weekend. Anyway, it must have worked, because I learned the following week that they had been short-listed for interview, and that they wanted me to attend Canberra the following week to participate in the presentation.

Before I knew it, I was boarding the long flight from Heathrow to Sydney, via Singapore, to meet up with the bid team in Australia. I had been to Australia before, but I had forgotten what a long slog it was to get there – and just how bad the jet lag was. Upon arrival in Sydney, I had no idea what time of day or night it was. I had to clear immigration and customs and then transfer to a domestic flight up to Canberra, where the meetings were due to take place.

Following an interview panel with a selection of Australian government representatives, we won the bid. I was deployed to Australia a couple of times thereafter, to provide some strategic advice to the implementation team. I can remember being called into a meeting with Mike Pezzullo during one of those trips, to be received with a very warm handshake and some delight that I was involved in the process. This reinforced my belief that there was an alumni of current and future Heads of Borders around the world who held a mutual respect for one another – and still do, to this day.

One of my lasting memories of my Australia experience was meeting Roman Quaedvlieg, who had been appointed as the first Head of the Australian Border Force. The local team felt that it would be best if I met Roman alone for lunch, and they booked an Italian restaurant in Canberra for the purpose. I hadn't met him before and had no idea what he looked like, so I asked the team to give me a brief description. One of the ladies there simply said "Tony, don't worry, you will know when you see him. He is an absolute dish".

So, there I was sat at a table in a busy restaurant looking around at the men in the room to see who might fit the bill. Fortunately, I recognised a tall dark handsome man coming towards me as the most likely candidate, although it's more likely the fact that he was a kindred spirit rather than a "dish" that enabled us to hit it off so quickly. Like me, Roman had risen through the ranks. He had a very strong operational background, although his experience was more in the police department than in immigration. But we both shared a passion to tackle and disrupt international organised crime, and still do.

I never spent as much time as I would have liked with Roman during his tenure, but we have kept in touch ever since. Indeed, it was the publication of his book *Tour de Force* – a signed copy of which now sits on my bookshelf – that prompted me to write this one.

CHAPTER 29

THE MALAYSIAN EXPERIENCE, 2015

Media and public interest in immigration and borders continued unabated as new challenges arose. As time went by, I found myself receiving an increasing number of bids from TV and radio companies to comment on border security and immigration related events. And there were plenty of those. One event that sticks out in my mind was the disappearance of flight MH370.

On 8 March 2014 flight MH370 took off from Kuala Lumpur bound for Beijing, with 227 passengers and 12 crew on board. 38 minutes into the flight, the air crew lost all contact with air traffic control – and the flight literally fell off the radar. The event hit national headlines all over the world, as the immediate aftermath revealed no trace of any crash site. All kinds of conspiracy theories were raised by a variety of aviation security "experts", but nobody was able to fathom precisely what had happened. One thing the Malaysian government was able to do was to release the flight "manifest" so that a hungry media pack could report the names and the nationalities of those on board, although where they were and what had happened to them all remained a mystery.

It was initially reported that some of the passengers on board were from EU countries, including one person from Austria and another from Italy. It was not entirely clear why these people were on a flight from Kuala Lumpur to Beijing, but there was a strong possibility that they would be seeking to transit there for an onward flight to Europe.

When their identities were revealed, it soon became clear that the rightful holders of the passports declared at boarding were in fact alive and well and living in Europe, and no doubt extremely surprised to discover that their names were being flashed across international media outlets as "missing presumed dead".

It subsequently transpired that two Iranian nationals, Pouria Noor Mohamed and Syed Mohammad Rezar Delawar, had in fact managed to board the flight as imposters, using the stolen passports of the EU nationals concerned. Now had either Malaysian Airlines or the Malaysian Immigration Officer looked closely at the photographs in the passports and compared them with the passengers, they might have spotted this. Better still, had the Malaysian government deployed e-gate technology at their outbound controls, then the fraud would almost certainly have been detected, given that modern-day biometric facial recognition systems are far better at detecting imposters than the human eye. Best of all, if either the airline or the officer had checked the passport numbers against the Interpol lost and stolen travel document database (LSTD) then they would have known that both these documents had been reported stolen by their rightful holders during a previous holiday in Bangkok, where they had been handed over as security for rental of motorcycles there and never returned.

This was a common scam known very well to those of us who worked in the border security business – if you can get past boarding checks with a fake passport or as an imposter, then you are over the first hurdle towards a passage to the West, where you will be able to claim asylum on arrival. There is a network of small-time villains in the Far East using tactics such as these to acquire genuinely issued valid EU passports, which they then sell on to organised crime groups (OCGs). The OCGs then hold them to sell to people wanting to smuggle themselves into the West, without having to go through the tortuous overland journey to Europe. This meant matching the supply of migrants with the stolen supply of passports to find the best "lookalike", then identifying the path of least resistance through the aviation network, to avoid detection. In this case via Kuala Lumpur and Beijing, where pre-boarding checks were weaker.

As this story broke, I was inundated with enquiries from BBC, ITV, Sky News, and anyone else who could get through to me wanting to know how this had happened. Were they terrorists? Had they blown up the plane? How did they get through security?

Of course, I was no better equipped than anyone else at that time to say what had happened to flight MH370. What I could say – with some confidence – was that it was not uncommon for migrants to try to board flights to the West in order to claim asylum, using lost and stolen passports as "lookalikes". I was able to explain on BBC Breakfast TV that there were about 800 million hits a year against the Interpol LSTD, but it didn't follow that all countries of the world were using it. 250 million of those hits were recorded in the US, and 120 million in the UK. The vast majority of hits were recorded against people who had reported that their passport had been lost or stolen, but had then forgotten to report that they had subsequently found it again. I met a few of them during my own time on the line, and it never ceased to amaze me that they somehow thought it was all my fault that they were being held up pending further checks on their identity.

So it didn't follow that all of these hits were against imposters. Furthermore, although no empirical data was available, I know from previous experience that the UK Border Force International Liaison Officers and airline colleagues around the world had offloaded about 50,000 inbound passengers a year – usually because they were holding improper documents.

Of course, there was no evidence to suggest that Pouria and Delawar were terrorists who had anything to do with the downing of flight MH 370. More likely they were simply migrants wanting to get into Europe with stolen EU passports in the hope of having a better life. Sadly, for them, they picked the wrong flight at the wrong time. But this didn't mean that we could ignore the potential link between inadequate documentary checks upon departure and border security. I knew from previous experience that terrorists had used weaknesses in international border security systems to travel for nefarious reasons in the past, a fact that would soon be evidenced elsewhere.

Not long after this, I was invited to assist the Malaysian government in the introduction of a new IT system for the Immigration Department there. The new system, known as SKIN, was to replace a lot of the outdated legacy systems currently in place at the Malaysian border. My engagement led to meetings with the Minister of Home Affairs, and I subsequently arranged for the Minister and his entourage to visit our National Border Targeting System (NBTC) in the UK. I was always very proud of the UK Border Force and our capabilities, and I know that in many respects we are the envy of the world in this field. I still receive a lot of enquiries from Border Agencies around the world wanting to learn from us, and I work closely with Border Force International to enable them to do so. I did prepare a draft border strategy for the Malaysian government at that time, which I hope has gone some way to help them to overcome some of the challenges they are facing there.

Meanwhile the mystery of what brought down flight MH370 was never solved. Different pieces of wreckage were found some time later far away from where the plane first vanished.

Conspiracy theories continue to abound. And imposters still try to use lost and stolen passports to try and emigrate to the West.

CHAPTER 30

THE EU MIGRANT CRISIS, 2015

Despite the best efforts of my friends in Frontex, 2015 became the year of the "EU migrant crisis". As the year drew on, we saw ever-increasing numbers of migrants crossing the Mediterranean Sea in order to seek refuge in the EU. By November, over one million crossings had been made – a four-fold increase on the previous year. This exodus had been driven partly by the increasing influence of the Islamic State of Iraq and the Levant (ISIL) driving refugees out of Syria into Turkey; and partly by an explosion in organised crime groups engaged in human smuggling from North Africa, and Libya in particular.

Broadcast media had reporters out in the Greek Islands showing scenes of unprecedented numbers of migrant boat arrivals. Sadly, more and more people were drowning, with bodies being washed ashore in Lesbos as the cemetery there became overcrowded. The image of a three-year-old Syrian boy, Alan Kurdi, hit the international media just as I was appearing on Sky News discussing the issue. Public opinion turned on a sixpence.

With a Conservative government having been elected in May 2015 on a ticket to hold a referendum on leaving the European Union, there had been increased rhetoric about "taking back control" of our borders and reducing net migration to the UK. Now it was clear that we had a humanitarian crisis on our hands. The drownings of innocent children had to stop. Surely the EU could not allow this situation to continue unchecked?

On 11 November 2015, EU and African leaders met to discuss what to do about the crisis. I was interviewed on "Good Morning Britain" by Kate Garraway and Susannah Reid. At the time, EU leaders were making public pronouncements about how many refugees they would take. France announced that they would take 24,000, Spain 15,000 and Germany 31,000. David Cameron announced that the UK would take 20,000 directly from refugee camps, over a four-year period. Of course, none of these gestures came anywhere near reaching the numbers arriving at the time. Although public opinion varied between Member States, it was clear that most EU countries were not prepared to open their borders to ever increasing numbers of refugees.

This led to chaotic scenes in the borderless Schengen zone, whilst EU leaders argued with one another. At one stage the Hungarian police surrounded Budapest station to prevent migrants boarding trains for Germany – only to discover hours later that Germany had agreed to allow them through. Similar scenes were recorded in Austria. At the external EU Frontier, Hungary was busily erecting fences to prevent migrants from getting in. There were even scenes of border guards chasing people and tripping them up in an attempt to stop them. I remember vividly chairing a conference in Budapest around this time where the Croatian Border Police gave us a first-hand account of the chaos that ensued there as vast numbers arrived at their border seeking to enter the EU, against patchy directions from Brussels about whether they should be allowed in or not, and on what terms.

I argued at the time that the only way to fix this problem was to work with source and transit countries to (a) control the flows and (b) deliver returns. Anything less would continue to fuel the supply chains feeding the OCGs, and lead to more drownings. Promises of open borders and unlimited uncontrolled migration would not be acceptable to the majority of voters in the EU, with many countries already walking a precarious tightrope with right wing parties gaining momentum by advocating tougher immigration controls.

Something had to give. On 20 March 2016, the EU reached a deal with Turkey to control the number of migrants using the "Eastern Mediterranean" route. Amongst other things, this involved moving migrants away from the Turkish coastline and back to Ankara, where they would be entered into the Turkish asylum system. The EU also agreed to pay Turkey three billion euros to help them manage refugees – a sum later extended by another 485 million euros in 2020, as the deal was extended until 2022. At the same time, any migrants seeking to cross the sea from Turkey to the Greek islands would be returned instantly to Turkey.

The EU-Turkey deal remains fragile to this day, and there is every chance that we will see another migrant crisis in the Eastern Mediterranean in the near future. I warn about this constantly, when asked about the latest migrant crossings to the UK from France. The only way to stop these entirely is to come to an international agreement with France, who should take back migrants immediately and resettle them away from the French coastline for processing in France. But that's another story.

CHAPTER 31

THE PARIS AND BERLIN ATTACKS, 2015-2016

Although migration to the West had become a major incident in 2015, Border Agencies were facing up to another problem which didn't involve the same numbers, but certainly involved the same risk. Arguably a higher risk still.

By the end of 2015, 30,000 foreign fighters were in Syria, fighting for ISIL. They came from all over the world to join the cause: 8,240 from the Middle East, 8,000 from the Maghreb, 5,000 from Western Europe, 4,700 from former Soviet Republics, 900 from South East Asia, 875 from the Balkans, and 280 from North America.

Identifying them at outbound controls was a hugely difficult mission for the Border Agencies. Many of them travelled by circuitous routes and in family groups. Some used the annual pilgrimage to the Hajj in Saudi Arabia as their reason for travelling. Many countries – including the UK and the US – did not have "physical" passport inspections at embarkation and had to rely upon targeted interventions against specific passengers. Given the nature of the business, the targets were primarily Muslim; but it would be unlawful, disproportionate, and unreasonable to target passengers on those grounds alone. The vast majority of Muslim travellers were entirely innocent, and found the activities of ISIL as abhorrent as the rest of the population. Meanwhile, TV and internet pictures showed more and more people being taken hostage and being publicly beheaded by ISIL. We needed to find a way to prevent terrorist travel, a concept that was not entirely alien to me.

On Friday 13 November 2015, just a couple of days after my appearance on "Good Morning Britain" discussing the EU Migrant Crisis, three groups of terrorists carried out multiple attacks in crowded places in Paris, killing 130 people and injuring over 400 more. The story broke on Sky News and I found myself on live television again the following day discussing how this could have happened, and whether there had been a breach of border security either in France or in the wider EU. Evidence was emerging to suggest that the attacks did have an international dimension, with reports of arrests taking place in Brussels and fingerprint checks from one of the terrorist corpses revealing that he had recently entered the EU posing as a Syrian refugee. Although it was early days, I took the view that this was indeed a well-orchestrated and carefully planned attack by a group of international terrorists, who had probably been travelling to Syria to work alongside ISIL and had crossed multiple borders along the way.

As it turned out, of the 12 attackers 10 were suicide bombers and only two survived. The two survivors were Salah Abdeslam and Mohamed Abrini. Abdeslam was a French citizen who had been born in Brussels and was one of the ringleaders who escaped. He lived in the Molenbeek area of Brussels, an area believed to be a high risk for terrorist sympathisers. He was stopped by police near the Belgian border just hours after the attack, and released. He had previous convictions for robbery and had also been arrested by police in Amsterdam in February 2015 for drugs offences. He was a childhood friend of Abrini, a Belgian national who was later identified as the "man in the hat" during the attacks on Brussels airport in March 2016. Like Abdeslam, he also lived in Molenbeek and escaped after the Paris attacks. Abrini is also suspected of having been to Syria to fight for ISIL, and he had visited the UK using his EU passport on more than one occasion. Abdeslam and Abrini are both now serving custodial sentences in Belgium.

Of the 10 attackers that died, at least seven are believed to have travelled to Syria to fight for ISIL and return to the EU undetected. All the attackers were known to the police – some for crime, some for terrorism, some for both. Two of the attackers had been fingerprinted at the Greek border six weeks earlier, posing as refugees in the migrant crisis. And most of the attackers lived in residential areas in Paris and Brussels, known to be breeding grounds for ISL.

I often use the Paris attacks as a comparator when delivering lectures on border security and terrorist travel. Many of the features identified here are similar to those identified 15 years earlier, on 9/11. The fragmented nature of intelligence both within Member States and between them was clearly a symptom of failure, just as it was in the United States. Although there are powers to close Schengen borders in times of crisis, such closures are unlikely to prove effective without adequate and timely sharing of intelligence between the key actors.

Another case I refer to in a similar vein is that of Anis Amri, also known as the "Berlin Christmas bomber". On 19 December 2016 Amri deliberately drove a truck into the Christmas market at Breitscheidplatz in Berlin, killing 12 people and injuring 56 more. He escaped during the confusion, whilst the German police arrested the wrong person. Amri was able to travel by coach from Germany to Holland and Belgium and then by train from France to Italy, without any passport check or search, despite having a handgun in his backpack. He hired a car in Italy and was stopped during a routine check in the middle of the night by police in Milan, whereupon he pulled a gun and was shot dead by an Italian policeman.

For students of border control, Amri's immigration and travel history are disturbing. Despite having a criminal record in his native country of Tunisia, he managed to travel to the Italian island of Lampedusa by life raft in 2011 and pretend to be a minor, by lying about his age. He was sent to a detention centre for temporary migrants, where he led a riot and set the premises on fire. He was convicted of arson and robbery and served four years in prison, but was nonetheless released by the Italian government without deportation in June 2015, because the Tunisian government would not co-operate with his return. He then travelled to Germany via Switzerland as part of the "migrant crisis" and claimed asylum on arrival in Germany in July 2015. He was refused asylum in Germany July 2016, but as they had also been unable to document him for return to Tunisia he was allowed to remain at large. He was known to German police for criminality and had also been placed under surveillance for terrorism by German police. During this time, he had also been arrested in Germany with a false Italian identity card and released.

The case of Amri features almost all the problems we face today in using our immigration powers to mitigate threats to our national security. He should not have been admitted to the temporary migrant centre in the first place, because he was not a minor at all. But he knew full well he would receive more favourable treatment if he could pass himself off as one. Despite committing criminal acts and receiving a four-year custodial sentence in Italy, he managed to avoid deportation back to Tunisia as a foreign national offender (FNO), simply by failing to comply with the documentation process. Having secured his freedom, he was able to travel freely across the borderless Schengen zone as an "asylum seeker" and gain entry to Germany as such, despite his criminal past. Once there he went on to perpetrate more criminal acts and – despite being under observation by the German authorities on both criminal and security grounds – he was once again able to evade deportation by failing to comply with the documentation process, even though he had by now been refused asylum.

There were multiple opportunities for the border and immigration agencies to intervene, but they had taken the path of least resistance. The failure to deport Amri back to Tunisia simply because he would not comply with documentation procedures indirectly led to the deaths of 12 people and the serious injury of 56 others, in the country that had been kind enough to offer him temporary protection in the first place.

I don't know which official had the task of reporting all this to their relevant Minister of State in Germany. I'm just glad it wasn't me. Theresa May would have had my guts for garters.

CHAPTER 32

BREXIT AND "TAKING BACK CONTROL", 2016

As a former Head of the UK Border Force, I suppose it was inevitable that I would be drawn into the debate about Brexit, especially given that I had maintained a very high media profile since my retirement – and had not been afraid to speak out publicly on border and immigration matters. In fact, I was contacted by both the "Leave" and the "Remain" lobbies, keen to get me to speak out publicly in support of their case one way of the other on what would be best for our border, immigration controls and national security. I was not alone there – I know many other former senior civil servants and police officers received similar approaches. Some spoke out, although I did not take up either invitation personally. It was clear that this was going to be a very divisive debate, which would split families, households, and communities in two across the country.

Clearly one of the main arguments behind "vote leave" was immigration. The official migration figures had been creeping up towards record levels. In November 2015, the BBC reported that the annual "net" migration figure (that is the number of people entering the UK against those leaving) had reached 336,000 – the highest total since records began. At the same time, it was reported that asylum intake figures were at their highest level for 12 years. Of the 336,000, more than half (180,000) had arrived from EU countries. The government had pledged to reduce the net migration total from six figures to five – although it wasn't entirely clear how they would do so whilst we remained in the EU. In fact, there were no meaningful immigration controls against EU nationals by now. An EU passport or identity card was just as valuable in securing entry, residency, and entitlement to services as a UK passport. Sometimes more so, in cases of family unification. Nigel Farage was having a field day with this as leader of the UK Independence Party, who swept to victory in the EU elections in 2014, making our presence at the EU Parliament little more than a disruption.

I was never a great fan of ONS immigration figures. I knew too well that they only told half the story. We have never had a comprehensive entry/exit system in this country, even going back to those early days of traffic index and white and yellow cards in Lunar House in the 1970s. There was widespread speculation that the true net migration figure was much greater than this, with suggestions that over a million people were now living here illegally, having either evaded border control altogether or overstayed their conditions of entry. Lots more data was now available on Home Office systems, but nobody knew the real answer. The one issue not in dispute was that we had indeed "lost control" of EU migration. David Cameron's impassioned plea to restore some form of control to us from the EU Commission was met by a brick wall. Freedom of movement was one of the four pillars upon which the EU was built. It was non-negotiable.

As referendum day drew nearer, I found myself becoming ever closer to Brexit commentators and politicians. This was a new phenomenon for me. As a lifelong civil servant, I had been fiercely apolitical. I had met a few MPs in my time, but I had never been particularly close to any of them. However, this changed after I retired. I wanted to give something back to my community in Sutton, and became involved in local community groups including things like Neighbourhood Watch and Safer Neighbourhood Team ward panels. I had always been a big fan of community policing and it was pretty clear that the local police needed all the help they could get from the public. In the course of this experience, I found myself volunteering to chair the local police ward panel in Sutton, which also comprised three ward councillors – two Liberal Democrats and one Conservative.

The Conservative was Tony Shields – a retired fireman who was (like me) not backward in coming forward, and later became a good friend. After one meeting Tony promptly whisked me off to the local Conservative Club to meet a few people and share a few beers – and that was that. My affiliation to the Conservative and Unionist Party was sealed over several pints of lager and a few war stories. I had found a new social outlet and a new direction in my life, which was very much needed at the time.

I started to pop into the Conservative Party office in Sutton during my down time to help with local leaflets, canvassing and the like. The Conservatives were being outdone by the Liberal Democrats in Sutton at the time, both at national level and at local level. The immediate target was the 2014 council elections; the next one was the 2015 General Election. I was invited to stand as a local councillor in Carshalton South and Clockhouse, alongside Moira Butt and Tim Crowley, who were already Conservative councillors in that ward. After a very long night at the Westcroft Community Centre in Wallington I found that I had failed by about 100 votes to secure my seat. What was more, the entire Conservative team had been wiped out, winning only nine seats of a possible 54.

Having had some involvement in the election's planning, it did strike me as chaotic and ill co-ordinated compared with the

Lib Dems. Whilst they seemed to have a well-oiled campaign team, we seemed to be all over the place – running around like headless chickens. Many of these wards were marginal. The key was to target our voters and get them out to vote on the day. We had failed to do that in spectacular style. As the beers went down in the post-mortem in All Bar One in Sutton, I let my feelings be known to the remaining councillor group and to the parliamentary candidate for the 2015 election, Paul Scully.

Before I knew it I was drafted into Paul's inner team, establishing a new command structure, and writing a campaign strategy to get him elected as the MP for Sutton and Cheam. In the course of all this I ran into a few senior Conservatives who remembered me from my time in government service, including Boris Johnson and Theresa May. Indeed, Theresa turned up at a Conservative dinner I attended, and upon seeing me said that she would have to change her speech now she knew I was in the room!

Against all the odds Paul Scully was returned as MP for Sutton and Cheam in 2015, with a 5.6% swing against Paul Burstow, the Liberal Democrat incumbent. Of course, this wasn't all down to me – Paul had a huge team supporting him at the time. But he was generous enough to give me significant credit for his victory at the celebration party. My relationship with Sutton Conservatives continued thereafter, and I helped them overcome some internal problems in the Federation with Carshalton and Wallington – and provided similar support to a young man called Elliot Colburn, who managed to unseat Tom Brake in the 2020 General Election, also against the odds. I have remained good friends with both Paul and Elliot to this day.

Paul was a keen Brexiteer from the start, and he had developed a close working relationship with Boris Johnson, who was leading the "Leave" Campaign. Boris came to Sutton on a number of occasions to present his case, which I thought was well made. I had personal experience of working with the EU institutions, and I did have some concerns that there was a significant and powerful drive there for political union which would – if left unchecked – undermine the sovereignty of Parliament. I also had some concerns that many of the immigration policies that successive EU governments tried to introduce were being undermined by extensions to EU law, often driven by judicial overreach in the European Court of Justice and the European Court of Human Rights. I was never anti-immigration "per se", but I was a strong advocate that immigration and border controls should be controlled in accordance with laws passed by the British Government, and not pervaded by case law made in Strasbourg or Luxembourg. Similarly, UK immigration policy and practice should be determined in Whitehall and Westminster, and not in Brussels.

That said, I knew that our relationships with EU Member States – and France in particular – were critical to the future of UK border control. We had agreed a great many bilateral treaties with our French colleagues going back decades, and it was important that these would be preserved after Brexit. The last thing we needed was another massive asylum influx from France, as we had seen in 2001. The only way to guarantee that this would be prevented was to ensure that we retained our juxtaposed controls in France.

Why so? Well, because Border Control can be described as a game of trumps. The starting point is that you can't come in without a proper passport and permit to do so. If you try to do that, you will be sent straight back whence you came. Likewise, if you do manage to enter illegally then you will be arrested and sent back either to your own country, or the country you arrived from, or some other country where you may be acceptable. These were the rules that I cut my teeth on back in the day.

However, your trump card is to find a way to get here, and then either claim asylum or human rights on arrival. Asylum and HR claims trump border control. You can't be sent back until your case has been fully considered – away from the border. Meanwhile, you will be allowed in temporarily and provided with accommodation and maintenance if you don't have any of your own. Once here there are a myriad of options available to you to prolong your stay, often to the point of no return. Indeed, some advocates argue that any person arriving at the UK border – no matter how – should be given a path to British citizenship. In other words, we should open our borders to the world and allow unfettered access to everybody. In over 40 years' service, I never once worked for a government of any colour that advocated such a thing. Indeed, most favoured stronger controls, rather than weaker ones.

So how do we trump this? Simply by keeping people out of the jurisdiction. If they can't get here, they can't claim asylum or human rights here. We demand that all passports and papers are inspected before passengers are allowed to board flights to the UK. Any airline bringing an inadequately documented arrival (IDA) to the UK would be fined £2000 per passenger. We demand that all lorry drivers check their load before boarding ferries to come here. Any driver failing to do so would also receive a substantial fine, should illegal immigrants be found in his vehicle. Plus, we operate our border controls before arrival wherever we can. Which includes at the juxtaposed controls in France. Therefore, it was imperative that our agreements with France survived Brexit. But would they?

I was approached by the BBC to spend a day with them in Dover, to discuss all this. After much procrastination on my part, they were able to establish that I was a Brexiteer. They wanted to film me with a Remainer – and to hold the conversation at sea with the White Cliffs of Dover in the background. As it turned out, the "Remainer" in question was none other than Charlie Elphicke, who was the MP for Dover at that time. As the elected representative for Dover, Charlie's main concern was indeed that the juxtaposed controls would be withdrawn after Brexit –

and this would lead to a repetition of the catastrophic scenes of 2001, with thousands of asylum seekers arriving on the ferries and flooding into the town.

After an extended interview on the topic, we exchanged business cards and Charlie asked me if I could help him with a paper he planned to write called "Ready on Day One". Despite being a Remainer, he took the view that there was a very strong chance that the country would vote leave – and if they did, the impact upon Dover and Kent more widely would be massive.

Around the same time, I was invited on another "media boat show" by Nick Ferrari, from LBC radio. Nick had interviewed me on several occasions during his breakfast radio show and wanted to do a podcast on UK border control after Brexit. They hired a launch and we set out from Dover harbour one sunny afternoon to discuss all this. One area that Nick was keen to point out to me was the risk that illegal immigrants could get round our border controls by crossing the Channel from France. He took me to various inlets and coves along the Kent coastline to demonstrate the point.

I told him that although this had appeared on our risk register over the years, we had never considered it to be a viable option. The vast majority of illegal entrants entering the UK were still concealing themselves in the backs of lorries. Apart from a few episodes of drug smuggling by OCGs, we had seen very little human smuggling across the English Channel. Indeed, we had taken advice from the Coastguard on this and had been assured that these waters were far too dangerous for that. These were busy shipping lanes with fierce cross currents and any attempt to cross in this manner would be foolhardy.

Famous last words. Little did we know what was to come.

After the referendum, chaos ensued in Westminster. Nobody at the heart of government thought this would happen. David Cameron felt he had no choice but to resign as Prime Minister, having instigated the referendum in the first place, and then led the "Remain" campaign against his old friend Boris Johnson. A new government was formed by my old boss Theresa May.

Similar chaos ensued in Whitehall. The UK Civil Service is an incredible institution full of highly talented individuals, but it is apolitical and as such struggles to make policy without a very clear steer from the government of the day, which was fiercely divided between a "soft" and a "hard" Brexit. There was talk of a variety of models, including membership of the EU Customs Union or the European Economic Area, but whichever model we chose, there would remain a strong EU influence over Westminster. That was something that the more ardent Brexiteers were not prepared to accept.

One reason put forward after the referendum for reversing the decision was the impact upon borders. This had been a major theme of the "remain" campaign. I was amazed at the sheer number of "border experts" that suddenly emerged on the scene, advocating that we would be unable to effectively keep our borders moving if we ended free movement of people and goods. Most of them had never worked in border control in their lives.

Whilst there was no doubt in my mind that the Border Force, HMRC and others would face significant challenges in ending free movement at the border, I did not believe that these were insurmountable. Save perhaps for Customs Controls in Northern Ireland, where a storm was brewing. I had voted to join the European Economic Community in the 1970s and it certainly had no immediate impact upon immigration controls from EU countries at the time. Assuming we maintained the Common Travel Area between the UK and Ireland – and Ireland retained the Schengen opt out – I did not foresee any major problem with people movements, although we would need a new Immigration Act to enable us to equalise controls between EU and non-EU citizens. What I didn't see coming was the Customs challenges, particularly if the UK (and Northern Ireland) were to diverge from EU Customs policy. But more of that later.

Charlie Elphicke wasted no time in enlisting my help for his "Ready on Day One" paper. He was indeed ahead of his time. He envisaged an immediate need for a huge investment in infrastructure in Kent to cope with Brexit. There was no room at the foot of the cliffs in Dover to conduct all of the Customs checks that would arise from Brexit. This was a "Ro-Ro" port where lorries full of EU produce literally "rolled off" the ferries and onto the M2 and M20 motorways, without stopping. Although we had powers to stop and search any vehicle arriving at Dover for contraband or dangerous and prohibited goods, we did not require any customs declarations from them – and we did not need to perform regulatory checks. In order to do this, we would need new Border Inspection Posts (BIPs) away from the port where further checks could be conducted. We also needed urgent work to widen the motorways serving the port – and (potentially) a new Thames Crossing to cater for goods heading to the North of England and beyond.

Charlie set up an All-Party Parliamentary Group (APPG) on this and even invited Xavier Bertrand and others from the regional council of Hauts de France to discuss how we might implement it. I found Monsieur Bertrand to be extremely collaborative and helpful throughout this exercise. He was pragmatic about Brexit and keen to clean up the Pas de Calais and the Hauts de France region by dismantling the criminal gangs and building new trade powerhouses to facilitate British investment in the region, where companies could still benefit from the Single Market. This gave me some hope that we could come to an accommodation with our friends and neighbours in France about dual management of our common border, notwithstanding the ending of free movement between us.

Unfortunately, Charlie's enthusiasm for government investment in his plan fell on stony ground with the Treasury. Although HMRC had set up a Border Policy Delivery Group (BPDG) to manage the post-Brexit border, it was pretty clear that the government of the day was not prepared to invest in major infrastructure projects such as this. His paper slipped off the radar. Sadly, Charlie also had personal issues of his own which eventually led to his losing the Whip and subsequent deselection. But despite all that I still applaud his vision, which would eventually start to take shape some years later.

CHAPTER 33

NEOM, A NEW WORLD WITHIN A KINGDOM – 2017

Although I was by now spending a good deal of my time wrestling with the various permutations that might emerge at the UK Border after Brexit, I had not taken my eye off the ball on the global borders picture. I attended many border conferences around the world, from Texas to Istanbul, from Brussels to Singapore, and from London to New Delhi, to keep abreast of border developments further afield.

One experience that stands out in my memory was an invitation to attend a "round table" event with other international Border Experts in Dubai, to discuss the creation of NEOM, a scheme for a vast development in the north-western corner of Saudi Arabia.

This came completely out of the blue. I had never heard of NEOM and had no real idea about what would be expected of me, but I knew that I could hold my own anywhere in the world if the subject matter was about future borders (far less so if it was about anything else). But having received assurances that this was indeed the case, I boarded a flight to Dubai to attend the event. Sadly for me, I somehow managed to lose my voice altogether en route, and there was a time on the eve of the event where I wondered if I would be able to speak at all. Which would be unfortunate, given that I was to deliver a presentation on border security there. In the end the hotel staff worked wonders with cocktails of honey and lemon, and all was well.

Although the event was held in Dubai, it was hosted by a senior official from the Kingdom of Saudi Arabia (KSA) where the NEOM project would be built. The ambition was to transform KSA into a vibrant society with a thriving economy. This would involve establishing three cities that would be recognised in the top 100 cities globally; increasing average life expectancy from 74 to 80; increasing spending on culture and entertainment from 2.9% to 6% of GDP; increasing private sector contributions from 40% to 65%; increasing rankings from #25 to #10 in the Global Competitiveness Index; and increasing non-oil government revenue from $43 billion to $270 billion. In order to do all this, a new "region" called NEOM would be built in the North West corner of the country covering an area of 26,500 square kilometres – 37 times the size of Singapore and 6 times the size of Dubai. This would be a pristine environment with rich marine ecology, world class regulation for people and businesses, committed new leadership and – wait for it – its own border management and security system.

Now I had visited Saudi Arabia a couple of times during my career and whilst some parts of it are very plush and well presented, others are not. As a tourist destination, it certainly didn't match up to Dubai or other parts of the region. Nonetheless it was clear that the Saudi government were serious about it, and they had already invested a good deal of money to set the ball rolling.

We were ushered into a lavish conference room full of cushions and sofas placed strategically in a circle, whereupon we were provided with the vision for NEOM.

My presentation focused mainly upon the areas I have covered in this book – the need for an overarching border strategy, the guiding principles of modern-day border management, and the options to introduce technology to manage immigration, customs, and security. It was clear to me that there were several large corporations involved in the project, but success or failure would ultimately depend upon a clear and consistent strategy, a properly resourced programme plan, a very clear scope and desired outcome, and strong consistent governance and leadership.

One thing that struck me at the workshop was their interest in innovation and technology. It was clear that the vision to build NEOM was a powerful one, to support external investment in Saudi Arabia as part of the plan for long-term economic growth in the region. However, apart from my involvement in this one-day workshop I never heard any more about it. This was often the case in my life as a global border security consultant. I would be whisked off to some far-flung place and placed in front of an audience to talk about borders, and that would be that. Whether NEOM ever becomes a reality or not is another thing. But sometimes it's good to dream of a better future somewhere in the world, for all of us to aspire to. And it was a welcome distraction from ongoing border-related problems at home.

CHAPTER 34

THE WINDRUSH
SCANDAL, 2018

Although I had by now been out of the Home Office for some time, I still had several friends and former colleagues in the Department, and a good idea of what was going on there.

Even before I retired, I had expressed some concerns that the cuts we were facing – and the consequential "ventilation" of a large number of long serving immigration officers from the business – could lead to a loss of corporate memory and knowledge of critical issues. Many of which are reflected in the early chapters of this book, as to how and when UK immigration controls were introduced and to what cohorts of immigrants.

The creation of the concept of "right of abode" in the UK and the development of UK citizenship laws following the introduction of the Immigration Act 1971, which came into force shortly after I joined the Department all those years ago, had become lost on the next generation of caseworkers. They had not been subject to the same extensive levels of training that I had when I joined. Knowledge and experience of the business lost its place in the pecking order, particularly in the upper levels of the Department, where voices were more likely to be heard.

We knew very well about the British Nationality Act 1948, and the rights it conferred upon Commonwealth citizens to emigrate to the UK. We also knew that a great many Commonwealth Immigrants were admitted after that, with no records being kept as to their date and place of entry, and that essentially any Commonwealth citizen who had entered the UK prior to 1 January 1973 was exempt from deportation.

I was also convinced that the extension of the "hostile environment" in 2013 – just as I was retiring – would lead to problems for some people who were residing lawfully in the UK but had no passport or permit to prove it. The fact that there was no record of them at the Home Office Immigration Department did not mean that they were in the UK unlawfully. Instead of introducing a National Identity Register when we had the chance in 2010, we had moved ahead with a policy that required employers and landlords to "check immigration status" and "copy documents", even though some people might not have them. I don't think this was a deliberate policy to harm people who had the right to live here; it was simply naïve of the policymakers behind it to ignore the possibility that this might happen. Employers and landlords were always going to err on the side of caution. If the person being checked could not produce the required documents shown on Home Office lists A and B – which were themselves riddled with complexities – then they were out. Worse still, when referred to Home Office caseworkers who really should know better, they were served with deportation notices rather than the residence permits to which they were entitled.

I watched aghast as a spat developed across the floor of the House of Commons over who had authorised the destruction of landing cards at the Home Office. The blame game was on. In response to a question from the leader of the opposition, the Prime Minister reported that the landing cards had been destroyed by the Labour government of 2009, and not the coalition government of 2010 – the implication being that Windrush would never have happened if the landing cards hadn't been destroyed.

I spoke to John Humphries on BBC Radio 4 the following morning to set the record straight. Landing cards were not taken from Commonwealth citizens prior to 1 January 1973; they were taken only from aliens. Thereafter some landing cards were retained and copied onto microfilm – but not all of them. The presence or absence of a landing card at the Home Office did not of itself clarify lawful or unlawful presence in the UK. Furthermore, it was not the landing cards that were destroyed in 2009. It was the old registry slips that indicated the existence of a Home Office file. Given that legacy Home Office files were now stored in a warehouse run by "Iron Mountain" – which I knew well, having been there myself – there was little need for retaining the old slips. They would not confirm lawful status either. In fact, the only Home Office records that would confirm lawful status were UK passport records, Home Office files or Biometric Residence Permits (BRPs) that were only issued to non-EU migrants after 2008 (against my advice at the time, as stated earlier).

In my view, the principal reason for the Windrush disaster was a lack of corporate memory, knowledge and experience of immigration law, history, and practice; coupled with an attempt to build a "hostile environment" for illegal immigrants without a national identity register to back it up. I was never approached or interviewed by Wendy Williams, who was given the task of investigating and reporting all this. Having read her report, I think it is a balanced and fair reflection of the facts. I did however take issue with some of the reporting by other journalists that Windrush was a deliberate act by a racially motivated Department. It was not.

There is no doubt that the Immigration Service I joined in the 1970s was politically incorrect in its culture and its behaviour. Calling inadmissible passengers "duffers" and headhunting refusals and removals was wrong. We were not alone in such things. The police and other enforcement agencies of that era – and even wider society – had a long way to go in developing values in public service.

But we weren't racists. As I said earlier, most of my refusals at Heathrow were white Europeans, because that was the nature of the traffic. At Terminal 3 it was more likely to be Asians. At Gatwick, Africans. Checks were not based on the colour of the skin, but on the nature of the passport and the entitlements contained therein, and by examination of the facts and the evidence. The same applied to Immigration Enforcement. Both the UK Border Force and Immigration Enforcement have been enriched by the diversity of their respective workforces. The suggestion that they are institutionally racist is simply not true.

However, the Home Office needs to think long and hard about its recruitment, retention, and training policies in the complex area of immigration at all levels if it is to avoid another Windrush disaster. Starting with the implementation of a national digital identity register which enables every person lawfully residing in the UK to prove it simply and easily, without any fear of being sacked, evicted, arrested, or deported from the country.

CHAPTER 35

ALTERNATIVE ARRANGEMENTS FOR THE IRISH BORDER, 2019

Meanwhile, back home the UK government was continuing to struggle with the repercussions of Brexit. Theresa May knew this would be the most difficult aspect of her tenure as Prime Minister. She said so many times. What did Brexit mean? It meant Brexit. How would we deliver it? Through strong and stable government. Was the government strong and stable? Er…

On 8 June 2017, the Conservative government decided to go to the polls. The odds were in their favour. Polling in April and May showed them significantly ahead of Labour with leads well into double figures and rising to 20% on some occasions. However, as polling day approached, the gap narrowed. Some polls were even predicting a swing to Labour, and a hung Parliament. Hardly the "strong and stable" government required to deliver Brexit, especially with widespread division within the Conservative party itself on the matter. I was out canvassing in Sutton and could see that our support was wavering on the doorstep – not least fuelled by a policy announcement from

CCHQ about funding social care for the elderly. This hit a sour note with many elderly Conservative voters, who felt social care should be provided by the government for those who had served the country in the past. It was a classic own goal.

In the end Labour gained 30 seats, the Lib Dems gained four seats and the DUP gained two, with the Conservatives losing 13 and the SNP 21. This meant that the Conservatives could only govern effectively with the support of the DUP. An agreement was reached, and a government was formed. But it was far from strong and stable.

The majority of people in Northern Ireland had in fact voted to remain in the EU, as had the majority of people of Scotland. They had been outvoted by majorities in England and Wales. However, this put much greater pressure on the Union than had previously been the case. Despite the arguments about EU membership, one thing that it had delivered was unity between the four nations of the UK and the Republic of Ireland behind the European project. This raised questions as to whether the United Kingdom could survive all this. Obviously, the DUP and the Conservative (and Unionist) Party were committed that it should do so, but Brexit had left the island of Ireland with a huge headache. How could Northern Ireland (as part of a United Kingdom) manage the land border with the Republic of Ireland (as part of the European Union) without introducing border controls there?

Now I am not an expert in the history of the Irish Border, but I did know that the peace agreement established on Good Friday 1998 had managed to overcome the "troubles" there for over 20 years. The mere mention of the word "border" in Northern Ireland conjures up painful memories for the communities living there. Yet here we were in the midst of a debate as to how the UK (and Northern Ireland) could possibly leave the EU without introducing border controls on the island of Ireland, at least for customs and trade purposes, if not for people.

I had by now become co-chair of the International Summit on Borders with my good friend and former CBP Commissioner Judge Rob Bonner. Rob was in fact the first ever Commissioner for US Customs and Border Protection, and we first met whilst I was working in Canada on the post 9/11 "Hands Across the Border" project. Like me, Rob had "stayed in the game" after his retirement and each year we would jointly host the Summit, which comprised of expert panels from border experts around the world to discuss topical matters of the day.

At one of the planning meetings we agreed that we should really look at the post-Brexit Irish border as a case study, and assemble a group of experts to discuss it at our next event. It didn't take us long to identify Dr Katy Hayward of Queens University Belfast as an expert commentator on the Irish Border. I contacted Katy, and she kindly agreed to participate in our event in Washington DC the following year. What's more, she invited me to attend an event she was hosting at Queens on that very topic, alongside a couple of other prominent speakers – Shanker Singham, who was an international trade expert and had been providing advice to the European Research Group on Brexit, and Lars Karlsson, a former Head of Swedish Customs and the World Customs Organisation, and also a member of the Advisory Board to the Summit.

Most of my presentation was restricted to the ongoing free movement of people within the Common Travel Area of The United Kingdom, Ireland and the Channel Islands notwithstanding Brexit. Although there were some concerns that the Irish authorities had overstepped the mark by checking passports on trains and buses going across the border into Ireland, this was not hugely contentious. On the other hand, Shanker spoke about customs and trade issues and regulatory options, which were significantly more controversial. Although I wasn't aware of it at the time, Shanker had been working with several parliamentarians on various permutations for border checks on goods moving between the UK and the EU after Brexit. One proposal was that a "backstop" could be placed on the internal UK border between Great Britain and Northern Ireland. This would avoid the need for physical checks and infrastructure on the Irish land border– unless or until "alternative arrangements" could be found. This idea had of course offended the Democratic Unionist Party (DUP), who were opposed to any form of border control between Northern Ireland and the rest of the United Kingdom. And after all, the DUP were propping up the Conservative government at the time.

Under the joint chairmanship of Greg Hands MP and Nicky Morgan MP, a Parliamentary Commission was formed to look into the concept of "Alternative Arrangements" in more detail. What were they? How would they work in practice? Could they replace the "backstop"?

Shanker was invited to form an "expert panel" to look into the possibility of "Alternative Arrangements" in more detail, and to report back to the Commission. He rang me one afternoon to ask if I would be interested in joining the panel. I pointed out that most of my experience was on the "people movement" and "border security" side of the house. I did have some knowledge of intelligence-led targeting for prohibited and dangerous goods, anti-terrorism, anti-smuggling, and customs controls, but I was not an expert in the finer detail of regulatory checks or checks on products of animal and plant origin and the like. Nonetheless we agreed that my areas of expertise would add value to the project – and that was that.

This led to a series of meetings, visits, and roadshows across Northern Ireland where we met a large number of community and business groups to discuss the challenge and potential solutions to it. It was clear that there was already a huge amount of good work being done there by people much closer to the problem than we were. Some (understandably) questioned why we were there at all – surely this was a local matter, and something that required a local solution? Many saw us as instruments of the Westminster government, who could never really fully grasp the reality of the problem there.

Although we met a great many experts on our travels, there was also a lack of understanding or knowledge about the implications of Brexit upon the Irish Border. It had already been agreed by both sides that the Good Friday Agreement and the Common Travel Area would prevail. Yet many people we spoke to in the border communities were convinced that they would now need a passport to cross into Ireland and back to get their shopping – or worse still, they would be subjected to questioning by an officer in uniform at a control post there. These were of course complete red lines to both sides, but either government outreach and communications had not accessed these groups - or they simply hadn't been believed.

In addition to our road trips to Northern Ireland we also attended meetings in Dublin, Westminster, and Brussels to talk about Alternative Arrangements for the Irish Border. The result of our work was an extensive report and two draft protocols, which proposed an alternative to the backstop through a combination of trusted trader/AEO+ schemes, technology, and checks away from the border at points of loading and unloading. Many of these measures were described by our opponents as "unicorns", but I already had first-hand experience of border technology systems that were capable of tracking a packet of fish from Paris through London and Liverpool to Belfast and Dublin without any need for physical checks and infrastructure at the border. Indeed, border controls were developing rapidly all over the world towards seamless travel and trade. I was convinced that regardless of the outcome in Ireland, other land borders around the world would be adopting these arrangements in years to come.

Although our report was widely heralded by the government at the time as a potential solution – and even shared with EU negotiators – it took a separate agreement between Boris Johnson and Leo Varadkar to achieve the breakthrough via the "Northern Ireland Protocol" which determines via a Joint Committee which goods will require Customs Declarations based on "risk".

It is fair to say that work is still progressing on this model. But the ambition is to enable Northern Ireland businesses to continue to enjoy "unfettered access" to the rest of the UK market; whereas goods moving from Great Britain to Northern Ireland will require declarations and inspections, in specific circumstances. Our work on "Alternative Arrangements" was consigned to history – but working on it was an experience I shall never forget, and another milestone on my remarkable borders journey.

CHAPTER 36

TURNING THE TIDE ON MIGRANT BOATS

Having told Nick Ferrari on LBC some years earlier that it was highly unlikely that we would see illegal migrants crossing the English Channel by boat, imagine my surprise when the first boats started to arrive on the Kent coastline in 2017. Between January 2018 and June 2020, the figures rose to 4,600. In all 8,000 made the crossing in 2020. On 7 August 2020, a total of 235 arrived on 17 vessels in one day alone. By mid-2021, figures had risen to around 500 per day in fair weather conditions.

I was a frequent commentator on BBC Radio Kent and was frequently asked about this issue. I had to say hand on heart that irregular migration by sea had not been an issue during my time in the UK Border Force, and that we had not seen this coming. Yes, we were frequently playing cat and mouse with the human smugglers on the French side, and had been for over 20 years. But in my time the favoured method of travel was concealment in vehicles. Clandestine entry by small boats was rarely seen.

In some respects, we had become victims of our own success.

By plugging the gap in our defences at the French ports, we had disrupted the smuggling gangs and reduced the numbers of successful concealments in vehicles to the point where they were resorting to more desperate measures. They knew that there was a never-ending supply of migrants in Europe who were desperate to get into the UK, and would pay well for the opportunity. They also had no regard for human life – they only cared about the money. In order to evade our security checks at the French ports, they had taken to the beaches and small boats – many unseaworthy – to pursue their mission. The illegal migration stories were compounded in October 2019 when 39 Vietnamese migrants were found dead in a trailer at Tilbury, having suffocated at the hands of human smugglers.

I wrote about this in various media channels, and gave oral and written evidence to the Home Affairs Select Committee. There was a good deal we could learn from the history of human smuggling into the UK, and how we had sought to manage it in the past. Through my experience in international border security, I also knew that there was a lot we could learn from other countries – notably the EU migrant crisis of 2015 (described above) and Operation Sovereign Borders in Australia.

I told the Committee that those who had said that these waters were too difficult to navigate in unseaworthy vessels had been proved wrong. We had seen arrivals in all forms of makeshift craft, even inflatables and canoes. So how could we turn the tide, and stem these illegal flows?

This is a complex problem. There are significant challenges raised by international law, including the 1951 Refugee Convention, the 1951 European Convention on Human Rights, the UN Convention on the Law of the Sea (UNCLOS), the Convention for Safety of Life at Sea (COLAS), and the Convention on Maritime Search and Rescue (SAR). Following media reports that French vessels were "escorting" migrant boats into British waters in May 2020, the Home Secretary announced that she would change the law to close the Channel loophole. But any change in international law would need international agreement, unless we could negotiate a bilateral agreement with France – which we had done many times in the past.

The UN Convention on the Law of the Sea encourages neighbouring states to establish regional arrangements for search and rescue at sea. Examples include joint patrol vessels, and the placement of officials from one jurisdiction on board the vessel of another. So, there is no reason in international law why the British and French governments could not introduce joint search and rescue patrols. They would have to meet the requirements on International Law; but – crucially – refugees and asylum seekers can be taken to any place where there is no risk of their life or freedom being threatened in accordance with Article 33(1) of the Refugee Convention, on the principle of "non-refoulement". In other words, not sending people back where they came from if they were likely to be persecuted there. So subject to mutual agreement, we could establish an integrated UK/French border patrol to rescue migrants at sea and bring them to a place of safety. As both countries are signatories to the 1951 Convention, that could be to a port on either side and not necessarily to the country whose vessel happens to rescue them.

Of course, this needed a political agreement with France. Some may say this is not achievable. Maybe not. But in 2002 the total UK asylum intake figure rose to over 100,000, with the vast majority arriving from France. To stem the flows, the UK and France agreed a bilateral Treaty (Le Touquet) to establish "juxtaposed controls" whereby officers would conduct passport inspections prior to boarding ferries. As these inspections were "extra territorial", asylum claims were excluded. This led to a far harsher reduction of asylum claims from France than the numbers we see on the migrant boats today. In my experience, successive French governments have been prepared to work with UK border enforcement agencies to disrupt and deter irregular migration on the cross-Channel routes. They don't like human smugglers any more than we do. This suggested that there was scope for further bilateral agreement to counteract the maritime threat.

Some ardent "remainers" argued that this was all a symptom of Brexit. If we had stayed in the EU then we would have been able to remove many of the migrants back to France for asylum processing under the Dublin Convention, which was designed to prevent "asylum shopping" in different EU countries. As a non-EU country, the UK was no longer part of the Dublin agreement and had therefore lost the capacity to deliver 'safe third country' returns to the EU. This argument carried only minimal weight, in my view. To return an asylum seeker to another Member State under Dublin, the receiving state had to prove that an asylum claim had already been made in the other state, or that they had entered the EU there. Although the migrants had clearly come from France, it was highly unlikely that they had entered the EU there. More likely they had crossed via the Balkans, or the Mediterranean route, and then made their way to France through the borderless Schengen zone. Given that nearly all migrants are undocumented on arrival, this evidence was rarely available, which accounts to a great extent for our very low returns rate under the Convention when we were still a party to it. In fact, the UK took more asylum seekers back under Dublin from other EU countries – mainly Ireland – than they returned. As the UK had now departed the EU, it would no longer be a party to the Dublin Convention anyway. A new "safe third" agreement with France and the wider EU was needed.

There will always be migrants in France who want to come to the UK. Some may have legitimate reasons for doing so – for example those with family connections here. To meet this demand, the UK government could offer a legitimate migratory route to the UK for specific categories of persons through our Embassies in Europe. But I resisted the argument put forward by many that we should open asylum application centres in Calais. This would simply fuel the human smuggling supply chains, and bring more migrants to the Hauts de France region. Furthermore, there was nothing to suggest that those who applied and failed would give up. More likely they would attempt the crossing anyway.

A much better arrangement would be to replicate the EU-Turkey agreement and to return the migrants to other cities in the EU where they could be properly processed through established EU asylum centres. This would also require EU agreement. But the only real answer to the problem was to stop the boats. And if we couldn't do that, to return the migrants immediately to France for processing. Anything less would continue to fuel the smuggling supply chains – and more lives would be lost.

Of course, my publicly stated position on this didn't land well with human rights activists and lawyers who were quick to call me ignorant, or racist, or both. They argued that everyone had a right to claim asylum or human rights at the border, under the 1951 Conventions, regardless of whence they came. Something the UK government is now seeking to change with the introduction of the Nationality and Borders Bill 2021.

As I have said many times before, I am not "anti-immigration" – and I am certainly not a racist. In my experience, immigration is broadly acceptable to most people, provided that it is "controlled". Clearly what we were seeing on the English Channel was "uncontrolled" migration, with the human smugglers getting the upper hand. If left unchecked, this would fuel community tensions similar to those we had witnessed during the asylum influx of 2001-2002. Many more people would drown. And the Home Office Immigration Department would be overwhelmed again.

There is certainly a global debate to be had about legal resettlement routes. The frustration of the UNHCR and refugee lobby is palpable. By refusing to open legitimate resettlement programmes for those displaced in source and transit countries, the Western world is simply encouraging more irregular migration across multiple borders. This has been demonstrated most recently by the rush of Afghan nationals seeking to flee the Taliban, and the chaotic scenes at Kabul Airport.

According to UNHCR there were 79.5 million forcibly displaced people in the world at the end of 2019, and 33.8 million of them were displaced outside their country of origin. Of these, 39% were hosted in five countries: Turkey (3.6 million), Colombia (1.8 million), Pakistan (1.4 million), Uganda (1.4 million) and Germany (1.1 million). Hundreds of thousands are in other countries close to unstable states, such as Iran and Ethiopia.

Meanwhile, despite pleas from UNHCR, the Western world has consistently reduced its contribution to refugee resettlement schemes. In 2019 countries previously renowned for a more generous approach to refugee resettlement reduced the numbers to a trickle. Of UNHCR submissions made to destination countries, 5774 came to the UK, the third highest behind the USA (21,159) and Canada (9,031) and higher than any other EU Member State.

Some commentators argue that other EU countries have a more generous approach to refugees than the UK does. It is true that some EU countries receive a greater number of asylum applications than the UK. According to figures released by the European Parliament the top five EU countries receiving the highest number of applications in 2019 were Germany (165,615), France (128,940), Spain (117,795) Greece (77,275), and the UK (44,835). In fact, the number of asylum applications in mainland EU countries far exceeds their political will to accept refugees. They have no choice, because the external EU border is porous and a great many irregular migrants have managed to penetrate it. Like us, they struggle to enforce failed asylum seeker (FAS) returns. Many applicants who do not qualify to stay in one Member State simply stay there without permission, or travel to another, encouraged by the borderless Schengen zone. Others will drift north and lodge asylum applications in those countries they see as more attractive (eg Germany and France).

Because the UK is not (and never was) in the Schengen zone, the final hurdle is the English Channel, and how to penetrate that. Given enforcement measures by successive governments of all colours they have found it ever more difficult to do so – at least until they discovered this latest loophole of getting out onto the waters and getting "rescued" by a British vessel.

These figures show that the UK is not as "unwelcoming" to refugees as some commentators argue. In terms of "regular" routes we are the third highest in the world, and the highest in Europe. In terms of "irregular" routes we are only fifth in the EU, and higher than Italy and Sweden.

Although the UK does provide a generous reception system for accommodating and supporting asylum seekers during the application process, this is less so once status has been granted. Under the Canadian system, Provinces are provided with specific funding from central government under the "settlement allocation model", to support refugees with language training and integration into local communities. This could form part of a new UK asylum and refugee strategy, although no UK government could go too far along this road until they had clearly demonstrated to the public that they had "taken back control" of irregular routes in the first place.

At the time of writing, the UK government is about to bring forward a new Immigration and Borders Bill which will try to address this problem by distinguishing those who arrive from "safe third countries" (such as France) from those who seek resettlement through legitimate routes (such as the Syrian project). The former will be returned immediately to pursue their applications elsewhere, or failing that, will be given a less generous temporary status, whereas the latter will be given automatic indefinite leave to remain on arrival. I have publicly supported these measures and will continue to do so, but I am sure the passage of this Bill through Parliament and particularly through the House of Lords will be a painful one, as the government struggles to resolve the conflict between national and international law in "taking back control" of our borders.

CHAPTER 37

Protecting public health – the COVID pandemic and border control, 2021

If I thought I had a tricky time during my career in the Home Office, I often spare a thought for my successors. Having already been hit hard by two major events – Brexit and the Channel migrant boats – along came COVID-19.

As the COVID pandemic raged across the UK in 2020, causing untold damage, a day rarely went by without me receiving a call from UK broadcast media asking me for my thoughts on COVID and the UK border. Why didn't we close the border earlier? Why are we doing it now? How will the Border Force manage it? Can hotel quarantine stop new strains getting in? Do we need vaccination certificates to travel? What about our summer holidays?

Once again I found myself writing several articles in the national media about this, and giving evidence to the Home Affairs Select Committee.

The three primary functions of border control are the

protection of public security, public policy, and public health. On security, we conduct thorough multi-agency checks on everybody entering the UK, both at point of booking and at point of entry. We are rather good at that.

On policy, the ending of free movement has given us a new Border Operating Model, a new Points-Based Immigration System, and a new UK Border 2025 Strategy – all published in the course of 2020. It will take us time to implement the new systems and processes at the border. We aren't so good at that yet – but we will get there.

But bottom of our report card is the protection of our national health. On that, we must try harder.

Once upon a time, we had a Port Medical Inspector (PMI) in every port of entry. Immigration Officers (as we were then) could refer any passenger to the PMI if they were perceived to be a health threat. PMIs were empowered to issue us with a form "Port 30" which gave us grounds to refuse leave to enter on medical grounds. New migrants coming to settle in the UK were routinely checked for communicable diseases before a visa was issued.

As passenger numbers grew, PMIs were gradually removed from our ports of entry on grounds of "efficiency". We stopped checking health credentials as a condition of entry. The greater threat was no longer the importation of disease; it was the importation of dangerous, harmful, or non-compliant people and goods. Health checks fell off our radar.

Between January and April 2020 Singapore, South Korea, Australia, and New Zealand all systematically introduced strict border controls to mitigate the importation of COVID at their borders. Travel to those countries was subsequently restricted to their own nationals and family members only, and 14-day quarantine at a designated location became mandatory on arrival. These countries have managed to control the spread of the virus much more effectively that has been the case in other countries, including the UK, Europe, and the US.

Although we introduced strict quarantine measures for passengers returning on evacuation flights from Wuhan in January 2020, no measures were introduced for flights or arrivals from other destinations – increasing the risk that the virus would be imported from other countries.

In June 2020 we started to ask inbound passengers to complete an on-line passenger locator form (PLF) to "self-certify" quarantine, but enforcement was "light touch" and there was no requirement to undergo a test, either before travel or upon arrival.

My recommendation to require airlines, ferry companies and rail companies to check health credentials for all passengers boarding flights, ferries, and trains to the UK (as they do with passports and visas) was finally implemented in January 2021, a year after COVID was first detected in Wuhan. This new requirement required the production of a completed PLF, and evidence that a negative COVID test had been taken within 72 hours of travel. Boarding should be denied to anybody unable to meet this requirement, but as yet no effective compliance framework has been set up between the UK Border Force and the airlines to establish whether or not this has been done. Meanwhile we have seen all kinds of "test certificates" turning up at our ports in various languages and scripts, some of which are clearly fake.

The new requirements have put an additional strain on the Border Force. Officers must now check PLF and negative test forms as well as passports; interview all passengers to determine travel history and purpose of travel to the UK; and now – where they identify a case of a UK citizen or resident arriving from a "red list" location who must self-isolate – liaise with local authorities and health agencies to enforce mandatory quarantine in nearby hotels.

Although the UK government published its UK Border 2025 Strategy on 17 December 2020, this did not focus specifically upon the pandemic. Many of the transformations therein are relevant (for example shifting to upstream intervention), but it does not specify how this would be done with regard to health checks.

I recommended that the government should develop a Counter-Pandemic Border Strategy (CPBS) to manage the second and subsequent waves of COVID-19, drawing upon lessons learned in other countries, as a matter of urgency. This should include the following factors:

1. The protection of Public Health is a key requirement of the UK Border, alongside the protection of National Security and Public Policy.

2. Departments should establish clear lines of effort between them to implement the CPBS.

3. Port Medical Inspectors and facilities should be reinstalled at UK ports of entry, to work in tandem with the UK Border Force in implementing the strategy.

4. "In country" pandemic threat levels should be translated into similar response levels at the Border, as they are for national security.

5. The government should work with international carriers and organisations to develop a new form of health pass which would meet internationally approved standards and would certify the health status of all international travellers at point of booking and check-in, in the same way as it does for passport and visa data.

6. The Home Office should conduct an urgent review on pre boarding/pre-clearance capabilities with international carriers to ensure they comply with requirements to check

health credentials prior to boarding, building upon the existing international liaison officer (ILO) network at key source and transit airports.

7. The Government should establish a Cross-Departmental Project Team to implement mandatory quarantine requirements for passengers arriving at UK ports of entry including tests for symptoms, safe and secure transport to designated locations, and in-country enforcement.

8. The government should conduct an urgent review of exit checks to ensure a co-ordinated response between UK Border Force, local police and carrying companies on requirements to check outbound travellers for permission to travel, and how this will be enforced in practice.

9. The Home Office should establish a national critical incident command and control infrastructure which can be stood up at short notice to respond to current and emerging health threat levels at the UK Border. This should include regular tests and exercises.

Of course, whether the UK government chooses to implement any of these recommendations is a matter for them. But either way they cannot continue to preside over a problem where passengers are queuing at the Border for over seven hours for health screening. Nor can they ignore the potential for some new strain or pandemic to enter the country in the future.

So far, this has been my latest engagement in the ongoing debate about border control and immigration. I doubt that it will be my last.

If I have learned anything about border control over the past half century, it is the unpredictability of it all. We never know what is around the next corner. But I can only end by repeating the immortal words of my predecessor TWE Roche in "The Keys to the Kingdom":

My special thanks go to all the rest of that great company of people who have been my colleagues in the Immigration Branch for more than a quarter of a century, who have moulded the very being of the Service to which I have been so proud to belong.

For me it's been nearly a half of a century – and the organisation has undergone many changes from the Immigration Branch to the UK Immigration Service, the Border and Immigration Agency, UK Border Agency, and the UK Border Force. But the sense of pride in the great company of people that have worked there in the past – and those that still do – will also remain in my heart forever.

POSTSCRIPT

I never quite knew when I started this book where it would end. My life in borders is not done yet, and I still don't know if I will ever fully "retire" from working in this extraordinary business.

On the home front, Mum passed away in 2015 after more heart valve problems, at the age of 84. Dad was devastated – they had been together for nearly 70 years, and he was completely broken when she passed. It wasn't until after her demise that we realised how dependent he was upon her. After one trip back from the hospital, Jill took him home and he wasn't able to find his pyjamas. It turned out that Mum had prepared his clothes for him every day and every night – he didn't even know where they were stored. He stopped eating and taking his medication, saying he just wanted to die. We spent more and more time with him, and I became increasingly worried about his welfare.

Jill, Sharon and I did all we could to keep him going – he had no other carers to rely upon, with my brother Michael having emigrated to Thailand many years earlier. Michael was himself financially dependent upon Mum and Dad to fund his stay in Thailand, which was an added complication, and a role that I had to assume as Dad became increasingly ill. Michael was himself unwell, suffering from lung disease and diabetes and increasingly asking for support to pay for his own medical treatment in Thailand.

In the end it became clear that Dad couldn't look after himself anymore and needed full-time care. The two options were to place in him a care home, or to move him in with us. I had always promised Mum and Dad that if anything happened to either of them, I would do my best not to put them into care and to look after them myself. We did not have enough space in our house in Sutton, so we pooled our resources and moved to a bigger house in Purley where we could have him with us and give him his own space.

I was proud to have been able to keep him going for a few more years. In that time, we managed to take him out to Texas (where I was attending Border Security Expo) to spend some time with his sister Marge, before she passed away herself shortly afterwards. Sharon also took him to Thailand to see Michael, and we took him on holidays to the Isle of Wight with us (where I ended up hiring a cottage to finish this book).

Mike's condition in Thailand continued to deteriorate to the point where I had to bring him home and locate him with us, at least until I could get him restored to reasonable health and properly cared for elsewhere. This placed an unreasonable burden both on Jill and the boys, who were essentially living with two invalids for some time before I could get Mike relocated into sheltered accommodation in Brighton.

Dad suffered a stroke in 2019 from which he never fully recovered. He developed vascular dementia and I placed him in the Sunrise of Purley care home, where he passed away peacefully in November 2020. During COVID I took up running at the ripe old age of 66 and managed to raise £1500 for the Alzheimer's Society by completing the London ASICS 10k run through London a year later.

Sharon continues to support me in my border security business, and my elder son Mark is now making a good career for himself in accounting. Daniel is approaching 21 and has sadly missed out on most of his first two years at Southampton University because of Covid, although he goes to France shortly to continue teach English as a foreign language. My youngest, Ben, finished school at Sutton Grammar this year with 3 Straight A's at Advanced Level, and has also fled the nest to read law at Nottingham University.

Jill is still working in the Home Office, currently managing the Immigration Compliance and Enforcement (ICE) teams across the country whilst simultaneously sending officers down to Kent to deal with the growing number of migrants arriving there. She is pursuing her own leadership journey there now.

What goes around comes around. There will always be another borders challenge for the next generation of Border Force Officers coming through the ranks. My thoughts are with them – it can be difficult work at times.

But when I look back through this book and my extraordinary lifetime in borders, I can't complain. For everyone that wants to unlock the kingdom, there will be others with a fresh set of keys. I wish them all well in their endeavours.

Answers to casework questions on page 221

1. Mike Tyson, US citizen. A professional boxer but convicted rapist, he sought entry to come to the UK to participate in a boxing match which would raise a lot of money for charity. The back pages of the tabloids were all for it. The front pages of some of the broadsheets were against. We had demonstrations from Women's Rights organisations outside the Home Office, and rallies in boxing communities around the country arguing the case. Although Tyson was inadmissible due to his previous conviction, the Home Secretary decided that he should be admitted exceptionally on this occasion. Tyson arrived in Britain on 16 January 2000 and knocked out his British opponent in the second round of the fight.

2. Martha Stewart, US citizen. Businesswoman, writer, and television personality but convicted of fraud. Sought entry to come to the UK to meet HM Queen Elizabeth as part of a promotion campaign to promote Wedgwood pottery in the United States. Widespread support from the Department of Trade; widespread opposition from the law enforcement community and campaign against fraud. Stewart was refused permission to enter the United Kingdom in 2008 on the

grounds of her criminal conviction and imprisonment for fraud four years previously, on the grounds that her presence in the UK was "non conducive to the public good".

3.   Nick D'Arcy, Australian citizen and international swimmer, former Australian champion and gold medal prospect. D'Arcy sought entry to compete in the London 2012 Olympics but was convicted of GBH. Widespread support from the Australian Government and the IOC. Widespread opposition from the law enforcement community and campaign against violence. D'Arcy's criminal conviction rendered him inadmissible to the UK, but following representations by the Australian team that he was a medal hope, he was granted accreditation to the London 2012 Olympics to compete in the Games. He was eliminated in the semi-finals.

Printed in Great Britain
by Amazon

79240965R00210